Direct Action, Deliberation, and Diffusion

What are the microlevel interactions and conversations that underlie successful and failed diffusion? By comparing the spread of direct action tactics from the 1999 global justice movement protests against the World Trade Organization in Seattle to grassroots activists in Toronto and New York, Lesley J. Wood argues that dynamics of deliberation among local activists both aided and blocked diffusion. To analyze the localization of this cycle of protest, the research brings together rich ethnography, interviews, social network analysis, and catalogs of protest events. The findings suggest that when diverse activists with different perspectives can discuss innovations in a reflexive, egalitarian manner, they are more likely to be able to incorporate locally new tactics.

Lesley J. Wood is an associate professor of sociology at York University in Toronto, Canada. She researches how social movements and state responses to those movements are changing in the current globalizing moment. She has published on this question in journals including *Mobilization, Qualitative Sociology*, the *Journal of World Systems Research*, and *Upping the Anti*. She has authored or coauthored book chapters on the control and surveillance of protest, summit protests, transnational social movement networks and coalition formation, the World Social Forum, deliberation, and nineteenth-century British social movements. She is the coauthor of the second and third editions of the late Charles Tilly's book, *Social Movements, 1768–2008/2012*. She is a regional editor for the international, peer-reviewed, online journal *Interface*, a journal for and about social movements.

CAMBRIDGE STUDIES IN CONTENTIOUS POLITICS

Mark Beissinger, *Princeton University*
Jack A. Goldstone, *George Mason University*
Michael Hanagan, *Vassar College*
Doug McAdam, *Stanford University and Center for Advanced Study in the Behavioral Sciences*
Suzanne Staggenborg, *University of Pittsburgh*
Sidney Tarrow, *Cornell University*
Charles Tilly (d. 2008), *Columbia University*
Elisabeth J. Wood, *Yale University*
Deborah Yashar, *Princeton University*

(continued after Index)

Direct Action, Deliberation, and Diffusion

Collective Action after the WTO Protests in Seattle

LESLEY J. WOOD
York University, Ontario

CAMBRIDGE
UNIVERSITY PRESS

CAMBRIDGE
UNIVERSITY PRESS

32 Avenue of the Americas, New York NY 10013-2473, USA

Cambridge University Press is part of the University of Cambridge.

It furthers the University's mission by disseminating knowledge in the pursuit of education, learning and research at the highest international levels of excellence.

www.cambridge.org
Information on this title: www.cambridge.org/9781107682641

First published 2012
First paperback edition 2014

A catalogue record for this publication is available from the British Library

Library of Congress Cataloguing in Publication data
Wood, Lesley J.
  Direct action, deliberation, and diffusion : collective action after the WTO protests in Seattle / Lesley J. Wood, York University, Ontario.
    pages cm. – (Cambridge studies in contentious politics)
  Includes bibliographical references and index.
  ISBN 978-1-107-02071-9 (hardback)
  1. Protest movements – Washington (State) – Seattle – Case studies.   2. Demonstrations.   3. Political participation.   4. Political activists.   I. Title.
  HM881.W66   2012
  303.48′409797772–dc23   2012003301

ISBN 978-1-107-02071-9 Hardback
ISBN 978-1-107-68264-1 Paperback

Dedicated to those who struggle for a more just and beautiful world

Contents

Figures and Tables

Acknowledgments

Any writing project, like any social movement campaign, involves a large number of people. First and foremost, I must thank my parents, Rosemary and Matthew Wood. I could not have done it without them. I also want to thank my academic mentors for their guidance, wisdom, and encouragement: Dana Fisher, Kelly Moore, Francesca Polletta, Jackie Smith, Sidney Tarrow, and the late Charles Tilly. I am extraordinarily lucky to have been able to draw on their combination of skills, knowledge, and passions. Participants in Columbia's Workshop on Contentious Politics rounded out my education by consistently asking the tough questions. I must also thank colleagues who acted as critics on early versions of chapters and papers: Sun Chul Kim, John Krinsky, Takeshi Wada, and Cecelia Walsh-Russo. Elisabeth Wood must be thanked for her advice on revising the manuscript, Irina Ceric for her legal advice, and A. K. Thompson and the editors at Cambridge for their editing help. I would be remiss if I forgot the people who helped me to attend graduate school; it was a collective project. I must thank Aunt Evelyn, Dyane, Linda, Poppet, Sally, Colin, Kirsten, and the Scott family. I need to thank the activists from DAN, Mob4Glob, More Gardens!, OCAP, OPIRG, and SLAM for taking the time to talk and read my scribbles when they had far better things to do. Last but not least, I must thank my partner in crime Mac Scott for taking care of wee Sidney and for his unflagging enthusiasm and support of my project, even when it meant that I stopped going to meetings, protests, and parties – at least for a little while.

I

Introduction

The year 2000 was an unusually busy one for many activists in Canada and the United States. At the time, I was living in New York City and attending three or four meetings a week. These meetings planned for two or three rallies, marches, and protest actions every month. I was not alone. Following the successful demonstrations of November 1999 in Seattle, new activists seemed to spring up as if from nowhere to form "anti-globalization" organizations.[1] Established groups began talking about trade and neoliberalism in new ways, and many activists talked about and experimented with the tactics and styles of organizing that had been so successful in Seattle. In New York, protesters at immigrant rights marches donned black bandannas in the style of the black bloc, and others brought giant puppets onto the picket lines of local labor disputes. Imitating demonstrators in Seattle, many activists pushed past the classic repertoire of marches and rallies and began to engage in direct action. They formed affinity groups, attended trainings in blockading, and experimented with jail solidarity techniques. "Seattle tactics" like black bloc, puppetry, blockades, and jail solidarity spread to activists across Canada and the United States.

At the end of that year, I returned home to Toronto for the holidays. Over drinks, I met with friends active in a local antipoverty organization with the hope of discussing plans for the convergence against the Summit of the Americas in Quebec City in April 2001. Instead, I listened as they dismissed those protests. "We need to stay local," they argued. During that week in Toronto, I heard activists who had been in the streets of Washington, DC, protesting the World Bank and the International Monetary Fund a few months earlier distance themselves from the anti-globalization movement, its tactics, and its participants. I became curious. In New York, some of the same conversations about the anti-globalization movement being too white and too disconnected from local struggles and too abstract were also

---

[1] Following the lead of the movement, I refer to the "anti-globalization movement" and the "global justice movement" interchangeably.

taking place. And yet, New York's anti-globalization coalitions were holding together. Activists there were still experimenting with the tactics associated with the Seattle protests. A year after the World Trade Organization (WTO) protests in Seattle, why did New York's direct action activists continue to experiment with the Seattle tactics when direct action activists in Toronto largely abandoned them?

On the surface, one would expect the activists in the two cities to respond to the Seattle protests in a similar fashion. After all, they learned about the protest from similar sources. A handful from each city had attended the convergence and returned home to regale others with stories, video footage, and photographs. Information about tactics like black bloc and organizational forms like affinity groups flowed through organizational networks like Reclaim the Streets and Food Not Bombs, trade union networks like the Canadian Labour Congress, and student activist networks like the Canadian Federation of Students. Activists experienced in movement tactics from organizations like San Francisco Bay area's Ruckus Society or Calgary's Co-Motion Collective traveled to New York and Toronto to run activist training workshops. These trainers told stories about the protests and taught local activists about blockading, puppetry, and jail solidarity tactics. In addition to local trainings, some activists made their way to events like the annual Earth First! Rendezvous gatherings or the National Conference on Organized Resistance (NCOR) in Washington, DC. News of the Seattle tactics also spread informally by way of traveling activists who told stories of the Seattle protests as they visited friends and radical projects in different cities.

Media also played an important role in spreading information about the protests and their tactics. Activists in New York and Toronto read the same Web sites, magazines, and newspaper articles discussing movement strategy. They were on the same e-mail lists. Internet communities operated as sites for debate and enabled the distribution of news and information about the use of various tactics. "Indymedia" and other forms of alternative media became key sources of information and discussion about the Seattle tactics. Activists in both cities also learned about the protests, the tactics, and their impact via the mass media. After all, the Seattle protests were nothing if not widely reported. Reflecting on her experience at the demonstration, movement activist and author Starhawk writes: "For once in a political protest, when we chanted 'The whole world is watching!' we were telling the truth. I've never seen so much media attention on a political action" (Starhawk 1999). This high level of visibility made the event a "best case scenario" for diffusion through mainstream media channels.

Activists in Toronto and New York had access to similar sources of information about Seattle; however, their emulation of the tactics used at these protests varied significantly. To understand this difference, we need to look at the relational dynamics that shaped the terrain on which organizations and activists operated in each city. These dynamics influenced whether or not activists could collectively deliberate about the tactics – whether they could interpret, evaluate, and experiment with them in ways that would make their incorporation possible.

Although the tactics used in Seattle spread widely during the months following the event, they did not spread everywhere. As McAdam and Rucht (1993:58) point out, "the real challenge is not so much in demonstrating the mere fact of diffusion ... but to investigate systematically the conditions under which diffusion is likely to occur and the means by which it does." This book recounts the findings of such an investigation. I argue that a particular set of structural conditions needed to be present in the receiving environment in order for diffusion of the Seattle tactics to be successful. Potential adopters need to be able to gather and talk about the tactics in a relatively reflexive, diverse, egalitarian, and open manner. Most of the time, however, categorical and relational inequalities and historical patterns of exclusion make deliberation and diffusion impossible. Because blocks to the diffusion of new ideas are a key reason that waves of protest collapse, this book offers one explanation of why the Seattle cycle dissipated so quickly.

RESEARCH DESIGN

To explain the conditions for relational diffusion, this project compares two very similar cases with different outcomes. I trace the diffusion of a cluster of protest tactics from one site to two others sharing a great deal in common. I hold the influence of factors associated with the "sender" site (Seattle and the direct action repertoire it spawned) constant and isolate the causal influence of factors that differentiate the reception process in the two "receiver" sites (New York and Toronto). By focusing on the characteristics of activist organizations and the past and present patterns of interaction and inequality within the two urban centers, I explain variations in the Seattle tactics' diffusion.

To compare New York City and Toronto, I examine their respective demographics and political economy and outline their relationship with the state/ provincial, regional, and federal levels of government. Such data shows the importance of some of the categorical inequalities of race and class within each city. To compare each city's respective dynamics of contention, I developed catalogs of protest events using *The Toronto Star* and *The New York Times*. These catalogs cover events that took place two years before and two years after the Seattle protests. In combination with interviews with activists and personal journal entries, these catalogs provide a sense of the actors, issues, targets, and networks that underpinned protest and deliberation in each city.

For both Toronto and New York City, I selected three organizations that would be the most likely adopters of the Seattle tactics. All six organizations have a history of engaging in disruptive protest, and all six cited the Seattle protests as having had an influence on their activities. In each city, I chose a global justice coalition, a student organization, and a group focused on local campaigns and issues. I examined the minutes (when available) and publications of each organization and developed timelines that traced four years of protest activity with Seattle as their midpoint. To understand each group's tactical decision making, I interviewed between four and six of its participants, totaling thirty-two people in all.

To determine how historical and ongoing relationships influenced deliberation and diffusion, I asked each activist about their political biography and about the tactics and strategy, structure, and decision making in their group. I also asked them about the interactions their organization had with both collaborators and other role models. Finally, I asked all respondents whether their organization would experiment with each Seattle tactic, and why they would or would not engage in such experiments.

To understand the way that the activists perceived the different tactics under review, I looked beyond the content of their explanations and considered the more widespread dynamics of particular debates and the practices of argumentation and storytelling that informed them. Like anyone, activists valued certain identities and strategies and dismissed others at particular times and places. Both the form and content of activist conversations influenced the future deliberation and tactical experimentation. As a result, in this book, I look at the stories that activists told while debating property destruction and summit hopping and recounting their subsequent use or rejection of the Seattle tactics. The content of these discussions influenced subsequent relationships and practices by valuing some identities and strategies, but not others. The form of these debates is also important. Therefore, in this book, I examine the evolution of debates around summit hopping and property destruction and argue that the way these two debates unfolded – both online and offline – has facilitated the building of some relationships but not others, influencing deliberation and diffusion.

By comparing the demographic, relational, repressive, organizational, and discursive conditions for deliberation and diffusion in each city, we can understand why activists considered using black bloc, puppetry, blockading, and jail solidarity in New York more than in Toronto. By locating these observations within an understanding of the two different contexts, I show why, unlike their more ragtag equivalents in New York, experienced and well-resourced activists in Toronto were neither interested in nor able to experiment with nor incorporate the Seattle tactics.

THE SEATTLE TACTICS

The tactics whose diffusion I am tracking became visible during the protests against the 1999 meetings of the WTO in Seattle. At that time, tens of thousands of protesters filled the streets and blocked WTO delegates on their way to meetings designed to further intensify global neoliberal trade. Activists hung banners off bridges and buildings, while puppeteers and musicians provided an air of celebration. As the day progressed and repression increased, activists wearing black bandannas smashed Niketown and

Starbucks windows. The police subsequently arrested hundreds of demonstrators and teargassed, pepper sprayed, and beat many others. All of a sudden, direct action protest in the United States was front-page news around the world.

Bringing together labor, environmental, and student movements, the protests in Seattle were a laboratory of innovation and exchange where North American protesters experimented with disruption, communication, and decision-making tactics. Successful in their attempts to shut down the WTO meetings and embarrass both local and national hosts, these protests marked a new wave of direct action activism. Like the waves of protest triggered by the success of the civil rights movement's sit-in tactics and the waves of civil disturbances in the late 1960s or the more recent wave of protest triggered by the Occupy Wall Street (OWS) protests, the effect of the Seattle demonstrations rippled outward to activists and observers in Canada, the United States, and beyond.

When I asked activists in New York and Toronto how the Seattle protests had influenced their local organizations and practices, they identified four types of effects. First, groups organizing around different issues began to form new multi-issue coalitions. In both cities, large coalitions explicitly identifying with the Seattle protests and the movement against the International Monetary Fund (IMF), World Bank, and World Trade Organization emerged. Second (and related), groups that previously had not worked together began to collaborate. Third, participation – particularly by younger activists – increased in social movement organizations both within and beyond the anti-globalization movement. As one Toronto antipoverty activist explained, "I think a lot of people were more excited about protesting." Finally, the Seattle protests inaugurated a period of tactical experimentation. During this period, organizations debated, adapted, and experimented with the tactics used in Seattle. These four effects make the connection between the rise and fall of a wave of protests and the diffusion of particular tactics clear.

In what follows, I focus on activist experimentation with the Seattle tactics. After the smoke had cleared and the crowds had dissipated, activists in many countries discussed the meaning and value of the Seattle tactics. Sometimes, they tried them out. This book looks primarily at the spread of black blocs, jail solidarity, blockades, and giant puppets; however, I also consider the spread of other "Seattle associated" practices, including Reclaim the Streets street parties, Radical Cheerleaders, the strategy of targeting corporations, and the adoption of organizational forms like the affinity group and the spokescouncil. Although no single group of activists took on all of these tactics – and global justice activists often expressed disagreement concerning their strategic value – many activists in North America attempted to incorporate one or more of them into their local protests between 2000 and 2001. Since then, whenever summit protests have occurred, black bloc activists, puppeteers, and blockaders have converged to emulate aspects of the Seattle repertoire.

Importantly, none of the tactics I've identified were new in Seattle. Nevertheless, their combined effectiveness during the protests recoded them as "successful," connected them, increased their attractiveness, and revitalized their meaning. As they spread to new contexts, activists adapted the tactics. Black Blocs in Seattle became Black and Pink Blocs in Prague (September 26, 2000); Shutting Down the World Trade Organization (WTO) in Seattle morphed into Shutting Down the Financial District in Toronto to protest government cutbacks to education, welfare, and health care (October 16, 2001). Activists who locked their bodies together in Washington DC at demonstrations against the IMF on April 16, 2000, repeated the tactic to save the DC General Hospital in 2001. Giant puppets and marching bands began to appear with increasing frequency at local protests for community gardens and on picket lines. Meanwhile, "Radical Cheerleaders" developed cheers and dance routines to address issues ranging from health care to queer sexuality.

Despite their proliferation, the extent of activist experiments with these tactics varied. Activists in New York experimented longer with the tactics than activists in Toronto. Although one might look to individual psychology or organizational histories to account for such variations, these approaches are unable to consider how actors in networks, organizations, cities, and countries actively influence the spread of ideas. In order to understand the flow and localization of direct action tactics from Seattle to Toronto and New York, I turn to diffusion theory, which addresses the spread of innovations most directly.

THEORIES OF DIFFUSION

Diffusion theory attempts to explain when and how ideas and practices travel. It developed in the eighteenth and nineteenth centuries in opposition to evolutionary theory. Whereas evolutionary theories saw social change developing from within an institution or society, diffusion theorists saw change in social practices as being stimulated by the transmission and reception of new ideas across boundaries and borders. Although diffusion has long been seen as a major source of change (Parsons & Shils 1951), increased travel and communication in the period of globalization has attracted new attention to the question (Chabot 2010; Kolins Givan et al., 2010; Tarrow 2005).

Over the past twenty years, many parallel diffusion literatures have developed in relative isolation from one another. One study counted thirteen different diffusion literatures within fields as disparate as rural sociology, clinical epidemiology, marketing, and organizational studies (Greenhalgh et al. 2005, 1). Each of these literatures has conceptualized, explained, and investigated the subject differently. There have, however, been some areas of agreement: innovations tend to be adopted within a population following a general "S" curve, with early adoption leading to a period of rapid adoption and then tapering off (Granovetter 1973; Katz 1999).[2] There is also general consensus that the successful diffusion of an innovation is dependent upon the transmitting context, the channels of communication, the context of the innovation's reception, and the character of the innovation itself (Hedstrom, Sandell, and Stern 2000; McAdam 1995; McAdam and Rucht 1993; Myers 2000; Oliver and Myers 1998; Strang and Meyer 1993). However, there is less agreement about the relative importance of each piece of the puzzle. Some research emphasizes the role of the transmitter and highlights the importance of visible and successful events to the diffusion of innovations. Other work emphasizes the importance of channels of communication and suggests that both strong (family and friendship) and weak (acquaintance) ties are important for the effective diffusion of information.

Like McAdam and Rucht (1993), I emphasize the role of the receiving context. In cases like the Seattle protests, the transmitter is widely recognized, and the ties connecting those demonstrations to direct action activists across Canada and the United States are relatively dense and consistent. As a result, differences in adoption must be explained by looking at differences in the characteristics of adopters and/or the patterns and processes of reception. We can begin by considering Katz's definition of diffusion because it allows us to focus both on the process of reception and on the way that diffusion is itself a collective process: "Diffusion ... [is] defined as the acceptance of some specific item, over time, by adopting units – individuals, groups, communities – that are linked both to external channels of communication and to each other by means of both a structure of social relations and a system of values, or culture" (1968).

Although it emphasizes reception, a definition such as Katz's underplays the process of contestation and interpretation that determines how an innovation's adoption takes place. In the past, theorists have often assumed that adopters imitate other users in a relatively unconscious fashion or, alternately, that they are able to engage in rational calculations of costs and benefits (Strang and Meyer 1993, 487). Research on fads and fashions tends to portray adoption as imitation. This school of thought argues that, under conditions of uncertainty, organizations will tend to imitate other organizations, especially when particular ideas are promoted by opinion leaders or used by those with prestige (DiMaggio and Powell 1983; Hirsch 1972; Majahan and Peterson 1985; Thompson 1967). Such processes lead to bandwagon effects, whereby an increasing number of adopters push "laggards" to join them (Granovetter 1978). Although this approach to analyzing the reception of innovations offers some useful insights into the influence of opinion leaders, it presumes their influence to be somehow automatic; however, such an emphasis neglects the interactive and interpretive struggles that shape how potential adopters

---

[2] Critics of this model note that, sometimes, receiving groups have no direct or even indirect contact with the transmitter, but adopt through a sense of cultural similarity. Sean Chabot adds that sometimes things spread from margin to center (Chabot 2002).

evaluate prestige. Moreover, it fails to consider the importance of the past actions and identities of such adopters.

Emulation and diffusion is more likely when potential users of an innovation see themselves as similar to past users of that innovation in some way. Rogers (2003) noted this and argued that imitation or contagion can be blocked through difference or disconnectedness, pointing out the importance of examining the role of demography on this process. Soule (1997) similarly found that university activists tended to imitate the tactics and strategies of activists at universities that they saw as similar to their own. When they identify with these past users in some way, diffusion becomes more likely.

Other research emphasizes the characteristics of the innovation itself. This work suggests that potential adopters evaluate the costs and benefits of an innovation in a rational manner (Abrahamson 1991, 587; Hedstrom 1994; Strang and Soule 1998, 266). Early work saw such evaluations as independent and made by individuals (or organizations acting as individuals) considering costs and benefits, profit, or impact. This approach often assumes that the criteria for such decisions are easily comprehensible and consistent. however, others argue that the costs and benefits that underlie decisions by potential adopters change throughout a diffusion cycle. Here, feedback loops influence the decision to adopt (Conell & Cohn 1995; Holden 1986; Rogers 1962, 154–5; Silverberg et al. 1988). While the presumption of a rational adopter has been useful inasmuch as it has highlighted the active nature of potential adopters, it presupposes a uniform and abstract rationality removed from its cultural and political context and agreed-upon goals that neglect the way that social categories – including categories of value – are constantly reorganized through processes of interaction and meaning making.

Despite the insights of these classic works, analyses of diffusion that presume either contagion, unreflexive imitation or utility-maximizing rational choice can't explain why activists in Toronto rejected the Seattle tactics while their New York equivalents continued to use them locally. In order to understand this puzzle, we must consider the subset of the diffusion literature that sees adopters and rejecters of innovations as active participants (both individuals and groups) engaged in meaningful social interaction.

Some of the earliest diffusion literature makes a similar emphasis. Both Coleman, Katz, and Menzel (1957) and Lazarsfeld, Berelson, and Gaudet (1944) argued that diffusion was a deeply social process. In their paper on "The Diffusion of an Innovation Among Physicians," Coleman et al. (1957, 269) showed that the spread of the drug Gammalin among doctors was dependent on social ties and social interactions under conditions of uncertainty. In their 1944 study of mass media's effect on voting behavior, Paul Lazarsfeld et al. found that the mainstream media had little influence on voting decisions. Instead, they argued that the influence of received ideas on existing practices, or diffusion was a "two step" process. "Ideas often flow from radio and print to opinion leaders and from these to the less active sections of the population (1944, 151)." While the first step is one of information transfer, the second step (from opinion leaders to followers) involves the spread of interpersonal influence (Rogers 2003, 304). Thirty years later, Czepiel (1974) found that such "word of mouth" processes were also crucial in the diffusion of major technological innovations. The recognition of the importance of opinion leaders in the process of adoption shows how social structure influences the flow of ideas. The processes by which opinion leaders exert this influence continue to be understudied. Snow et al (1986) argued that successful diffusion by opinion leaders depends upon their capacity to frame the practice to be adopted as meaningful by using local symbols that facilitate transmission (Snow et al. 1986). Although this characterization of the process depicts diffusion in "top down" fashion, later studies have shown how the process is influenced by both the knowledge, attitudes, and beliefs of opinion leaders *and* the networks in which those opinion leaders participate (Spalter-Roth, Fortenberry, and Lovitts, 2007).

In recent years, more emphasis has been given to the processes and mechanisms that enable diffusion. In a landmark work, Sidney Tarrow (2005) describes three paths of diffusion and identifies the mechanisms that underlie each. According to Tarrow, there is *relational* diffusion, which relies on close relations of trust; *nonrelational* diffusion, which relies on media; and *mediated* diffusion, which relies on brokers that link transmitters and receivers. Most cases of diffusion involve a combination of paths. In this study, I emphasize relational diffusion among organizations in two cities and the way that activists see themselves as similar to or different from the earlier users of the tactic, the protesters in the Seattle protests of 1999. I look briefly at the way local opinion leaders mediated the localization of the tactics from the Seattle protests. Then I examine the way that activists who receive information about the tactics through nonrelational sources (i.e., mass media, independent media and Web sites) theorized about them collectively (Strang and Meyer 1993, 284). Deliberation underlies relational, mediated, and nonrelational diffusion (Rogers 2003, 284).

This emphasis builds on the approach of Sean Chabot. In his examination of the spread of Gandhian nonviolence from Indian anti-colonial movements to the U.S. civil rights movement, Chabot (2010) considers how the microlevel dynamics of peer-based dialogue underpin diffusion. His study reveals how dialogue allows new ideas to be translated, interpreted, and altered for new contexts. According to Chabot, understanding the form and content of such dialogue will allow us to understand how diffusion takes place. Unlike Lazarsfeld's portrayal of opinion leaders "spreading the word" to potential adopters, Chabot defines dialogue as "involving two or more active participants who are willing and able to contribute their viewpoints and to engage in rounds of questions and responses aimed at learning from others and expanding horizons" (2010; 104). Here, dialogue reveals itself to be unlike other forms of communication because of its exploratory, pedagogical, and reflexive character. For Chabot, dialogue is crucial to diffusion because it allows potential receivers to translate, experiment with, and integrate innovations (2010; 106).

Although Chabot's approach usefully identifies the importance of dialogue for mediated diffusion, it doesn't consider *the context* that facilitates or limits the possibility of such dialogue. In addition, Chabot dialogue is a kind of communication that is transformative, experimental, and open ended; however, his account illustrates how this happens between individuals, but gives little attention to how this might play out within organizations. For organizations to consider altering their routine practices and adopting new ideas, they must balance organizational histories, practices, identities, and strategies with deliberation – conversations that are relatively equal and reflexive, and diverse, especially if those organizations value collaborative decision making. Consequently, to understand how practices diffuse among organizations, we need to understand when and how such deliberation occurs.

The deliberation underlying a new tactic's adoption by an organization might be seen as an additional "third step" in Lazarsfeld's diffusion model. If the first step of diffusion is from transmitter to opinion leader, and the second is from opinion leader to followers, the third step in diffusion would be among participants within a collectivity considering adoption. Indeed, deliberation appears particularly important for diffusion among the kind of collective actors to be found in many non-hierarchical social movement organizations. This "third step" of deliberation allows participants to decide whether an innovation should be considered appropriate or useful, and whether and how to adapt it for use by their organization.

Such a "third step" of deliberation may not be essential for the reception of new ideas by all organizations; however, it *is* crucial for those with three characteristics – all of which are commonly found within social movement organizations. First, organizations that are non hierarchical do not rely on small numbers of decision makers to direct their strategy and choose their tactics. Instead, and regardless of whether their participation is formal or informal, larger numbers of participants are involved in making these decisions through deliberation and broader discussion. Voluntary organizations often fall into this category. Second, organizations and networks engaged in activities that involve some risk to their participants (whether physical, political, or social) also tend to rely on discussion to strengthen the collective identity required for such action. Social movement organizations that use direct action are examples of this. Third, groups that are pursuing goals that are "fuzzy" also tend to require more discussion than groups whose goals are immediately apparent and shared by all participants and observers. Social movement organizations often incorporate one or all of these characteristics. As a result, their process of experimenting with, adapting, and adopting an innovation relies less on opinion leaders and more on "third step" deliberation. However, such deliberation is most likely under particular conditions.

RELATIONAL CONTEXT OF DIFFUSION

Certain relational conditions facilitate diffusion. Two findings appear to be particularly important. The first is structural equivalence – potential adopters that have the same structural position as earlier adopters are more likely to be able to emulate those adopters (Burt 1987, Soule 1997, Strang and Tuma 1993). Following this approach, Walton and Seddon showed that social movements that had a structurally equivalent relationship to authorities such as the WTO engaged in similar levels and forms of mobilization against that authority (Walton & Seddon 1994).

But as Sarah Soule notes, structural equivalence is an interpretive process and not simply an automatic one. In her study of protest tactics in the anti-apartheid movement at U.S. universities, Soule found that activists in universities of similar size and academic reputation were more likely to act similarly when adopting an innovation from elsewhere. For Soule, this was because students at universities that saw their institution as similar to specific other universities, and this process of identification influenced their behavior. Structural equivalence facilitated this process of identification. Categories of race, class, and other divisions also influence this process. Consequently, potential adopters are more likely to act in similar ways to those with whom they feel aligned as a result of categorical identities perceived to be held in common (Wood 2007). As with common political and economic systems, common cultural practices facilitate diffusion (McAdam and Rucht 1993, Soule 1997). These commonalities make it easier for potential adopters to develop a shared identity with earlier users of a tactic, facilitating experimentation in the shared practices.

The second relational condition that facilitates diffusion is derived from Granovetter's concept of "the strength of weak ties." Social networks consisting of both strong and weak ties are more likely than those containing strong ties alone to be able to spread new information between clusters of actors (Gould 1991; Granovetter 1973; Rude 1964). These clusters can then deliberate on their use and incorporation. Weak ties between dense cliques allow information and innovations to spread easily through social systems. (Granovetter 1973)

The "weak ties" argument corresponds with the third relational condition that facilitates deliberation and diffusion. Actors in less centralized local networks will be more likely to be able to perceive, deliberate about, and incorporate innovations. According to Ronald Burt, "a system is centralized to the extent that all relations in it involve a single actor." This actor can be a single dominant organization or coalition that can develop significant control over a network. Actors in networks centralized around a small number of actors will have less opportunity to access new information, or deliberate and experiment autonomously with new tactics. In such a network, actors are much more likely to be influenced by the activities, or opinions of the prestigious actors than by the other actors in the network (Burt 1980:117).

Structural equivalence, weak ties, and decentralized networks facilitate diffusion. They do this because they help people with different experiences interact in relatively egalitarian and open ways. But while these findings suggest the relational conditions for diffusion processes, they do not yet constitute a close investigation of the meaningful interactions within and between activists and organizations considering a new tactic. In order to understand when and why a particular relational context facilitates diffusion, we need to look at how deliberation among potential adopters of an idea unfolds.

DELIBERATION

Deliberation is a particularly productive form of conversation. Often associated with democratic or civic engagement, deliberation brings together diverse actors with different opinions to exchange ideas in a relatively egalitarian and reflexive manner. Because it is tied to conscious and reflexive decision making (rather than merely reacting to situations or following routine), it is central to decisions that collectively and intentionally change practices. In his study of the California farm-workers movement, Marshall Ganz showed that activists had more "strategic capacity" to evaluate new innovations when they could participate in regular, open, and authoritative deliberation about strategy (Ganz 2000, 1005). This does not mean that deliberation is simply rational calculation writ large, as some of its proponents have suggested. For Francesca Polletta (2006), deliberation must be conceptualized as being both deeply meaningful and meaning making – involving stories, debate, emotion, and rationality. Such talk is more than a mechanical evaluation of alternatives; it is a collaborative process through which people tell stories, make arguments, and define and redefine their identities and strategies. In the midst of such conversations, an activist may explain who they admire, who they refuse to work with, and where and when a particular tactic emerged. Deliberation includes stories and arguments that make claims about who "we" are and who "they" are, what "we" do and what "they" do. Ultimately, these claims allow an organization or network to decide whether to adopt or reject a particular tactic.

Deliberation is also a particular form of conversation that occurs among participants who have relatively equal power and influence within the group. Of course, the key qualifier here is "relatively". Complete equality is unlikely in any group, or at any meeting. Even "leaderless" groups have informal leaders (Freeman 1970). But because deliberation requires that multiple and different perspectives are considered equally, relative equality is a key feature of deliberative conversations. Unlike Habermas' description of the ideal speech situation, deliberation is not simply about the interplay of different ideas. In the way that I speak about it here, deliberation requires that different types of people, with different cultural and political experiences, and different relational positions are participating in these conversations.

I follow Habermas (1981) in this. I see certain types of communication as being particularly powerful for changing political and social knowledge. For these conversations to be influential on collective behavior they have to allow for a certain level of reflexivity about past practices, and reflexivity about the discussions about these practices. This reflexivity means that activists within collective decision-making spaces will be able to discuss the effectiveness and meaning of past practices and tactics, and the effectiveness and meaning of the process of discussing these tactics. But this emphasis on reflexivity is not simply about talking politics and wrestling with ideas. Deliberation is about action. For the organizations I'm studying these conversations are about making decisions about action and tactics, in ways that facilitate their actual implementation.

RELATIONAL CONTEXT OF DELIBERATION

As I've defined it here, deliberation is more likely to occur in a particular relational context where relatively diverse groups of people with different opinions but similar levels of influence might interact in ways that allow them to consider innovations in a relatively reflexive and egalitarian manner. Like the ideal relational context for diffusion, the ideal situation for deliberation arises when clusters of strong ties exist among people with relatively diverse backgrounds and perspectives interacting in a relatively egalitarian and reflexive fashion.

There is a paradox here. The strong ties that facilitate deliberation are much more likely to arise between actors sharing common characteristics or practices (Strang and Meyer 1993, 488). Dense cliques of individuals or organizations that are similar and linked by strong ties tend to discuss ideas more easily and adopt innovations more quickly than those who are more heterogenous (Morris 1981; Strang and Soule 1998, 272). However, such cliques are less likely to consider information or adopt innovations from outside their own circles. Paradoxically, when a social system consists primarily of weak ties among diverse actors with different perspectives, although they have access to a wide array of ideas and practices, the possibility that they will have the strategic capacity to engage in sustained, reflexive, discussion decreases.

Relatively decentralized networks facilitate diffusion by increasing the possibility of deliberation among clusters of diverse and relatively equal participants. Relatedly, the ideas and actions of opinion leaders in a centralized network have a disproportionate influence. If these opinion leaders are reluctant to innovate, they may constrain diffusion across the network by discouraging deliberation of locally new tactics. And sometimes, networks can be centralized around two dominant and competing organizations or actors. Actors in such networks can become enmeshed in competitions that harden boundaries and break weak ties. This outcome also makes open, reflexive, egalitarian, and diverse deliberation about new tactics much less likely.

Because deliberation requires that diverse participants with different ideas come together in a relatively equal and reflexive manner, it benefits from the same conditions that facilitate diffusion; a combination of weak and strong ties within a relatively decentralized network. Under these conditions, actors are more likely to introduce and discuss outside ideas. But because such conversations both produce and are a product of social relations, deliberation is often blocked by inequalities of power and control over resources. These categorical inequalities of race, class, gender, and so forth structure interactions and can limit the diversity of interactions by creating or reinforcing boundaries between potential collaborators. These inequalities may also limit the reflexivity of participants about the conversations themselves.

Such inequalities will also make the process of identification difficult. By identification, I mean the process by which an individual or collective sees themselves as having a similar identity to a transmitting individual or collectivity. Sidney Tarrow argues that such a process of identification or "attribution of similarity" is the central mechanism that underlies relational diffusion, the type we have been examining. Indeed, As McAdam and Rucht note, "all instances of diffusion depend on a minimal identification of an adopter with a transmitter" (McAdam and Rucht 1993, 60; Strang and Meyer 1993).

McAdam and Rucht specified three conditions that facilitated this process of identification: a common institutional locus, adherents from the same strata and a common language (1993:71). Sean Chabot built on this list by emphasizing the way that these conditions are enacted, "Identification is most likely when organizations see themselves as compatible, and share common meanings, a mutual sub-cultural language, and are alike in personal and social characteristics" (Chabot et al., 2002, 699). Such identification occurs most easily between like-minded organizations, but may also take place between opponents who value particular skills or attributes like endurance, strategic thinking or creativity, even when they may be traditional opponents such as protesters and police.[3] Clearly, categorical boundaries of race, class or location within a particular relational context can make identification more difficult.

The relational context in the two cities made it easier for New York City activists to deliberate about the Seattle tactics than for their Toronto equivalents. However, relational contexts cannot explain all the variation between the two cities. One also needs to look at the influence of the organizational context on both deliberation and diffusion.

ORGANIZATIONAL CONTEXT

Some types of organizations thrive on deliberative conversations while others typically discourage them. Such an observation seems obvious; however, it has remained a marginal part of theorizing around deliberation and diffusion. Andrew H. Van de Ven and Everett Rogers (1988) argued that the intersection of organizations and innovations is a productive site for research (in Rogers 1995; 391). They argue that the characteristics of organizations influence their receptivity to innovations in a manner over and above the aggregate influence of individual members (ibid, 391). "Organizations are often seen in this research as constraints or resistances to innovations, at least to the extent that many problems are usually encountered in attempts to implement an innovation in an organization." (Van de Ven and Rogers 1988 in Rogers 1995, 391)

---

[3] L. A. Kauffman notes that by the time of the protests against the World Bank and IMF in April 2000, activists had adopted paramilitary lingo: tac (meaning tactical), com (meaning communication), scouts, and recon (meaning reconnaissance).

Earlier material offers some hints that help to explain why certain organizations were more open to the Seattle tactics than others. As Marshall Ganz argues, the strategic capacity of an organization is greater if "a leadership team includes insiders and outsiders, strong and weak network ties, and access to diverse, yet salient, repertoires of collective action" (Ganz 2000: 1005). Such organizations will deliberate more easily, and be more able to incorporate new practices. In contrast, research has found that formalized, bureaucratic and centralized organizations have a tendency to follow their routines, become instrumental and avoid risky innovations (Ekvall 1986, Weber 1947). Formalization is the degree to which an organization emphasizes rules and procedures for participants. The degree to which an organization is bureaucratic is measured by formalization (Rogers 1995; 377). Due to its emphasis on routine and hierarchy, formalization inhibits consideration of outside innovations but facilitates implementation (ibid., 380, Zmud 1982).

Researchers argue that a centralized institution's ability to incorporate innovations is due to the way that its resource levels and legitimacy facilitate trusting relationships with potential adopters (c.f. Tolbert and Zucker 1983). It may also be because centralized organizations are able to avoid factions and maintain continuity more easily than other organizations (Gamson 1975).

However, although such an organizational structure may facilitate adoption, its organizational identity as formal and hierarchical is likely to prevent organizations from considering the Seattle tactics as appropriate. Indeed, it was less hierarchical organizations in both Toronto and New York City that were interested in considering the Seattle tactics.

DELIBERATION IN TORONTO AND NEW YORK CITY

Deliberation and diffusion are facilitated and constrained by both the relational and organizational contexts of the two cities. In what follows, I outline how these contexts affected the willingness and ability of three organizations in Toronto and New York City to deliberate about and incorporate the Seattle tactics. To be clear, I'm not arguing that these tactics were more effective than previous ones or that organizations in Toronto, New York, or anywhere else *should* have incorporated them. Any tactic is only effective at particular times and in particular places. Instead of arguing that these different organizations should have adopted the Seattle tactics, I am interested in the *processes* that led some organizations to be able to consider incorporating and experimenting with them. I argue that the organizations who were most willing and able to incorporate the new tactics were also those who had an opportunity to discuss them in an open and reflexive manner among diverse participants with different perspectives. Most of the time, however, such deliberation was blocked due to historically rooted categorical inequalities and longstanding struggles for power in each city. These dynamics made identification with the Seattle protesters more difficult and experiments with their tactics less likely. This was particularly true in Toronto.

Deliberation was blocked in Toronto in four ways. The first way was tied to differences structured by racial and class inequalities rooted in national and local political economies. These differences meant that many activists saw themselves as different from the Seattle protesters, and thus were less interested in discussing or copying their tactics. They also meant that groups of activists of color, poor activists, middle class activists, and white activists were less likely to gather to discuss the Seattle tactics than were more homogenous, especially white and middle class groups. This dynamic operated in both New York and Toronto but was more significant in Toronto. I'll discuss this dynamic in Chapters 7 through 11.

The second reason deliberation was blocked in Toronto arose from the historical pattern of relationships among local organizations and alliances. In Toronto, the recent national history of movements against free trade and cutbacks to social spending that formed during the 1990s yielded a cluster of relatively strong unions, community organizations, and student associations that were used to organizing together. In Toronto, this enduring cluster of large, formal organizations dominated local protest networks. As Ganz (2000) would state it, these organizations had resources, but not resourcefulness. Due to their formal and somewhat risk averse orientation, these organizations didn't identify with the Seattle protesters and were (at least initially) uninterested in discussing or experimenting with their tactics. I'll discuss this in Chapters 5 and 6.

The third reason that deliberation about the Seattle tactics was blocked in Toronto was that local protest networks were not only centralized around a small number of organizations but also polarized between formal and relatively well-resourced organizations and a small cluster of direct action organizations. In the past, a competitive relationship had developed between these two poles. As a result, deliberation between activists on one side or the other was extremely unlikely. Indeed, Seattle's success hardened the boundary between the two clusters. This blocked deliberation about the Seattle tactics from occurring between the clusters as well as within them. I discuss this in Chapter 6.

The fourth reason that deliberation about the Seattle tactics became blocked in Toronto had to do with the influence of the police and courts. After some initial post-Seattle experiments, repression and the fear of repression constrained discussion and experimentation. By increasing the cost of protesting and by targeting (and thus isolating) groups considered uncooperative or unpredictable by police, repression worked to block identification and limit deliberation and diffusion. I look at this in Chapter 10.

For these four reasons, deliberation about the Seattle tactics was blocked in Toronto more than in New York. Without deliberation, Toronto activists were less able to consider, adapt, and experiment with the innovations.

Without deliberation, activists were more likely to simply reject the Seattle tactics and maintain the existing repertoire. Curiously, because a lack of deliberation also meant that adaptation was less possible; sometimes activists uncritically imitated activists they identified with, a practice known by activists as "tactical fetishism." Without adaptation to the local context, such emulation tended to be short-lived.

In sum: this project looks at the conditions that facilitated the diffusion of the Seattle tactics to social movement organizations in Toronto and New York City. I found that conversations among diverse potential adopters that were relatively reflexive and egalitarian were essential for successful diffusion. For diffusion to be successful, such conversations must allow participants to see themselves as similar in some way to previous users. The conditions for such deliberation are influenced by past and present patterns of interaction at the transnational, national, local, and organizational level. By looking at these conditions, we can understand why the Seattle tactics spread more effectively to activists in New York than they did to their Toronto equivalents.

Understanding the conditions under which tactics and practices diffuse among social movement organizations is important both theoretically and practically. Many activists want to better understand what conditions allow organizations and movements to be more strategic, effective, and sustainable. They want to know how to help their organizations take advantage of the most exciting tactics and strategies available. This analysis is intended to help to answer this question and better facilitate strategic, effective, and sustainable movements.

OUTLINE OF THE BOOK

This book asks why the Seattle tactics spread more easily to New York activists than to their Toronto equivalents. At first glance, one might assume that Toronto's activists would be the more likely adopters of the Seattle repertoire. They had a stronger recent history of direct action, a deeper engagement with global trade issues, and stronger, more well-resourced organizations fighting free trade and cutbacks to social programs. Nonetheless, New York activists experimented more with the Seattle repertoire than did their Toronto counterparts.

My research suggests that, where relatively equal and reflexive deliberation among diverse participants with different perspectives took place in organizations, so too did experimentation with the Seattle tactics. This finding offers a corrective to existing diffusion theory – and even diffusion theory that looks at diffusion among groups – because such theory often neglects the micro level interactions that underlie the reception of innovations, and the conditions that facilitate these interactions. By highlighting the importance of deliberation in diffusion, and by looking at how and where deliberation becomes blocked due to inequalities and perceptions of inequality in the relational context, I suggest that there are certain conditions that facilitate both deliberation and diffusion. In Chapter 2, I show the global wave of protest that was made visible by the Seattle protests. I look especially closely at the events that took place within the United States and Canada during this period in order to track the diffusion of five tactics within this wave. In the third chapter, I outline the history and use of these tactics. In Chapter 4, I introduce six direct action activist organizations who seemed likely to adopt the Seattle tactics and highlight its history and major activities. In order to deepen the comparison between Toronto and New York, I include one local, one student, and one anti-globalization organization from each city.

Chapter 5 looks at how the relational context in Toronto and New York City influenced diffusion. To do this, I analyze catalogs of all protest events covered in each city's major newspapers between 1998 and 2002 in order to evaluate differences in the locations, participation, issue orientation, targets, and tactics of protests in the two cities. Based on this analysis, I argue that the combination of fragmented political networks that isolated the cluster of direct action organizations from outside influences in New York ironically facilitated deliberation and experimentation with the Seattle tactics. In contrast, a small number of organizations dominated local protest networks in Toronto and limited deliberation about locally new innovations. As a result, New York activists were more likely than their Toronto counterparts to deliberate about the tactics and experiment with them locally.

Chapter 6 highlights how the relational context and the membership of local anti-globalization coalitions operating as opinion leaders influenced the reception of the Seattle tactics in each city. New York's Direct Action Network (DAN) and Toronto's Mobilization for Global Justice were the anti-globalization movement's local opinion leaders and flagship organizations. Drawing on meeting minutes, documents and press statements, interviews with organizers, and journal entries along with the event catalogs presented in Chapter 5, I argue that – because Toronto's Mobilization for Global Justice was operating in a more centralized context and was composed of larger, formal organizations – it was less interested in discussing the tactics and engaging in what were thought to be risky tactical experiments. In contrast, DAN-NYC was largely made up of small, informal, and marginal organizations with few comparable reservations. Counterintuitively, the organization with fewer resources was more willing and able to experiment with the new tactics.

Chapters 7 through 11 look at the form and content of the movement's deliberation and debates in the period immediately following the Seattle protests. I use the minutes from organizational meetings, journal entries, and archived listservs to explore how online and face-to-face deliberation facilitated reception of the Seattle tactics by allowing activists to redefine them and adapt them to local contexts. I analyze the relational and organizational context effected movement debates and evaluate how deliberative discussions about the Seattle tactics in Toronto and New York really were. Chapter 7 traces the debate around "summit hopping" and finds that that periods of deliberation were often brief and that they were threatened by a tendency toward polarization. When debates about summit hopping became polarized, deliberation ceased. At this point, the likelihood that the Seattle tactics would be adapted and adopted radically declined. I find that, although summit hopping was debated by activists in both cities, more deliberation took place among direct action activists in New York City than among their equivalents in Toronto. This deliberation facilitated New York activists' ongoing experiments with the Seattle tactics.

Chapter 8 examines the effect of the anti-globalization movement's debates about property destruction on the localization of black bloc tactics. I show how activist organizations in New York and Toronto formulated their own strategy by reacting to polarized discussions taking place both nationally and in nearby cities. Rooted in the relational and organizational contexts of their cities, this meant that although they avoided the divisiveness of movement debates about violence, they also blocked the local diffusion of the black bloc tactic and of coordinated property destruction to their organizations.

In Chapter 9, I look at how discussions about the identity of the Seattle protesters influenced discussions about the Seattle tactics in the two cities. Immediately after the Seattle protests, local activists in both Toronto and New York temporarily identified with the radical, militant, and creative character of the Seattle protesters. This identification facilitated deliberation and diffusion. However, influenced by the relational contexts and local histories, local activists gradually began to activate boundaries of race, class, and strategy in order to distance themselves from an "anti-globalization" identity of "white, student, anti-globalization activists." Unsuprisingly, this boundary activation reduced many activists' interest in discussing or experimenting with the Seattle tactics.

In Chapter 10, I look at the effect of police repression on deliberation. I highlight four incidents that activists in the two cities identified as having influenced their subsequent strategy and tactics. These incidents suggest that repression interrupted New York and Toronto activists' identification with the Seattle demonstrators in particular and the global justice movement more generally. They also show how repression impeded potential adopters' strategic capacity by reducing the availability of human and organizational resources and fragmenting relationships limiting the possibility for deliberation and diffusion.

In Chapter 11, I look at the way that the September 11 attacks on the World Trade Center and Pentagon interrupted the spread of the Seattle tactics. I show how a serious political shock to political and economic regimes can influence diffusion by forcing activists to re-articulate their identities and strategies for the new context. As a result of these discussions, many of the activists and organizations in New York and Toronto saw the post-9/11 moment as being significantly different from the one in which the Seattle tactics emerged. Practically speaking, this meant a partial retreat from confrontational direct action and a new emphasis on the problem of white dominance within the global justice movement. These conversations expedited the global justice movement's fragmentation and subsequently restricted its tactical influence on the emerging antiwar and immigrant rights movements.

In the last chapter, I conclude that it is a combination of external context and internal relationships that influence whether or not deliberation is possible, and how this affects social movement organizations' ability to reflect strategically and incorporate locally new tactics. Patterns of interaction among movement organizations and activists interrupted the diffusion of the Seattle tactics to New York and especially to Toronto by disrupting activists' ability to trust one another and to discuss, consider, and adapt the locally new tactics in reflexive and egalitarian ways. By being cognizant of the impediments to deliberation we can understand how and why tactics might fail to diffuse even if they are appropriate and potentially useful. For those interested in the building of creative, strategic, and successful social movements I finish by suggesting that categorical inequalities and struggles for power both inside and outside organizations can limit diffusion in ways that are sometimes unseen and unacknowledged.

MY POSITION AS A SCHOLAR ACTIVIST

By now it should be clear that I am not an objective observer studying these organizations from on high. I became an activist long before I decided to do this project. My research was influenced by this history and by my ties to many of these activists and organizations. I grew up in Toronto as a white, working class, suburban kid and lived there until I left to travel, work, and attend university. I returned to Toronto and lived there full-time between 1994 and 1998. During that time, I was active in a range of projects and campaigns against cuts to social spending, against free trade and neoliberalism, and promoting cycling, sustainable transportation, First Nations solidarity, prisoner support, cooperatives, and alternative media. When I returned to Toronto in 2003, I began attending actions organized by the Ontario Coalition Against Poverty (OCAP). I joined that organization after the first stage of this research was completed in 2004.

My partner worked with OCAP when I met him, and – like me – has been on the executive committee of the organization at various times. I have a less extensive relationship with OPIRG Toronto, although I've worked with many OPIRG activists on prison, community organizing, and sustainable transportation projects. Friends and housemates have been (and continue to be) staff, members, or on the Board of Directors.

After completing my first year of graduate school in New York, I returned to Toronto for the summer of 1999. During that summer, I was employed by OPIRG Toronto to develop the infrastructure for a student-run not-for-profit vegetarian cafe. When I returned to New York, I continued to get frequent updates about OPIRG's activities. Of the six organizations studied, I had the least direct contact with Toronto's Mobilization for Global Justice. The group was active while I was living in New York and, by the time I returned to Toronto, they had ceased meeting. I contacted them through their Web site, and asked my initial contacts to recommend other participants who had different perspectives to interview. Since then, I have worked with a number of key Mob4Glob organizers on campaigns including the recent mobilization against the G20. In this analysis, I rely on personal accounts, interviews with organizers, and associated documents.

After moving to New York in 1998, I became active in a number of organizations including Bronx United Gardeners, a community gardening group. While we were independent of More Gardens, both groups worked together on a citywide campaign to save New York's community gardens. As an individual, I participated in More Gardens! Coalition actions and events and socialized with its members. I became a member of New York's Direct Action Network from the time of its formation in 1999 until its collapse in 2002. I attended weekly three-hour meetings, participated in actions, and worked on various committees. Friends of mine were involved in the Student Liberation Action Movement at Hunter College. As a member of the Direct Action Network, I worked with SLAM in the August 1st Coalition that mobilized for protests against the Republican National Convention in Philadelphia in 2000. I began this project in 2002, at the end of my engagement with DAN-NYC, and at the end of the period studied here.

This "insider" position mostly benefits my research. Because of it, I had a better sense of the dynamics within each organization than I would have otherwise. This allowed me to select interviewees who represented a range of positions and perspectives. It also allowed me to engage in conversations to which outside researchers may not have had access. Movement concerns direct my questions. I hope this will make the results more useful for activists and more interesting. Because I am a participant as well as a researcher, and because I continue to be accountable to the activists I've studied, I believe I am less likely to distort either the interviews or my observations. I have shared an executive summary of the results of this research with the organizations and activists discussed here.

Of course, my position as an insider brings potentially negative consequences as well. My respondents may have been tempted to frame their answers to correspond to what they perceived my preferences or loyalties to be. Furthermore, my own perspective on tactics, goals, and organizational dynamics will inevitably influence my understanding of these organizations. I try to minimize these distortions by sampling a variety of activists and by drawing upon movement documents, secondary literature, and media coverage.

When I interviewed activists, I had to be aware of the significance that timing played in informing their perspectives. By the time I began my interviews (Sept – Dec 2003 in New York and Jan-March 2004 in Toronto), OCAP and OPIRG activists were already resistant to discussing the Seattle protests. For this reason, I emphasized the larger question of tactical decision making and ordered the questions so that discussion of the Seattle protests took place at the end of the interviews. Although most of the activists I know are not interested in diffusion as an abstract process, they are deeply interested in finding out what can make their actions more effective. Similarly, they recognize that there have been moments at which they have been more creative, more strategic, and more open to new ideas. I continue to write about these findings. They are intended to be useful for those interested in building stronger and more effective movements. For the full list of interview questions, see Appendix A.

This book is a comparative analysis of diffusion from a single point to six organizations in two cities in North America. However, analysis of the particularities of these two trajectories will be useful to scholars and activists interested in more general questions that seem particularly relevant given the wave of protest currently (2011) sweeping across world. Why is it that – at particular moments – successful high-profile protests will spark revolutions while at other times, they yield only disappointment? High-profile protests have sometimes been the stimulus for much larger and longer-lasting events. Speaking about the effect of the protests against the 1968 Democratic National Convention in Chicago, Jerry Rubin explained:

The year after Chicago, there were more demonstrations on college and high school campuses than any other year. And I would say it was directly and psychologically related to Chicago, the memory and myth of Chicago. People sang "I miss Chicago." There was a riot in Berkeley the week after Chicago. Chicago reached people through the media. It became a myth in their own heads, it became exaggerated way out of proportion. And they tried to act it out in their own situation thanks to Chicago. (Gitlin in Goodwin and Jasper 306)

While Rubin saw the impact of the Chicago protests being transmitted through psychological processes, this book looks to deliberative and relational dynamics to explain the effect of Seattle. After Seattle, many activists in North America felt like they could make a difference. Everything seemed possible. Activists believed that they had the creativity, the tactics, and the numbers that could make real systemic change (Thompson 2010). Unfortunately, while some small successes can be celebrated, the movement cannot claim to have deeply affected the global capitalist system. Eleven years later, it is obvious that – at least in North America – the cycle of protest identified with Seattle has waned. And yet, its trajectory has altered the landscape of direct action in Canada and the United States. Recent protests against of the Occupy movement are testament to this transformation. Although they are sometimes transformed, one continues to see aspects of tactics and forms of organization made famous in Seattle in many of these demonstrations.

This is not a postscript to recent movement history. It's a comparative analysis of a process that has happened before and continues to occur. In the past few years, we've seen the tactics of those opposing global neoliberalism spread to activists operating outside of the zones in which they emerged. In North Africa, the Middle East, Spain, and Greece we've seen pro-democracy movements experiment with the tactic of occupying public squares. And in the student protests across the United Kingdom, we have seen black bloc tactics, climate camps, and giant puppets. With each wave of protest, tactics and frames spread like that proverbial wildfire.

The form and content of decision making at meetings can have important implications for the power and potential of social movements. By limiting or speeding the spread of tactical innovations – whether they are barricades, bombs or banner drops – deliberative dynamics can push movements toward revolutionary challenges, or toward stagnation. Such an argument has implications for movements across time and space, but at a time where political innovations, symbols and slogans are spread at lightning speeds by electronic media and social networks among movements around the globe, the question of diffusion, and the dynamics that underlie it, have never seemed more relevant.

2

The Seattle Cycle: 1998–2002

Meeting, rallying, and marching – protest repertoires have remained relatively stable since the rise of the modern nation-state in Western Europe at the beginning of the nineteenth century (Tilly 1995, 1997). Those organizing the majority of public claims making efforts in democratic states select from a short list of tactics. However, as transnational institutions become more powerful, as new technologies burgeon, and as ties of collaboration and communication between domestic social movements across borders become denser, a new transnational regime emerges, and correspondingly, many observers suggest that a shift in repertoire may be underway. For many, the Seattle protests were emblematic of this shift, a shift toward network forms of organization and direct action. (Amoore 2005; McDonald 2006; Smith 2001a; Smith 2001b; Starr 2000; Tarrow 2005; Tarrow and Imig 2001; Tarrow and McAdam 2005; Wood and Moore 2002; Yuen, Katsiaficas, and Rose 2004).

In this chapter, I examine how the Seattle protests influenced protest tactics in Toronto and New York. We know that cycles of protest are tied to the diffusion of new or revitalized tactics (McAdam 1995; Tilly 1997). Periods of intense mobilization foster new coalitions, increase tactical innovation, and further the diffusion of innovative practices and tactics to new sites (Tarrow 1998, 146). During such periods, network relationships undergo sudden expansions in scale, density, and complexity (Ikegami 2005, 47). In contrast, periods of movement decline are associated with factionalization and institutionalization. During these periods, movements retreat into existing routine although, sometimes, these patterns are combined with brief experiments in militancy (Koopmans 1993). Similar patterns are evident when we look at the diffusion of the Seattle tactics and the cycle of protests' subsequent collapse.

Successful protests encourage sympathetic observers to test the limits of social control in their own sites (Tarrow 1998, 24). Such confrontations reveal authority's weak points and allow claimants to become aware of their strengths. They invite even timid social actors to align themselves with challenger or opponent (ibid., 24). Events like the Seattle demonstrations broadcast political opportunities and stimulate a wave of protest while boosting the diffusion of tactics and frames associated with the landmark event. In this way, the scale of protest shifts from a local event to the national or international arena (Tarrow 2005). In this way, the protests of 1999 in Seattle launched a wave of protest partly because the demonstrations were understood to be successful. Protesters in Seattle stopped delegates from attending planned WTO meetings and forced President Clinton to acknowledge that the protests caused the summit to end early. According to the *Seattle Weekly*, the protests "helped inspire Third World delegates to rebel against the U.S. party line and inspired hundreds of millions around the globe, including left-leaning governments in South America." All told, the event was "a shot in the arm that has led to further gridlock for the WTO and multilateral trade agreements. In the United States, the WTO protests created a debate where little debate had previously existed" (Parrish 2004). In the *San Francisco Chronicle*, Europe's chief trade commissioner Pascal Lamy argued that the street protests showed that the talks were in trouble. "I think what's happening outside has an influence on the negotiations. The U.S. position is even less possible after the demonstrations than before, because the public has social concerns that need to be addressed" (Collier 1999).

As a coordinated transnational actor, the global justice movement became visible to media outlets in the global north during the World Trade Organization's first meetings in 1998. Before this period, North American and European activists interested in global economic policy predominantly engaged in lobbying through nongovernmental organizations (NGO). A class of experts had emerged and worked to influence institutions like the United Nations, the World Bank, the International Monetary Fund, and regional transnational authorities like the European Union (Smith 2001b). Largely restricted to conferences and policy documents, such actions were rarely disruptive. As Rucht (2001) has noted, transnational social movements during this period were far less likely to use even routine protest tactics like public demonstrations than were their national social movement counterparts.

In 1998, however, meetings of international financial institutions became targets for "global days of action" against neoliberalism. Both locally rooted and globally coordinated, global days of action (made easier by increasing Internet use) facilitated networking and diffusion. The strategy of a global day of action (GDA) encouraged activists to connect local campaigns and issues to global targets and themes. "Calls" for days of action were distributed through online and offline social movement networks and the independent media. One such call announced worldwide protests on November 30, 1999, the second day of the WTO summit in Seattle. According to the call, the day of action:

Would be organized in a non-hierarchical way, as a decentralized and informal network of autonomous groups that struggle for solidarity and co-operation while employing non-authoritarian, grassroots democratic forms of organization. Each event or action would be organized autonomously by each group, while coalitions of various movements and groups could be formed at the local, regional, and national levels. A strategy that may be useful at the local level is that various groups co-operate in creating a surrounding atmosphere of carnival and festivity as a setting for their various actions (N30 Global Day of Action Collective 1999).

TABLE 2.1. *Global Days of Action against International Financial Institutions,*
1998–2001

Date	Summit Location	# events/cities protest
1. May 16–May 18, 1998	Group of 8 (16th) in Birmingham, WTO (18th), Geneva	43/41
2. June 18, 1999	Group of 8, Koln, Germany	58/54
3. November 30, 1999	WTO in Seattle, USA	111/97
4. September 26, 2000	IMF and World Bank in Prague, Czech Rep	98/88
5. Nov. 9 2001	WTO in Doha, Qatar	157/152
	TOTAL	467/432

Source: Wood 2004.

Even though global days of action are not new, the strategy has increased dramatically in use – both geographically and in terms of the range of issues addressed – as a result of expanding electronic communications networks and the growth of global institutions (Tilly and Wood 2008). Since 1998, various organizations and networks have called for global days of action on a wide range of topics. In the past year (2011), there have been global days of action against climate change, austerity budgets, corporate greed, the repression of Egyptian pro-democracy protesters, nuclear weapons, military spending and Israel's treatment of the Palestinians, to name only a handful. Over time, participation in global days of action has become broader and more diverse. Table 2.1 illustrates changes in the scale of global days of action between 1998 and 2002.[1]

Starting in 1998, activist networks called for global days of action to coincide with the meetings of international financial institutions. Although the number of cities mobilized for each event varied, activists in Toronto and New York consistently participated. The Ministerials of the WTO (GDA 1, 3, and 5) appear to have inspired the greatest level of mobilization, possibly as a result of the efforts of multiple networks seeking to take advantage

[1] This chapter uses activist reports of 467 contentious events, over the five days, collected from Internet sources. Contentious events are defined as gatherings of ten or more people – outside of formal government routines, in publicly accessible places, and making claims that, if realized, would affect the interests of their targeted object (Tilly 1995, 63). I included events if they affiliated themselves with a global day of action through speeches or signs, or if they submitted a report to those who compiled lists of the global day of action protest activities against transnational institutions. Events included rallies, a guerrilla attack on a police station, leafleting the public, marches, street parties, property destruction, street theater, civil disobedience, riots, occupations, banner hangs, and the disruption of offices, businesses, and streets. Organizational meetings or conferences were excluded. See a more detailed analysis of this data in Lesley Wood, 2004. "Breaking the Bank and Taking to the Streets" *Journal of World-Systems Research*. Special issue: "Global Social Movements Before and After 9/11," pp. 3–32.

of potential opportunities made possible by a relatively new institution. Participating events took place on all continents, and although the majority of demonstrations (69 percent) took place in Europe, the United States, and Canada, the largest events took place in Asia and Latin America.

The protests that took place on these global days of action were linked through a number of social movement networks. Newly formed or significantly strengthened by the advent of electronic communication, these networks allowed activists to work together and communicate more easily (della Porta and Tarrow 2006b). Even before the Seattle protests, activists in the United States and Canada were learning about new tactics and developing shared identities through these networks. Reclaim the Streets (RTS) stands as perhaps the perfect example of a key player in this emerging movement. RTS London was the Western European convener for the Zapatista-inspired, anti-neoliberal People's Global Action network. Consequently, the organization had contacts with social movement organizations worldwide. Starting in 1995, RTS organized illegal carnivalesque street parties in the United Kingdom to draw links between neoliberalism, environmental concerns, and the politics of urban space. Between 1995 and 1998, the "street party as protest" tactic spread rapidly from activists in the UK to those in Canada and the United States, including those in Toronto and New York City. After the success of the first anti-neoliberal global day of action in 1998, Reclaim the Streets London called for "Carnival Against Capitalism" actions to take place on a global day of action called for June 18, 1999. Although the call for action did not explicitly request that the street party tactic be used, it brokered new ties by linking activists in different cities and provided communication and information channels that enabled many protestors to experiment with its use. The Reclaim the Streets network was also one of the channels through which the disruptive tactic of "Critical Mass" bicycle rides spread from San Francisco (where it began in 1992) to cities throughout North America and beyond. At the same time, the Jubilee 2000 network was working to diffuse the "debt chain" tactic (in which activists encircle and join hands around international financial summits) to activists internationally. All three tactics became part of the cluster that would be associated with Seattle and known to activists in Toronto and New York City.

The global networks underlying the Seattle wave of protest included the International Confederation of Free Trade Unions (ICFTU),[2] Jubilee 2000,[3]

---

[2] The most established global network in our data is the ICFTU, which was set up in 1949 and as of 2001 had 231 affiliated organizations in 150 countries and territories on all five continents, with a membership of 158 million. The events organized primarily by ICFTU make up approximately 10 percent of our dataset.

[3] Jubilee 2000 emerged from religious communities in 1996 and its petition gathered 24 million signatures from more than 60 countries. Its main goal was the cancellation of debts of the poorest countries by the year 2000. Since that time, as Jubilee South, it has expanded its focus and works more generally against neoliberalism. Jubilee 2000 can be identified in the public leadership of approximately 3% of our events.

ATTAC (Association pour la Taxation des Transactions financière et l'Aide aux Citoyens),[4] and People's Global Action (PGA).[5] Each network had its own goals, tactics, targets, ideology, and culture. In the United States and Canada, ICFTU and PGA were the most visible global networks tied into the Seattle protests. Their ideological and tactical orientations both facilitated and constrained the spread of the Seattle tactics. In general, ICFTU members in Canada and the United States engaged in marches, rallies, and work stoppages targeting international financial institutions, while PGA activists were more likely to target local corporations using direct action. Along with national and regional networks like Public Citizen, 50 Years Is Enough, and Global Exchange, these groups constructed some of the relational links that would underlie the global justice movement in Canada and the United States.

Looking at global days of action protests in Canada and the United States reveals an increasingly broad wave of contention. Until September 11, 2001, participation in each of the global days of action increased in size and breadth. Each fostered innovation and diffusion of direct action tactics and forms of organization. Nine U.S. and Canadian cities participated in the first global day of action in 1998. A year later, fourteen cities participated. By the time of the anti-WTO protests in Seattle, thirty cities participated and, nine months later, thirty-seven cities participated in protests against the IMF and World Bank. After September 11, the number of cities shrank to twenty-three during the actions against the WTO from November 9 through 11, 2001. This trajectory is similar in both countries, with the exception that – in the United States – confusion and repression demobilized activists more dramatically after the attacks on the World Trade Center. The global days of action data only show the rough outline of the wave of protest as manifested by the summit protests. As I'll show in Chapter 5 local grassroots protest was following a similar trajectory. First, however, I want to turn to the protests most identified with this wave of protest, the demonstrations against the World Trade Organization that took place at the end of 1999.

[4] Founded in 1998 by Bernard Cassen and Susan George of the socialist monthly Le Monde Diplomatique, ATTAC (Association pour la Taxation des Transactions financière et l'Aide aux Citoyens) formed an international organization in 1999. By 2001, ATTAC had established local chapters in more than thirty countries (primarily in Europe) and included 80,000 members. The network worked in alliance with the labor movement and used marches and creative nonviolent protest to work toward the democratic control of financial markets and their institutions. The events organized primarily by ATTAC make up 16% of the dataset.

[5] Launched in 1998 in Geneva, the PGA is a decentralized collaboration that has no formal membership, but linked existing organizations that have endorsed the hallmarks. In 2000, the network was active in approximately forty countries, particularly in Latin America, Asia, and Europe. Participants include well-known movements including the Sandinistas, Zapatistas, Philippine, Brazilian, and Indian Peasant Movements and the European direct action movement including Britain's Reclaim the Streets and Italy's Ya Basta. The demonstrations organized by groups identified as part of the PGA (through inclusion on the PGA Web page) make up 53% of our dataset. http://www.nadir.org/nadir/initiativ/agp/en/index.html. Accessed November 30, 2011.

THE SEATTLE PROTESTS

November 30, 1999, the second day of the Seattle protests, was the third global day of action against an international financial institution. When news of the successful disruption of the World Trade Organization's meetings began to spread, a wide range of activists became interested (Danaher and Barbach 2000; Hardt 2002; Shepard and Hayduk 2002; Smith and Johnston, 2002; Wood and Moore 2005; Yuen et al., 2004). The energy unleashed by these protests was something like what George Katsiaficas (1987) described as the "eros effect" of the 1968 global wave of protest - stimulating protest worldwide.

Because the story of Seattle is well-known, the following account will highlight the networks and movement entrepreneurs that made it such a successful transmitter of the direct action tactics under review here. Shortly after the World Trade Organization announced that it would hold its Ministerial Summit in Seattle, Washington, international, national, regional, and local groups began to mobilize. Some of these organizations had worked on trade issues for years. Others had worked on labor, environment, or human rights issues that would be impacted by WTO decisions.

The groundwork for the anti-WTO mobilization in Seattle had been laid under particular circumstances. It began in 1995, when labor and environmental groups began to painstakingly build alliances in coalitions like the Alliance for Sustainable Jobs and the Environment (Rose 2000). Local Teamsters and International Longshore and Warehouse Union (ILWU) activists had long been committed to a politics that went beyond traditional "bread and butter" workplace issues. For example, on May 1, 1999, the ILWU staged a one-day walkout in support of political prisoner Mumia Abu Jamal. Anarchist networks were also significant. In June 1999, anarchists in nearby Eugene, Oregon, held a conference and affiliated themselves with the People's Global Action and Reclaim the Streets networks. They held a Reclaim the Streets protest targeting corporations to coincide with the second global day of action. The event ended in clashes and property destruction, with police arresting fifteen activists and deploying teargas. For years, the Pacific Northwest had also been home to networks of radical environmentalists organizing against destructive logging. Because of their links to Earth First!, many of these activists had acquired direct action and blockading skills. The convergence of these different networks would provide a context rich in possibility.

Another factor that proved to be important was Seattle's proximity to Vancouver, Canada. In 1997, activists there had mobilized against meetings of the Asian Pacific Economic Community (APEC). In a federally directed attempt to limit visible demonstrations, police came down hard on protesters by using pepper spray and even abducting a key organizer.[6] The subsequent political

---

[6] Pepper spray was increasingly used as restraining technique by police during the mid-1990s. In Ottawa, the rate of pepper spray use by the local force jumped from 61 incidents in 1996 to 111 in 1997 (Anderson 1998).

and media furor resulted in a federal investigation, increased militancy on the part of activists and increased interest in targeting the summits of international trade agreements. The history of struggles against free trade in Canada also ensured that Canadians were present in disproportionate numbers at the Seattle protests. According to Mark Lichbach, Canadians made up almost 10 percent of the demonstrators (2003). This was in part a result of infrastructural support and public education provided by more activist-oriented trade unions like the Canadian Union of Postal Workers and the Canadian Union of Public Employees.[7] Veterans of the anti–free trade campaigns in Canada, these unions were experienced in showing the links between trade issues, jobs, and social spending. They organized a traveling caravan that visited twenty-one Canadian cities to promote the protests in the months before Seattle.

By 1998, political networks were beginning to coordinate in new ways. Studies of political networks suggest that social movement practices shift when the patterns of relationships in which they are engaged become altered (Gould 1995; Mische 2003; Steinberg 1999b). By 1998, two such shifts occurred. First, although they traditionally had different targets, some issue-based networks focused on poverty, the environment, and labor began to see that their interests were shared and started targeting international financial institutions, including the World Trade Organization. Second, local and national social movements began to collaborate more frequently across national boundaries, sometimes forming new networks. Facilitated by the Internet, both types of collaboration contributed to the configuration of social movement networks within the global day of action on November 30, 1999.

In addition to these local, labor, and NGO networks, anarchist networks have – since the end of the Cold War – become increasingly important to Canadian and U.S. protest politics. These networks were actively involved in the Seattle protests and include those linking radical Food Not Bombs food provision projects, which had contacts in more than 20 Canadian and 200 U.S. cities (2006 figures). Other networks included those developed to provide solidarity with the Zapatistas, Anti-Racist Action (which had chapters in twenty cities across Canada and the United States in 2006), and bicycle activists participating in monthly Critical Mass bicycle rides (which, by the summer of 1997, were taking place in thirty-six cities in the United States, and five cities in Canada) (Carlsson et al. 1997). Networks between anarchists made possible by the Active Resistance conferences in Chicago (1996) and Toronto (1998) were also important. At both events, the groundwork for Seattle was laid. The Chicago conference featured CounterMedia, a precursor to activist-led Indymedia web networks. At both conferences, activists from the Art and Revolution Network provided training in radical puppetry techniques to activists from across Canada and the United States.

---

[7] The Canadian Union of Postal Workers (CUPW) acted as the secretariat and mailing address for the People's Global Action Network.

In the lead-up to Seattle, these activists began to shift away from routinized protest tactics, which had begun to feel increasingly banal and ineffective. These experiments reflected a desire to impact the targets of demonstrations in real ways. As one Toronto activist I interviewed explained:

Movements in the eighties felt like they couldn't win. That they were diminishing, and that they were going to lose. I think the nineties was a decade where a lot of movements spent overcoming that, and rebuilding the use of tactics that were based on winning, not just either accommodating the state or feeling good about yourself. And I think that Seattle was the culmination of that work.

Like earlier summit protests, the Seattle demonstrations acted as a hothouse for tactical innovation by bringing together networks and organizations. Forming the core of direct action organizing in Seattle, the Direct Action Network brought together activists from anarchist, environmental, antinuclear, feminist, anti-sweatshop, queer, community arts, and other networks. When on the day of action on November 30, 1999, the Direct Action Network and others successfully disrupted the summit, they all celebrated their success.

Panicked, Seattle Mayor Paul Schell proclaimed a civil emergency. On the morning of December 1, he created a militarized zone around the summit. Any sign, symbol, or activity that suggested dissent was not allowed in this zone (ACLU 2000). Police attempts to limit protest escalated both inside and outside of the zone and hundreds of people were arrested and teargassed and had plastic projectiles fired at them. Some were beaten.

Mainstream coverage of the events was extensive and featured regular comparisons to the protests of the 1960s (Friedman 1999; Gumbel 1999; Working 1999). After a long hiatus, street protest was heralded as "back" in the United States. According to a Factiva search of international news media between November 20 and December 5, 1999, more than 2,000 newspaper articles mentioned the protests. This mass media coverage helped information about the protests to spread widely. As well, alternative and independent media spread the news. The activist Indymedia Center became a key transmitter of protest information. A collaborative effort of alternative and independent media organizations and activists, Indymedia also became a physical hub from which media activists published a daily newspaper and hosted a Web site with text and audio segments and live streaming radio and video. The Web site logged more than two million hits and was featured on America Online, Yahoo, CNN, BBC Online, and numerous other sites (Indymedia 2011). Some of this material was later used to create video documentaries including "This is What Democracy Looks Like" and "The Battle in Seattle." In the weeks after Seattle, protest participants returned home and gave presentations about their experiences. Activist, advocacy, policy, and policing organizations hosted events to discuss what should happen "after Seattle." There was a sense that – locally, nationally, and globally – the landscape for protest had changed. As one Toronto activist explained, "There was a buzz and excitement about what was possible to do in an urban landscape with a mass protest against a bank, a multinational. And people were psyched and people were pumped and there was a collective bolstering of confidence." The stage was set for activists across the United States and Canada to try to replicate the successes of Seattle in their own local arenas.

THE SEATTLE WAVE IN CANADA AND THE UNITED STATES

The Seattle protests were influential worldwide; however, they were especially influential for activists in Canada and the United States because they lived in cities that were more similarly positioned in relation to national and transnational authorities than were activists on other continents.[8] Their histories and political economies meant similar types of regimes. As a result, activists in Canada and the United States were more likely to see themselves as similar to the Seattle protesters than activists on other continents. Activists in Canada and the United States were also more deeply affected by the protests because there were denser ties between themselves and the protesters in Seattle than activists in other countries. Finally, the protests were more influential on activists in Canada and the United States than they were on others because the preexisting repertoires of protest in Canada and the United States were more similar to those used in Seattle than were the repertoires used elsewhere. As a result of all these conditions, direct action activists in Canada and the United States were more likely to identify with the Seattle activists and to change their tactics after the Seattle protests than were direct action activists elsewhere. This becomes apparent when looking at the global days of action data shown in Figure 2.1. There, one can see that in the global day of action after the Seattle protests, there was an increase in the use of black bloc, blockades, puppetry tactics at global day of action protests in U.S. and Canadian cities, at least until the attacks on the World Trade Center on September 11, 2001.[9]

The diffusion of the Seattle tactics pushed the wave of protest. Between 1998 and 2002, this wave rose and fell most dramatically in Canada and the United States. Even immediately after the Seattle protests, receptivity to the Seattle tactics was not homogenous or universal. As I discuss in subsequent chapters, relational and organizational contexts, helped to explain why direct

---

[8] The pattern I found in the targets of global days of action protest in earlier work confirms this finding. I found that activists in countries that are part of the core of neoliberal institutions, those countries that have a "structurally equivalent" position in relation to the WTO, and the group of eight most powerful governments are most likely to target corporations. Of course, the mere existence of ties does not result in similarity. This process also depends on active interpretation by participants. I will explain more about this in Chapters 7 through 11.

[9] Jail solidarity was not tracked globally because it was a tactic that took place after the protests were over, and was frequently not included in activist or media coverage of the protest events.

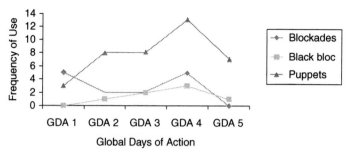

FIGURE 2.1. Seattle Tactics at Global Days of Action in United States and Canada.

action activists in New York were more willing to deliberate about and experiment with the Seattle tactics than their Toronto equivalents. Before considering these patterns of diffusion, however, it is necessary to consider the tactics themselves and to familiarize ourselves with the organizations most likely to adopt them.

3

The Seattle Tactics

At the protests against the World Trade Organization in Seattle, activists formed black blocs, engaged in jail solidarity, built and marched with giant puppets, blockaded roads and buildings, danced at street parties, rode in Critical Mass bike rides, performed Radical Cheers, and used affinity groups and spokescouncils to make decisions. After these protests ended, many of these tactics spread to activists across the world. Although none of these tactics was new, each was reinvigorated as a result of its association with activist successes in Seattle. In what follows, I consider the diffusion of black bloc, giant puppets, blockades, and jail solidarity to activists in six Toronto- and New York-based organizations. I have selected these tactics because they were each clearly associated with the Seattle protests and because activists used them at subsequent protests associated with the antiglobalization or global justice movements. I also chose them because, as a result of their drama and novelty, they were the tactics most likely to be referred to by activists in media and protester reports.

BLACK BLOC

As a set of street tactics, black bloc involves dressing in black and masking one's face (often with a black bandanna), moving in tightly packed groups, and protecting members of the group from police encroachment through evasive maneuvers. The rationale of black bloc is to avoid arrest, to inspire other participants, and to raise the cost of "doing business" for corporations or governments through disruption or property destruction. Tactics sometimes include spray painting or breaking windows and throwing Molotov cocktails at targets. They also sometimes include defensive maneuvers like "unarresting" or freeing protesters from police custody.

Originating in Germany in antifascist and autonomous movements of the 1980s, black bloc tactics spread to North America through the antifascist/antiracist network of Anti-Racist Action (ARA). They first appeared in the United States in 1991 during anarchist-affiliated protests against the Gulf War and in protests against Columbus Day in San Francisco. In Canada, the tactic was first used by Anti-Racist Action protesters in Toronto who took part in a citywide day of action against the Provincial Conservatives in 1996. ARA activists also used the tactic during a march against local Holocaust denier Ernst Zundel. Despite these initial experiments, the black bloc remained rare in Canada and the United States until it was popularized by the Seattle protests (Dupuis-Deri, 2003). In Seattle, a section of the black bloc explained their rationale in a communiqué released shortly after the action, where they argued:

When we smash a window, we aim to destroy the thin veneer of legitimacy that surrounds private property rights. At the same time, we exorcize that set of violent and destructive social relationships which has been imbued in almost everything around us. By "destroying" private property, we convert its limited exchange value into an expanded use value. A storefront window becomes a vent to let some fresh air into the oppressive atmosphere of a retail outlet (at least until the police decide to tear-gas a nearby road blockade)…. After N30, many people will never see a shop window or a hammer the same way again. The potential uses of an entire cityscape have increased a thousand-fold. The number of broken windows pales in comparison to the number of broken spells – spells cast by a corporate hegemony to lull us into forgetfulness of all the violence committed in the name of private property rights and of all the potential of a society without them. Broken windows can be boarded up (with yet more waste of our forests) and eventually replaced, but the shattering of assumptions will hopefully persist for some time to come. (Acme [ACME] Collective 1999)

The tactics prompted a flurry of debate, and this debate furthered the spread of information about the tactic. After Seattle, activists used black bloc tactics more frequently at protests against international financial institutions and policies in cities across Europe, North America, New Zealand, and Australia. Despite the increasing frequency of its use, the black bloc only appeared at a small proportion of demonstrations. Of the 467 protests that took place during the global days of action, black bloc tactics were only used at 18. The tactic's spread was most obvious in Canada and the United States where, in the months following Seattle, black blocs appeared at protests in cities including Washington, DC; Columbus, Ohio; Los Angeles, California; New York City; Chicago, Illinois; Toronto; and Montreal.

For some protesters, the black bloc tactics became a part of protest in a number of North American cities, at least in the context of large, militant actions. In 2010, there was a large black bloc at the protests against the G20 in Toronto and at protests against the Olympics in Vancouver. Protests against the 2008 Republican National Convention (RNC) similarly involved a black bloc. When asked whether the black bloc would be at the Republican National Convention protests, event organizers put the following response on their Web site: "Black blocking is a tactic, not a group, association, or corporation. Black blockers dress alike in order to minimize the targeting of individuals. Insofar as they further our struggles for autonomy, peace, and liberation, we stand for black bloc tactics" (RNC Welcoming Committee 2007). More than a decade after Seattle, black bloc tactics continue to occasionally be used in large protests in Canada and the United States – including the 2011 Oakland protests called by the Occupy movement; however, its form and features have often been adapted to the local context.

PUPPETS

The protests in Seattle are often associated with giant puppets. The puppets were used to communicate protestor demands in an accessible, nonthreatening way. A number of street puppetry troupes built puppets for the Seattle protests. Some of these troupes were linked through the Art and Revolution Network. That network began in Chicago during the 1996 Active Resistance anarchist gathering that coincided with protests against the Democratic National Convention. Inspiration for the tactic arose in part from the activities of Vermont's longstanding Bread and Circuses puppetry group and the Wise Fool Puppet Intervention from the San Francisco Bay Area, both who had been training Canadian and U.S. activists in puppetry techniques for years.

When asked about the use of puppetry in protest, Wise Fool Puppet Intervention's David Solnit explained:

It was an effort to find new language and use culture to articulate ideas and inspire ourselves and other people. The key is to bring creativity into movements so the point is not to expand a predictable formula and go, "Yeah, okay, now we add puppets into the predictable formula," but to be like a boxer, to always be on our toes and find new ways of doing things. Puppets are one way but there are a million others. (Renz 2005)

Puppetry was mentioned in almost 25 percent of protest reports on the global day of action protests (107/467) (Wood 2004; 2005). It was found primarily in Europe, Canada, the United States, New Zealand, and Australia. Like the other tactics, puppetry's popularity increased immediately after Seattle and declined again after the attacks on September 11, 2001. During this period, activists in New York and Toronto – especially those concerned about public space, community gardens, corporate power, and police brutality – experimented with puppets.

A few years ago, giant puppets began to be mocked by activists who decried their use as cliché and associated them with the now "old" Global Justice Movement. Today, although activists in some cities continue to use puppets, they are rarer. In the summer of 2011, environmental activists in Salt Lake City used them to mock a court decision they disagreed with – but I found few other examples before the wave of protest associated with the Occupy movement.

LOCKBOX BLOCKADES

Blockades may simply involve activists holding onto each other to form "soft blocks." At other times, activists lock their bodies to each other or to objects to form "hard blocks." Although blockading tactics have a long history, the "hard blockade" version I am interested in here emerged from the radical environmental movement, and especially Earth First!, which gained popularity through antilogging campaigns in the Western United States during the 1990s. The tactic was promoted by the Ruckus Society, which was formed by Greenpeace veterans in 1995, and held camps where activists could receive training in how to blockade a target. The Direct Action Network, which coordinated much of the direct action in Seattle, was formed at such a camp in 1999.

The tactic is also associated with the carnivalesque Reclaim the Streets movement in England. Reclaim the Streets activists used lockboxes to blockade roads during mid-1990s. Animal rights activists in the United Kingdom also used them to disrupt businesses that sell fur and other animal products (No Compromise 1999). In Seattle, hard blockades featuring lockboxes were used to block WTO delegate vehicles from entering the convention site area. Lockboxes come in different styles. Recounting protests against the August 2000 Republican National Convention in Philadelphia, one activist described lockboxes used there in the following manner:

In this case, they were four-inch PVC pipe, though stronger ones are made with metal. A metal rod had been drilled through the pipe, and the blockaders chained their arms to the rod. (A small karabiner made up one link in the chain, just in case the blockader needed to get out fast.) Chicken wire was wrapped around the pipe, and the whole contraption was covered in duct tape. The only way that the police can remove people from this is to saw through the pipe. The chicken wire means that the police will need to use heavy-duty saws. (Josiahag 2000)

After successfully keeping delegates out of the Seattle summit meetings, the blockading tactic spread. During global days of action between 1998 and 2002, some form of hard blockade was used at events in Europe, North America, New Zealand, and Australia. Forty-five protest events within the global days of action catalogue mentioned using some form of blockade, although most were not lock boxes.

Activists in Canada and the United States (including those in New York) experimented with lockboxes in the months following Seattle. In February 2000, New York activists (some of whom had attended the Seattle demonstrations) used lockboxes to defend a Puerto Rican community garden in the Lower East Side. In Toronto, only environmental activists connected to Earthroots have used lockboxes, and that was in 1996.

According to media coverage, in the last six months of 2011, lockboxes were only used in an anti–gas pipeline protest in Montana. Their use appears to have declined since the beginning of 2008 when they were found in Boston, Massachusetts; rural North Carolina; Florida; Pittsburgh, Pennsylvania; Minnesota; Vermont; Montreal, Canada; and San Francisco, California.

JAIL SOLIDARITY

Jail solidarity is a set of tactics in which protesters refuse to cooperate with authorities during arrest and processing. This noncooperation may include collective decision making to formulate demands, physical noncooperation like going limp, the withholding of identification to defy processing and release procedures, and impromptu annoyance tactics like singing badly (Thompson 2007). This noncooperation has a number of goals, including symbolically denying the legitimacy of – and actually disrupting the functioning of – the police and courts, protecting more vulnerable arrestees by keeping the group together, building a shared identity, reducing the severity of charges faced by protesters, and gaining access to lawyers or medical care.

One pamphlet explains the way this solidarity works:

> The leverage for solidarity arises because jails and courts, in order to run smoothly, rely on people to be passive and obedient. Jails expect prisoners to get in line and march where they're told. Courts expect defendants to sit quietly and give up their right to trial. Neither of these systems is set up to deal with large, organized groups of people who simply say, "No, I won't." So when people non-cooperate and negotiate as a group, the authorities may be forced to agree to their demands. (Just Cause 2004)

These tactics have been used in various forms for years in the United States and, to some extent, in Canada (most recently in the antinuclear movement of the 1980s). Activists with ties to this movement in the Midnight Special Legal Collective did legal support in Seattle and heavily promoted the tactic to protesters there. Jail solidarity was cited by activist trainers with the Ruckus Society as the reason that so many activists arrested at the Seattle demonstrations and, at subsequent demonstrations against the IMF and World Bank in Washington DC, were released without charges. In the period following the Seattle protests, activists experimented with the tactic at mass demonstrations across North America. Activists from New York and Toronto had the opportunity to participate in many of these demonstrations.

The police quickly learned to limit the disruptiveness of the tactic by separating activists and detention using larger facilities. By the end of the summer of 2000, the noncooperation aspects of jail solidarity ceased to be effective in achieving activist demands of release, reduced charges, or better treatment. Consequently, activist legal trainers in Toronto and New York stopped instructing activists to refuse to give their names; although, over the next ten years in both New York and Toronto, a small number of activists arrested at protests continued to engage in jail solidarity by refusing to identify themselves. By 2011, jail solidarity that involves refusing to identify oneself had almost completely disappeared in Canada and the United States.

Are the Tactics a Cluster?

Activists formed black blocs, blockaded doorways and roads, built and displayed puppets, and – once arrested – engaged in jail solidarity at the Seattle demonstrations. Each tactic became associated with those successful protests, and this association facilitated their spread. The success of those protests helped activists to transcend the divisions – and, indeed, antagonism – between the users of black bloc and the users of some of the other tactics in Seattle. This doesn't mean that the tactics were all subsequently used together. Nor can it be said that they always appealed to the same activists. Nevertheless, accounts of the Seattle protests bound the tactics together and, for the months following the event, subsections of protesters in New York, New Jersey, Toronto, and elsewhere attempted to use them in concert. These activists often referred to the tactics themselves as the "Seattle model." As time passed, protesters tended to incorporate some, but not all, of the tactics. They were less likely to be used at events that were seen as being unlike the Seattle protests in size, diversity, or focus.

Activists adapted these tactics to suit the contexts in which they found themselves. As I have noted, black blocs became black and pink blocs in Prague and "snake marches" in Toronto and New York City. The meaning of jail solidarity initially became narrower before coming to denote general support for those in jail. Blockading tactics changed in both their content and their use. As time passed, and as activists discussed and experimented with the tactics in new locations, additional tactics became identified with the cluster. At times, divisions between users of the different tactics became more pronounced.

Today, the Seattle protests are receding into collective memory. Mobilized around war and occupation, around immigrant rights, poverty, corporate greed or austerity many new activists see the Seattle protest wave as ancient history. The tactics are now associated with the antiglobalization movement rather than the Seattle protests. Gradually, the tactical cluster of tactics dissolves.

For a brief period of time, however, activists in New York and Toronto seemed particularly likely among their North American counterparts to experiment with the tactics – but there was some difference between the two cities. In neither city did the four tactics become widely accepted. However, in the post-Seattle period, activists in New York repeatedly experimented with all four tactics, whereas activists in Toronto only experimented in any significant way with puppetry, and even then, it was to a much lesser extent than in New York city. This difference can partly be explained by the relationships amongst social movement organizations, communities, and authorities within each urban context.

4

The Organizations Most Likely to Adopt

There were six organizations in Toronto and New York that seemed particularly likely to adopt the Seattle tactics. The four that had predated the Seattle protests had all used disruptive direct action in the previous two years. All six had some similarities with the Seattle protesters: They involved young people, were relatively new, and were critical of capitalism. To compare the diffusion of the Seattle tactics to the two cities, I selected an organization that primarily focused on local issues and targets, a student organization, and an organization that opposed international financial institutions. Despite these similarities, the organizations varied with respect to their issues, targets, memberships, and organizational structures.

NEW YORK ORGANIZATIONS

More Gardens! Coalition

A local organization dedicated to defending New York's community gardens, the More Gardens! Coalition, has organized demonstrations, festivals, and fundraisers since 1999. Seen by many as the direct action wing of a larger community garden movement, the group has – especially since 2000 – also engaged in community organizing, lobbying, and educational work. The More Gardens! Coalition formed in response to Mayor Rudolph Giuliani's attempt to sell off the community gardens private citizens had developed in the vacant lots since the 1970s. Active throughout the city, "More Gardens!" was most visible in Manhattan's rapidly gentrifying Lower East Side where the organization became well known for its struggle to defend the Esperanza Garden. Esperanza, which had been developed by local residents for more than a decade, was one of the most active community gardens in the area. The city first threatened the garden in August 1999 when it offered to sell it to a real estate developer. The struggle gained prominence when activists built a hollow fifteen-foot tall coqui frog, a native species of Puerto Rico, in the garden as a symbol of the struggle (Mikalbrown 2002, 230). Supporters began to camp out in the garden (and in the frog) despite the winter weather. By Valentine's Day 2000 (shortly after the Seattle protests), 150 community members had gathered to defend the garden. Many of these people used lockboxes similar to those made famous at demonstrations in Seattle. By the time the garden was bulldozed and thirty-one people were arrested, the More Gardens! Coalition activists had become front-page news (Will 2003).

The same day the developer bulldozed the Esperanza Garden, New York's Attorney General declared a temporary stay against any further destruction of community gardens. More Gardens then worked to get a public referendum on whether the community gardens should be made permanent and part of the city's Parks and Recreation properties. Although it managed to collect 20,000 signatures, it was still short of the required number. Consequently, the referendum did not proceed to the public. Although the majority of gardens have now been saved in part to the contributions from a private trust, More Gardens! Coalition continues to defend those under threat.

Between 1999 and 2002, the group had a small but stable core of two or three volunteer organizers, a fluctuating membership of ten to twenty active members, and many more supporters. Gardeners across the city took part in meetings when their gardens were threatened. Mostly young and white – and often identifying with anarchist, punk, and hippie subcultures – More Gardens! Coalition members acted in support of the predominantly African American and Latino gardeners. The active membership met once every two weeks at potluck dinners in the Lower East Side in order to discuss issues and make decisions about ongoing campaigns using a process of informal consensus. Between meetings, many members were actively involved in the gardens they sought to defend.

Because of its connections to the radical environmental movements that influenced the Seattle demonstrations, More Gardens! Coalition had experimented with puppetry and blockading in small ways before the Seattle protests. On April 11, 1999, Reclaim the Streets – NYC held an illegal street party on New York City's Broadway aimed in part at drawing attention to the struggle to defend community gardens.

More Gardens! Coalition members participated in the Seattle protests and were enthusiastic about the energy that erupted afterward. One member explained: "I think what happened in Seattle was really inspiring and people took a lot from that and got a lot of energy and inspiration and ideas were totally spread around at Seattle." Another member argued that Seattle had brought energy to local campaigns: "The movement against globalization brought a lot more people our way. A lot of the people that started to move around the planet to stop globalization would end up here. And they needed a place, and More Gardens would provide the place and they would get fired up about the gardens."

After Seattle, with an influx of new people, the scale and nature of More Gardens! tactics shifted. These activists began to use puppetry and blockading in a more confrontational way. The group became local experts in the use of these tactics and shared them with activists in other movements. During this period, More Gardens ! Coalition used a number of strategies, which ranged from lobbying local politicians to stop the destruction of particular gardens to occupying and dressing as plants and insects as it disrupted meetings of City Council and its various committees. A promotional pamphlet issued by the group around 2002 includes sections on community organizing, media work, puppetry, and civil disobedience. As its mission statement explains: "By using fundamental democratic tools such as community garden sponsored voter registration drives, legislative strategies, judicial actions and direct action, we shall reclaim our government and eventually affect its highest levels" (More Gardens! Coalition, undated). Newspaper coverage of protests in New York between 1998 and 2002 reveals that the *New York Times* often identified More Gardens! by name when reporting on its protests; however, it also identified these activists as garden supporters, protesters, and community activists. Since 2003, the organization has partly shifted its emphasis away from direct action and toward community consultation, education, media work, and lobbying.

Student Liberation Action Movement

The Student Liberation Action Movement (SLAM) was based at Hunter College in the City University of New York (CUNY) and at other public universities in New York City. Intentionally created as a women of color-led student organization, SLAM's main task has been to fight budget cuts and tuition hikes at CUNY. It has also fought to increase welfare rates, to develop and fund ethnic studies programs, to fight police brutality, and to oppose the police presence on campus. The group emerged out of a campaign against tuition increases and cuts to accessibility at the CUNY schools. That movement organized massive protests in 1995. One founding SLAM activist explained:

I recently described it as Seattle coming early to New York and it gives as a useful way of looking at it. It was 25,000, insanely young, blacks and Latinos. It was the biggest demonstration of young Blacks and Latinos in New York City history. It was huge. It was really militant in its objective and didn't succeed in just marching from City Hall to Wall Street. It was anti-capitalist in spirit kind of demonstration.

A year later, SLAM ran for student government at Hunter College and won. It controlled Hunter College's student government between 1997 and 2003 and thus secured the resources required to become a hub of protest activity with offices, computers, and paid staff. Decisionmaking within SLAM used consensus process, in contrast to the decisionmaking within the larger student government. SLAM began campaigns challenging the power of campus security guards and continued campaigns opposing the elimination of remedial education in public universities. By 1999, the group had begun to organize increasingly around criminal justice issues that were outside of traditional student concerns. It participated in protests against Mumia Abu-Jamal's ongoing imprisonment and planned execution in Philadelphia (July 1999) and again in Washington DC (February 2000).

From its inception, SLAM used a wide range of tactics, including direct action. SLAM members disrupted CUNY board of trustee meetings and graduation ceremonies to oppose cuts to remedial education. It held rallies, cultural events, and marches. It engaged in pamphleteering and ran the student newspaper and a high school organizing program. In February 2003, SLAM members occupied the offices of Hunter College's President (Freedom Road Socialist Organization 2006). SLAM also had a strong emphasis on political education and put a great deal of effort into training its organizers.

The demonstrations against the World Trade Organization influenced SLAM. Some members argued there was an increase in enthusiasm for protest after the demonstrations against the WTO. One member explained: "There was actually a march for Mumia December 14th or 15th 1999, and it was just a march in Philadelphia. But people were really pumped up by Seattle. What was the chant we had? 'Ain't no freedom without no battle! Power to the People from Philly to Seattle!'"

In the wake of those protests, SLAM reached out to other organizations (including the Direct Action Network, DAN) to form the August 1st Direct Action Coalition. The coalition aimed to highlight issues of criminal justice at the protests against the Republican National Convention scheduled to take place during the summer of 2000 in Philadelphia. As one member explained, "We wanted to be doing [the tactics] that DAN was doing." After that summer, things changed dramatically for the organization. Many of its core organizers graduated, and the group subdivided into a "student" and a "community" organization. New members ascended to leadership positions within the student organization, and the group concentrated on student government and student access issues. It also occasionally participated in antiwar mobilizing. In 2003, after seven years in office, SLAM lost the student government election and subsequently reorganized itself. In April 2006, SLAM celebrated its ten-year anniversary. It continues to organize campaigns on a number of issues including tuition fees, open admissions policies, and police brutality.

Although SLAM had more than one chapter at various points in its history, I focus on the chapter at Hunter College because the other chapters were mostly dormant by 1998. SLAM was never mentioned by name in the *New York Times* during this period, but the protests it is involved in often get covered. These articles refer to students, student activists, CUNY students, and Hunter College students.

Direct Action Network – New York City

Initiated by activists who had participated in the Seattle protests, Direct Action Network – New York City was New York's contribution to what became a network of more than a dozen DANs across the United States during 2000.

From its inception, it was affiliated with the People's Global Action network discussed earlier. Immediately after the Seattle protests, 150 people attended weekly DAN meetings in New York City. Over the next two years, this number gradually shrank to about fifty attendees. Participants at meetings made decisions using a formal process of modified consensus. Most DAN members were white and in their late twenties or early thirties. In its early days, DAN operated as an informal coalition of New York activist groups. Many of the groups that participated in DAN were small radical organizations based in Manhattan. These included the East Village Greens, More Gardens!, Reclaim the Streets, Jobs with Justice, Radical Faeries, Free Mumia Coalition, Rainforest Action Network, the Industrial Workers of the World (IWW), and others. In some cases, DAN-NYC provided opportunities for radicals in different organizations to work with others who valued direct action. Occasionally, small organizations used DAN to build support for their campaigns or to connect with other communities. Although the number of organizations affiliated with DAN was large, these organizations tended to be informal and small.

For many DAN members, the protests in Seattle deeply affected their political engagement. One experienced antipoverty activist who became involved in DAN explained how things had changed for him after the Seattle protests:

I joined groups that I would have never gone near before like Direct Action Network. I think I was more willing to do some coalition building. I mean, I think at that point in my life I was pretty devoted to community organizations, but I think because of Seattle I got involved in DAN which wasn't a community organization. I met some really good people. I think that there was more coalition building just in general, in the United States and in New York City after Seattle. I would say that the two big things in the United States that changed was coalition building and a more widespread belief in fighting battles to win, not just for the symbolic ability to say that we did something. I think those were the big changes. I think that those were changes that were building throughout the nineties but I think that Seattle coalesced them in the United States.

DAN's structure was explicitly and formally antihierarchical. When a spokesperson was needed, the individual was elected, and the position was temporary. However, despite numerous formal mechanisms designed to combat the centralization of power, inequalities around access to information and decision making emerged (Graeber 2009; Polletta 2001b). DAN's main activity involved mobilizing for protests against transnational institutions like the International Monetary Fund and the World Bank. It coordinated transportation, training, and support for New Yorkers protesting in Washington DC, Quebec City, and elsewhere. Although DAN organized only a small number of protests in New York City, its working groups on police brutality, labor issues, and genetic engineering represented DAN-NYC at labor pickets and at police brutality, environment, anti-sweatshop, and immigrant rights demonstrations. DAN activists also participated in protests around community gardens and public space. They brought the Seattle tactics of puppetry, black bloc, radical cheerleaders, blockading, and affinity group organizing to these movements and their protests.

Although the group was never identified by name in the *New York Times* during the period, coverage of its events referred to its members as anti-globalization protesters, protesters, activists, and young protesters. After September 11, 2001, many DAN-NYC members shifted their attention to the wars and occupations taking place in Afghanistan, Iraq, and Palestine. At that time, meetings became less frequent. Although it continues to operate as a listserv, DAN-NYC ceased to meet in 2002 after its members organized a new coalition called Another World is Possible to confront the New York meetings of the World Economic Forum. In 2003, some of these activists formed an antiwar coalition called No Blood for Oil, partly in an attempt to bring a more explicit anticapitalist analysis and direct action tactics into the antiwar movement.

TORONTO ORGANIZATIONS

Ontario Coalition against Poverty

The Ontario Coalition Against Poverty (OCAP) emerged from struggles around welfare reform during the late 1980s. Since its founding conference in 1990, the direct action antipoverty organization has campaigned against government policies that negatively affect poor and working people. It has also mobilized support for individuals fighting eviction, termination of welfare benefits, police harassment, and deportation. Funded primarily by organized labor until 2001 and – since that time – by individual donations, OCAP makes policy decisions at biweekly general membership meetings or at biweekly meetings of its executive. The organization's executive and its two or three staff are elected by the membership at an annual general meeting. Although the group's demographics have shifted over the years, its active members between 1998 and 2001 were mainly welfare recipients, people collecting disability support payments, and youthful supporters. Since 1999, younger people – some of whom are students – have begun to make up an increasingly large proportion of the organization's active membership.

Organizing under a banner that reads "Fight to Win," OCAP often uses disruptive direct actions to pressure authorities to concede to their demands. OCAP organize the majority of the protests in which it participates. Its large events receive a relatively high level of media coverage. It organizes numerous small delegations to welfare and immigration offices, employers, and landlords in order to quickly resolve members' problems. OCAP's use of direct action tactics began long before the protests in Seattle. It was even experimenting with the Seattle tactics prior to the event itself. This was due in part to its contact with organizers and networks that took a lead in the Seattle protests. During the Active Resistance Anarchist Conference in 1998, OCAP experimented with puppets while working with visiting puppetry activists.

In 1999, OCAP's friendship networks with people involved with Reclaim the Streets Toronto led it to adapt the street party tactic for an antipoverty protest. Although some members have argued that the Seattle protests had little effect on their work, others insist that the antiglobalization movement deeply influenced the organization. One member explained that, although not everyone in the organization was even aware of the Seattle demonstrations, they nevertheless brought a series of young people with an enthusiasm for militant direct action into the organization:

People came in whose first entry point into activism was around anti-globalization. Obviously there was a large group of particularly, youth who were brought into activism and a surge of activism around it and some of it transferred into more people getting involved and excited about OCAP. It had an impact on us tactically, that got played out in the June 15th demonstration and it had an impact in terms of people's willingness or interest in engaging in militant conflict.

OCAP became front-page news in Toronto when its demonstration at the Ontario Provincial Legislature turned riotous on June 15, 2000. Upon being refused entry to the Legislature to address the government, protesters began to pull down police barricades. The response by riot cops – some on horseback – was violent. Activists and police both suffered injuries. Several arrests took place both during and after the protest. After this event, OCAP faced increasing repression by authorities. After a flurry of debate in the mainstream media and condemnations by politicians, OCAP – having continued to stage confrontational protests – lost its office and a great deal of mainstream support. Nevertheless, according to organizers, support from the poor, the homeless, and students dramatically increased. Indeed, from 2003 to 2004, OCAP operated a second office. Today, although direct action is less common, OCAP continues to organize raucous protests against all levels of government and to be the organization most frequently identified in newspaper coverage of protest in Toronto. When not identified directly, OCAP is also referred to as homeless activists, antipoverty activists, antipoverty protesters, and homeless.

Ontario Public Interest Research Group – Toronto

The Ontario Public Interest Research Group (OPIRG) Toronto is a student group at the University of Toronto with a mandate for action, education, and research on environmental and social justice issues. It is part of an international network of Public Interest Research Groups (PIRG) that includes eleven in the province of Ontario. The organization has a volunteer board and is funded by University of Toronto student fees. It organizes primarily on campus and often focuses on issues related to accessible education; however, between 1998 and 2002, OPIRG Toronto had working groups addressing globalization, sweatshops, native issues, animal rights, and poverty issues. Activists energized by Seattle were involved with OPIRG. They were most active in the newly formed anticorporate action group, as well as the anti-sweatshop, fair trade, and Latin

American solidarity working groups. Each working group made decisions by consensus and sent a representative to annual general meetings.

The anticorporate action group emerged in the months after Seattle protests and organized buses to the protests against the World Bank and IMF in Washington, DC in April 2000. It helped to organize trainings in the Seattle tactics of affinity group organizing, as well as puppetry and blockading. Anticorporate action group tactics at protests targeting right wing conferences and corporations were not particularly confrontational but emphasized creative disruption. In 2000, some OPIRG activists looking for opportunities to use some of the more radical tactics they had learned helped to form an affinity group called Resist! This group helped organize the first Southern Ontario summit protest since Seattle, the protests against the Summit of the Organization of American States in Windsor, Ontario. Although OPIRG Toronto is never referred to by name in articles about demonstrations appearing in the *Toronto Star*, it can be identified in coverage as students, student activists, antiglobalization protesters, and protesters.

Mobilization for Global Justice – Toronto

Commonly known as Mob4Glob, Toronto's Mobilization for Global Justice emerged from the WTO Action Coalition in the summer of 1999. The new Mob4Glob was created in anticipation of the anti-WTO demonstrations in Seattle. Mob4Glob became the largest and most well-known organization in Toronto explicitly affiliated with the antiglobalization movement. It was composed of representatives from local and national political, labor, and social justice groups including Oxfam, the Canadian Auto Workers, the Canadian Federation of Students, the Council of Canadians, the International Socialists, and others. It organized a Toronto-based solidarity demonstration for the November 30, 1999, the global day of action that coincided with the events in Seattle. A number of participants and leaders in the group attended events in Seattle.

After Seattle, most members saw the main task of the coalition as being a space in which existing social movement organizations could organize against corporate globalization (Rutherford 2003). Participants were politically diverse and included socialists, anarchists, and social democrats who often endorsed a range of differing tactical approaches and goals. Between 2000 and 2002, the coalition coordinated demonstrations and teach-ins against corporate globalization. One member explains that things in Toronto changed after Seattle: "There were certainly changes in the way people approached things tactically.... But the main thing that happened was that it was just bigger. Everything that we did here was bigger and broader than it had been before and that was the most significant change post-Seattle." Some participants in Mob4Glob also argued that trade union and NGO engagement also radically increased after Seattle.

Like DAN-NYC, Mob4Glob participants made decisions at large weekly assemblies using a loose interpretation of consensus-based decision making

(Rutherford 2003). The size of meetings ebbed and flowed; however, they were at their largest around the time of the Quebec City protests against the Free Trade Area of the Americas (FTAA) in April 2001. Before these protests most participants represented organizations. Afterward, the number of unaffiliated activists' increased significantly. Like DAN-NYC, one of Mob4Glob's main activities involved coordinating transportation and logistics for Torontonians attending protests in Ottawa (G8), Quebec (FTAA), Washington (IMF and World Bank), New York (WEF), and Kananaskis (G8); however, Mob4Glob also organized a small number of protests in Toronto. These included one against a Finance Ministers meeting held shortly before the FTAA summit in Quebec City. It also organized blockading, puppetry, media, legal, medics, and jail solidarity trainings. Participants were mostly white, middle-class, and ranged in age from twenty to thirty-five (Rutherford 2003). Never referred to by name in either the *Toronto Star* or *Toronto Sun*, the group was identified by references to antiglobalization protesters, protesters, student activists, and activists. Like DAN-NYC, Mob4Glob ceased to meet in 2002.

RELATIONSHIPS AMONG THE NAMED ORGANIZATIONS IN EACH CITY

There was much more overlap and collaboration between the organizations in New York than there was amongst their Toronto equivalents. When I asked activists in each organization about their past activism, which organizations their organization worked with, and which organizations had been role models for their own organization, activists in New York reported many more shared influences. They also had more experience collaborating and their movement biographies were more similar. In contrast, relationships amongst the Toronto organizations were more competitive. The only linkages involved shared collaborations with the labor movement. There were very few influences shared by Mob4Glob and OCAP activists despite the fact that the number of influences identified by participants in each group was large. I'll discuss this more in the next chapter.

All six organizations studied here were influenced by the Seattle protests; however, their response to those protests varied. Some organizations facilitated the diffusion of the Seattle tactics more than others because of their histories, structural positions, relationships, and culture. These differences affected whether activists in these organizations were able to deliberate freely about the Seattle tactics. When such deliberation was possible, as it was in New York, experiments with the new tactics were possible. When it was less possible, there were fewer experiments.

5

Regimes on Repertoires

New York and Toronto activists' varying levels of openness to the Seattle tactics was tied to the particular structure and history of their national and local ruling regimes. As Charles Tilly has noted, regimes (including central governments) influence contentious repertoires in the following ways:

1. by imposing limits on collective claim making within the regime; and
2. by constraining or facilitating particular patterns of communication among claimants (actual and potential) that pool information, beliefs, and practices concerning what forms of claim making work or don't work. (Tilly 2008, 149)

Following Tilly, we can anticipate how Canadian and U.S. regimes influence protester repertoires in their respective countries. Both regimes impose similar limits on protest. When compared with other states, both are relatively democratic, relatively liberal, and have relatively high capacities. It is not surprising that protest looks similar in both countries. However, the Canadian and U.S. regimes are marked by differences: their political histories, political economies, and relative capacities. These differences influence communication among claimants and thus shape their collective identities and practices. By looking at how national and local regimes influence patterns of interaction among local protesters (and among direct action protesters in particular), we can begin to understand why New York activists incorporated the Seattle tactics more easily than they did those in Toronto.

HISTORICAL DIFFERENCES IN NATIONAL REGIMES

Differences in the national political regimes of Canada and the United States underlie distinct responses to the Seattle protests. To be sure, there are similar limitations on collective claim making. Moreover, although they are enacted differently, the U.S. Constitution and the Canadian Charter of Rights and Freedoms allow for a similar repertoire. Differences in terms of limitations on protest thus tend to be based on local bylaws and their interpretation or on innovations that have yet to be contested in court.

As Tilly (2008) noted, regimes also shape particular patterns of communication among claimants (actual and potential). These patterns affect the ways that people mobilize, communicate, and frame their issues. It is, therefore, significant that the historical organization of political structures differs in Canada and the United States. The United States developed as a decentralized alliance among elite opponents of British rule. In contrast, Canada was a centralized colonial project of elites engaged in a commercial enterprise. Nevertheless, over the past hundred years, the national government in the United States has become relatively more powerful, while Canada has devolved more power to the provinces. By the 1980s, 56 percent of total government expenditures took place at the federal level in the United States, while in Canada, only 34 percent of government spending was federal (Watts 1987, 777). This difference is tied to both geography and to economic dynamics. The larger area of Canada, with its smaller and more spread out population, has led to the maintenance of particularly distinct regional cultures, obviously between Anglophone and Francophone provinces, but also between other provinces as a result of patterns of immigration and economic development. Unlike the United States, where the economy is a large, national one, Canada's economy is a collection of regional economies, strung across the country (Watts 1987). In this context, there are challenges in mounting a truly national social movement for social and economic justice.

CANADIAN RESISTANCE TO FREE TRADE

Long before the Seattle protests, Canadian political actors were actively engaged in debates about neoliberalism, free trade, and the restructuring of welfare state. The struggles against free trade in Canada are deeply connected to more general struggles for Canadian autonomy against U.S. domination. This history goes back to the founding of the Dominion of Canada in 1867 and – before that – to the War of 1812, when U.S. forces attempted to invade Upper and Lower Canada. Many Canadians share a historical sense that closer economic integration with the United States would threaten Canada's political independence (Ayres 1998, 22). In 1969, Prime Minister Pierre Trudeau famously summed up Canadian feelings about its relationship with the United States when he said, "Living next to you is in some ways like sleeping with an elephant. No matter how friendly and even-tempered is the beast, if I can call it that, one is affected by every twitch and grunt" (Trudeau 1969). As a result of this political geography, both the Canadian Left and Right have grown accustomed to checking the influence of U.S. government and business decisions on Canadian policy; therefore, certain differences – publicly funded health care, the relationship with Britain (and sometimes the monarchy), multiculturalism, bilingualism, and others – have long been rhetorically celebrated.

The U.S.-Canada Free Trade Agreement (FTA) was the "most controversial agreement of its kind in Canadian history" and dominated the 1988 federal election. Both before and after it passed, left-wing groups across the country mobilized around demands for sovereignty, the environment, labor rights, and culture (Ayres 1998). Many of the organizations involved in these early battles against the FTA and the subsequent North American Free Trade Agreement (NAFTA) later joined the wave of protests against the subsequent cuts to social services, health care, education, and labor rights in the mid-1990s.

At that time, the federal transfer payments to the provinces to pay for social services were sharply reduced. Established in 1995, the Canada Health and Social Transfer (CHST) reduced federal funding by some $2.5 billion in 1996–97, and an additional $2 billion in 1997–98. Because social services are funded provincially, most subsequent struggles around cutbacks targeted provincial governments (Stilborn 1997). However, because transfer payment cuts affected a wide range of organizations and communities, a political opportunity for alliance building arose among networks that had not previously worked together (Ayres 1998). Moreover, debates about free trade and cutbacks between federal and provincial parties allowed more information to be released publicly. In this way, divisions among authorities became more apparent and provided a political opportunity for those opposing the restructuring.

Through these struggles, certain networks, organizations, and individuals developed high profiles among national and political social movement networks. Some of these actors were relatively strong and well resourced. The Pro-Canada Network and Action Canada Network brought together Canadian left-wing nationalists with popular-sector coalitions that included religious organizations and networks, women's networks like the National Action Committee on the Status of Women (NAC), trade unions, student organizations, and local and provincial governments (Ayres 1998, 31). In contrast to their U.S. counterparts, a large proportion of these groups received government funding.

The Council of Canadians (COC) has consistently been a key organization in these networks. Formed in 1985, the organization is most well-known internationally for having helped to abolish the Multilateral Agreement on Investment (MAI), which would have allowed corporations to challenge national laws (even those related to environmental and labor regulations) if they hurt profits. During the mid-1990s, the COC shifted their emphasis from nationalist demands for sovereignty to critiques of corporate globalization. This shift coincided with its rapid membership growth. By 1998, the COC had 100,000 members across the country (Ayres 1998, 139).

Also at the forefront of the movement against free trade in Canada were national trade unions. Boasting 3 million members, the Canadian Labour Congress (CLC) is a relatively powerful body in Canadian politics. Both the CLC and its member unions have historically provided significant resources to protests against international financial institutions and free trade. They have also been critiqued by grassroots activists for pushing the movement toward

social democratic electoral politics and for seeking inclusion in decision making rather than rejecting neoliberalism outright. Nevertheless, the CLC's
importance and commitment to social unionism has meant that Canadian
grassroots movements potentially have a powerful ally.

In Ontario, between 1995 and 1997, labor unions mobilized their members to oppose the provincial government's neoliberal reforms. There were
rotating general strikes across the province. In October 1996, the Metro
Toronto Day of Action shut down the city and brought a quarter of a million teachers, civil servants, industrial workers, and others to the center of
the city the following day (La Botz 2011). In 1997, cutbacks to health care,
education, and the public sector led to long strikes by teachers and postal
workers and to job actions by hospital workers and others. However, tensions began to emerge between popular-sector activists and the trade union
leadership as the cutbacks continued. These community activists accused
union leaders of abandoning the interests of the larger community in favor
of maintaining collaborative relationships with government (Ayres 1998,
49). As neoliberal restructuring proceeded, trade unions like the Canadian
Union of Public Employees, the Ontario Public Service Employees Union,
the Canadian Auto Workers, and the Canadian Union of Postal Workers, as
well as organizations like the Canadian Federation of Students, the Ontario
Coalition Against Poverty, and the New Democratic Party, could not agree
upon how to move forward.

In contrast to the significant mobilizations that took place in Canada, U.S.
mobilizations against free trade during the 1990s remained piecemeal. The
Democratic Party controlled the federal government, the economy was boom-
ing, and unemployment was low. Between 1993 and 2000, the United States
exhibited its best economic performance of the past three decades (Frankel
and Orszag 2002). Although U.S. labor, environment, religious, and consumer
groups opposed NAFTA, their opposition never became widespread. Indeed,
the highest profile opposition to NAFTA at the time was associated with
Ross Perot's presidential campaign. In that campaign, Perot argued against
NAFTA by describing the "giant sucking sound" that would inevitably arise
as employment and dollars rushed out of the United States and into Mexico's
coffers. Although these campaigns collectively raised a degree of awareness
about the trade agreement, they did nothing to link opposition to NAFTA to
struggles against welfare reform or public sector downsizing; therefore, they
did not encourage the development of broad left-wing coalitions as happened
in Canada.

However, some left NGOs, social movements, and trade union networks
did lay the foundation for later movements against neoliberalism in the United
States. Formed in 1987, the Jobs with Justice coalition organized union-
led social and economic justice campaigns. The Citizens Trade Campaign,
founded in 1992 as a coalition of environmental, labor, consumer, family
farm, religious, and other civil society groups, was also an early player.
Consumer group Public Citizen, trade activists Global Exchange, and

solidarity movements like CISPES (the Coalition in Solidarity with the People of El Salvador) were also central to the early opposition to free trade, as were others who consistently argued an anti-imperialist, anticapitalist line.

During the 1990s, in both Canada and the United States, activists mobilized against cuts to social services, deregulation, and neoliberal free trade policies. Given the more extensive history of engagement with questions of neoliberalism and free trade in Canada, one would expect that Canadian activists would be eager to participate in the protests against the World Trade Organization in Seattle. After all, negotiations at those meetings were meant to extend free trade and its associated neoliberal reforms internationally. However, although Canadian activists participated in greater numbers on a per capita basis than did their U.S. counterparts, differences in the two national regimes, local regimes, and political histories meant that Canadian activists were less interested in experimenting with the Seattle tactics than their U.S. counterparts.

COMPARING NEW YORK AND TORONTO

Within these broader national contexts, differences in local context can give us some clues about why the New York global justice movement was more willing to experiment with the Seattle tactics than its Toronto equivalent. The local regimes were different, influencing patterns of communication, meaning that New York City activists were more likely to identify with the Seattle protesters and see themselves as fighting the same battle than their counterparts in Toronto.

In 1999, Toronto's and New York's changing regimes shared similarities. Both cities were relatively central in the world system. An attempt to categorize and compare cities was made in 1999 by the Globalization and World Cities Study Group and Network (GaWC). The roster was outlined in the *GaWC Research Bulletin* and ranked cities based on provision of "advanced producer services" – like accountancy, advertising, finance, and law – by international corporations. The GaWC inventory identifies three levels of world cities and several subranks. New York was identified as one of only four "full service world cities," and Toronto was ranked a "major world city" (Beaverstock et al. 1999). But both are the largest cities within their countries, are financial and cultural centers, and are ethnically diverse and deeply tied into the global economy. In part because of neoliberal economic policy implementation, they have also experienced similar transformations in recent years.

In the 1990s, a new urban regime (which had begun in the 1960s) moved to consolidate its hold on New York and Toronto. By the 1970s, gentrification was restructuring urban spaces. Manufacturing jobs were disappearing and, concurrently, so-called FIRE employment (finance, insurance, and real estate) increased. Because of these trends, the urban geography of both cities underwent a massive restructuring (Smith 1996, 39). As cities found themselves competing on the global market, these economic shifts were often paired with political shifts. Increasing privatization of public services, cutbacks to social welfare spending, and increasing inequalities of wealth became hallmarks of the new "global city" (Sassen 1991; Smith 1996).

In 1993, New York Mayor Rudolph Giuliani was elected on a platform of "improving the quality of life, the business climate and education system while fighting crime." He remained in office until the end of 2001. During his time in office, he made massive cuts to welfare rolls, reduced rent control, and privatized public services. He also used police to displace homeless people and disrupt existing street life. New York's public assistance rolls were cut by more than half, from 1.1 million in July 1995 to 497,113 in July 2001 (Smith Nightingale et al. 2002). Boosters attributed the decline to economic prosperity and policies enacted by the mayor's Human Resources Administration that restructured application procedures and created stringent work requirements; however, a closer look at conditions affecting the city's poor called the actual success of these measures into question. Food stamp participation decreased by 35 percent between January 1996 and March 1999 as a result of welfare reform (New York City Bar 2001). At the same time, requests for emergency food aid increased by 36 percent between January 1998 and January 1999.

As welfare and social services were cut and poverty increased, the city began to place an increased emphasis on law and order. In this context, more people began to take note of the New York Police Department (NYPD) and its actions (Shalom 2000). Both the 1997 rape and beating of Haitian immigrant Abner Louima and the 1999 shooting of West African immigrant Amadou Diallo led to massive protests against police impunity and brutality.

With eight million residents, New York has one of the most racially and ethnically diverse populations in the United States. In 2000, only 45 percent of New Yorkers identified as white. Meanwhile, 36 percent of New Yorkers were born outside of the United States (Area Connect 2000; Beveridge 2003). However, like most U.S. cities, race and ethnicity remain significant in the production and maintenance of major social boundaries. Most neighborhoods and many institutions continue to be dominated by a single racial or ethnic group. Social movements and protest in New York City have long reflected these racial and ethnic divisions. During the latter half of the twentieth century, the black community, the Puerto Rican community, and the Chinese community each engaged in significant but separate mobilizations around housing, poverty, public schools, and civil rights.

The response of New Yorkers to changes in their city remained divided along the lines of ethnic communities, neighborhoods, and issues. Passionate critics engaged in marches, rallies, and direct action. Students protested cuts to education. AIDS activists blocked tunnels protesting cuts to services. Squatters defended their homes. Community gardeners, cyclists, and housing activists fought the city for control of urban space; however, a large multiethnic and multi-issue campaign explicitly targeting restructuring itself never emerged. Activists did not explicitly connect the shifts in the city to free trade or neoliberalism. Falling with the purview of NGO activity, such macroeconomic issues remained peripheral to street protest in the 1980s and 1990s.

Within fragmented local political networks, New York is host to the headquarters of many national NGOs. It also boasts an active trade union movement along with reams of ethnic social movement organizations and small left-wing groups of various stripes. However, this fecundity has not usually led to collaboration. Outside exceptional moments (like the police shooting of Amadou Diallo in 1999, or the Occupy Wall Street movement of 2011), groups engaging in disruptive direct action mostly remain within particular neighborhoods, ethnicities, issue areas, or political ideologies. This fragmentation limited the impact of different groups on the political networks in the city; however, it also paradoxically allowed for more experimentation with tactics and new forms of organizing.

TORONTO

Like New York, Toronto is its country's largest city. With a population of three million, the city is also diverse. In 2001, 43 percent of Torontonians identified as visible minorities, and the city is a major receiving center for new immigrants. Forty-nine percent of Torontonians were born outside Canada (Government of Canada 2001). Toronto is also the capital of the province of Ontario. Two years after Rudolph Giuliani became mayor of New York City, Mike Harris was elected as premier of Ontario. He defeated the social democratic New Democratic Party (NDP) that held power between 1990 and 1995. Beginning in 1995, Harris pursued similar reforms to those enacted by Giuliani. The Ontario Works Act cut welfare payments by 21.6 percent. Welfare income was then frozen at this reduced level. Increases in inflation and cost of living meant that by 2001, the real value of those cuts became 30 percent (Shapcott 2001, 9). Under Harris, rent control legislation was rewritten to favor landlords, large swaths of public housing and social services were privatized, and Toronto began to emulate New York's style of aggressive street policing. Evictions and homelessness increased rapidly. Although he proceeded with less power and ideological fervor than Giuliani, populist Mayor Mel Lastman devoted himself to overseeing these changes during his tenure between 1998 and 2002.

Initially, the social movement response to the restructuring in Ontario and Toronto was much more centrally coordinated than it was in New York. As I've mentioned, relying on national networks and one of the highest levels of unionization in the country, the Ontario Federation of Labour organized rotating "days of action" or general strikes. Social democratic party organizations, NGOs, trade unions and community organizations focusing on the changing nature of urban space, racism, poverty, car use, housing, and consumerism also participated.

By the time of the Seattle protests, activists in both Toronto and New York were drawing links between local struggles and changes in the operation of global capitalism. Despite sharing similar points of entry into the global justice movement, both differences in the national and local regimes and

political economies meant that, in New York, political networks were fragmented along issue, race, class, and neighborhood lines, while Toronto's
political networks were centralized and dominated by a small number of
powerful organizations. In Toronto, the cluster of direct action organizations
competed, but did not collaborate, whereas in New York City, the cluster
shared similar influences and collaborated frequently. These differences led
to differences in the structure of political relationships in each city and subsequently affected the way local activists responded to the Seattle protests, and
the global justice movement.

CENTRALIZATION OF LOCAL POLITICAL NETWORKS

According to Everett Rogers, the level of *centralization* in a network is determined by the degree to which power and control are concentrated in the hands
of a few individuals or organizations. Research suggests that participants will
be less likely to be innovative or open to new ideas when a system is dominated
by a few strong leaders (Rogers 1995, 380, 411). Correspondingly, actors less
influenced by central leaders are often more likely to innovate. Considering the
diffusion of policy innovations in nineteenth-century United States, Elizabeth
Clemens noted that "the potential for innovation was concentrated at the
peripheries of American politics, where marginalized actors mastered alternative forms and dominant institutions were less firmly established, providing
opportunities for experimentation" (Clemens 1997, 91–92).

There are different ways to evaluate the relative centralization of political
networks. In this study, I compared the characteristics of protest in Toronto and
New York by analyzing event catalogues of protest events from 1998 to the end
of 2001. These catalogues included all public protests of more than ten people
that took place locally and that were reported in the main local newspapers,
the *New York Times* or the *Toronto Star*. Coverage of marches, rallies, direct
actions, delegations, and other such events was included. I did not include organizational meetings or press conferences. I used the Lexis-Nexis search engine
to search for references to protest, protesters, protests, rallied, demonstrated,
and demonstrators. Although media coverage is limited, it is relatively consistent in its limitations, tending to cover the biggest and most dramatic protest
events. Based on past research, I estimate that this coverage accounted for less
than 20 percent of the actual protest events that took place during this period
(Wood 2004). The *Toronto Star* and the *New York Times* are the main liberal
papers in their respective cities; however, there are differences in profile and
coverage. While the *Toronto Star* is read across Southern Ontario, it does not
share the *New York Times'* ambition of being a national newspaper.

From this material, I identified the claimants or protesting organizations, as
well as their targets, and the locations of protest in each city. Overall, I found
significant differences between the two cities. I divided the four years into
two time periods: before and after the Seattle protests. Using formal measures
of centralization, I found that the Toronto networks were more centralized

before Seattle than the New York networks. This is not surprising and can be largely accounted for by differences in the size of the two cities. Consequently, there were more targets and locations and a larger number of collective actors in New York than in Toronto. Between 1998 and 2002, my analysis of *New York Times* coverage identified 221 different collective actors participating in 251 protest events. In contrast, coverage of protest in Toronto identified only 141 different collective actors who participated in 163 events. Protests in New York City tended to be bigger than those in Toronto. However, the differences I noted are not reducible to scale and the characteristics of protest. The relations between organizations and between organizations and available targets are also different.

I evaluated the structure of protest networks in each city. I did this by looking at the frequency with which particular actors, issues, targets, and locations appeared in the protest reporting over the four-year period. Per capita, Torontonians protested more than New Yorkers in the two years prior to Seattle (1998–1999) and were more disruptive when they did so, even though New York City has more than four times the population of Toronto, it has only one and a half times the number of reported protests. However, Toronto protests were less likely to end in arrests. The issues that Torontonians were most likely to protest during the 1998–2000 period were cuts to funding for education, social services, health care, local poverty, police brutality, and homelessness. When they protested, they were most likely to target some level of government – especially the provincial government. During the same period, New Yorkers were most likely to protest about gentrification, AIDS, cuts to funding for education, and labor issues. They were most likely to target corporations or the local government with their claims. Even though activists in New York and Toronto both engaged with a range of local, national, and international issues, a larger proportion of protests in Toronto than in New York concerned international issues.

This difference may be tied to immigration patterns or to the level of incorporation each city demands from its new arrivals. Far more than New York, Toronto is a city of immigrants. More than half of its population was born in another country (Toronto 2011). Its residents and government are necessarily attuned to international politics and economics. In contrast, U.S. global dominance means that, despite its participation in global networks, it is more able to act unilaterally. After the Seattle protests, Toronto's networks became less centralized, while New York's became more centralized around a small number of actors. In both cities, people were most likely to engage in protest as part of a labor or ethnic organization. In Toronto, ethnic affiliations underlay slightly more associations than organized labor, while in New York, organized and unorganized labor accounted for slightly more activity than ethnic organizations overall. Looking at the number of named organizations in each city reveals more interesting differences.

In Toronto, a small number of organizations appeared to dominate protest networks throughout the period in question. The OCAP and the

Canadian Union of Public Employees (CUPE) were respectively identified at fifteen and eight events. Other frequently identified Toronto groups or categories included students (twenty-one times), Serbians (five times), parents (six times), and teachers (nine times). The coverage located OCAP at 10 percent, and CUPE at 5 percent of events covered during the period. The dominance of a few named organizations in the Toronto social movement field reflects the history of recent struggles and has a number of consequences. The visibility of named organizations in a social movement field suggests their dominance as opinion leaders and their influence on other collective actors.

In New York, no named organizations visibly dominate protest networks. The most commonly identified collective actors (top 4 of 221) were all general categories: people (15 times), protesters (14 times), students (11 times), and garden supporters (8 times). None of these actors are particular organizations – although the Reverend Al Sharpton's organization, the National Action Network, was relatively prominent during the period, it was only named in the coverage of six events. Indeed, in the general categories, the only category identified with a specific issue was garden supporters, who were in fact organized into a small number of organizations including the More Gardens! Coalition. Other than Al Sharpton (4 percent of events), and possibly garden supporters, no collective actors appear on a regular basis in the New York protest coverage over a four-year period. This suggests that there are no collective actors consistently engaged in protest on a particular issue that are visible through the media. Of course, these differences may also be partly owed to the differences in the reporting style of the newspapers.

In terms of the targets of protest, government is much more frequent target in Toronto than in New York City. The top three institutional targets in New York are local government, police, and corporations, while in Toronto, most claims are directed at government: whether provincial, foreign, or federal. In part, this reflects the fact that Toronto is a provincial capital; however, it may also confirm the traditionally more prominent role that governmental institutions play in the lives of Canadians. In contrast, New York City activists are more likely to target corporations.

Relative to the overall number of protest events, Toronto activists also protested in a smaller number of locations than their New York counterparts. If we ignore the protests that took place in the downtown streets of both cities without any particular site as a target, we find that the 251 events in New York took place in 169 locations (an average of 1.48 events per location). The most popular locations were City Hall (twenty-six events), Police Headquarters (twelve events), Union Square (six events), Times Square (six events), and the United Nations Headquarters (six events). In Toronto, the 163 protests took place at 88 locations (an average of 1.85 events per location). The most popular locations were the Provincial Parliament (thirty-two events), City Hall (fourteen events), the U.S. Consulate (seven events), and the Toronto District School Board (seven events). With this difference, one can easily see how protest is spatially concentrated in Toronto, despite having more protests per capita.

Overall, when compared to New York, even when controlling for the size of the two cities, a smaller number of activist organizations, targets, and locations dominate the political networks in Toronto. Toronto's political networks are more centralized and this centralization may limit the possibility of deliberation about new tactics and strategies. At the time of the Seattle protests, leading activists had a clear sense of "how to protest." Dominant political players could easily dissuade other local activists from experimenting with locally new tactics. In contrast, although there are hundreds of social movement organizations in New York, their networks were more often fragmented along lines of race, class, neighborhood, and issue. Paradoxically, this increased direct action activists' receptivity to innovations by providing small spaces to experiment. Because they were less influenced by other local activists, New York direct action activists could discuss and experiment with the tactics. The combination of a shared national regime and fragmented local networks helped create a context that made identification by and deliberation amongst New York City activists easier. Deliberation of the new tactics also required a context of intensive interaction where diverse actors could discuss, evaluate, and adapt practices for the local context. This was facilitated by interconnectedness among the potential adopters likely to use direct action.

INTERCONNECTEDNESS BETWEEN THE ORGANIZATIONS MOST LIKELY TO ADOPT THE SEATTLE TACTICS

As I have discussed, regimes affect repertoires partly by influencing the way different claimants can interact and communicate. The structure of these flows of communication can be partly understood by looking at how regimes structure relationships among different races, classes and neighborhoods. These patterns influence activist and social movement interconnectedness. By *interconnectedness*, I mean the degree to which units in a social system are linked by interpersonal networks. As Rogers states, "New ideas can flow more easily among the members of an organization or cluster of organizations if it has a higher degree of interconnectedness." In a less interconnected system, clusters of participants are more isolated from one another. In contrast, when ideas can travel more easily between clusters and actors, organizational innovativeness and diffusion increases (Rogers 2003, 412). One can evaluate interconnectedness in a social system or network by looking at the extent to which groups, communities, neighborhoods, and organizations are tied to one another.

To understand the relationships among direct action activists in Toronto and New York, I asked participants in the six "most likely to adopt" organizations about the influence that other organizations had on their own group. Given that collective identities are a combination of patterns of relationships,

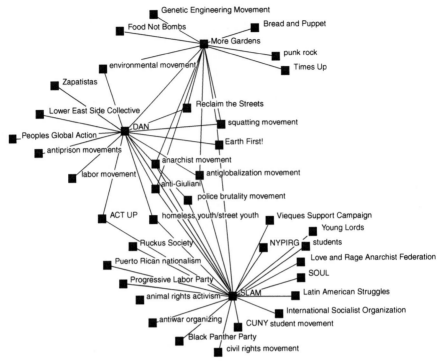

FIGURE 5.1. Influences on Organizations – New York City.

stories, and boundaries, organizations that share similar influences are both more likely to see themselves as similar and are also more likely to be interconnected. Organizations that are more interconnected are thus more able to collaborate and to discuss locally new tactics. Following this logic, I built a relational profile of each organization. When organizations shared similar influences on their identity, agreement on tactics and strategies became more likely. As a result, responses to ideas from elsewhere also became more similar. To evaluate how this takes place, I asked the thirty-two respondents in the six organizations about their individual participation in different groups, their organization's role models, and the organizations they identified as collaborators and coalition partners. Influences that were identified by two or more respondents were included in the relational profile. In this way, I mapped the organizational identities of the six organizations most likely to adopt the Seattle tactics in New York City and Toronto (see Figures 5.1 and 5.2).

Direct action activists in both cities shared some similar influences, but there was much more interconnectedness among the three organizations from New York than there was among organizations in Toronto. Although no formal membership organizations influenced activists in both cities, activists from all six organizations cited the anarchist movement in general as an influence. Activists from five groups cited the environmental movement and

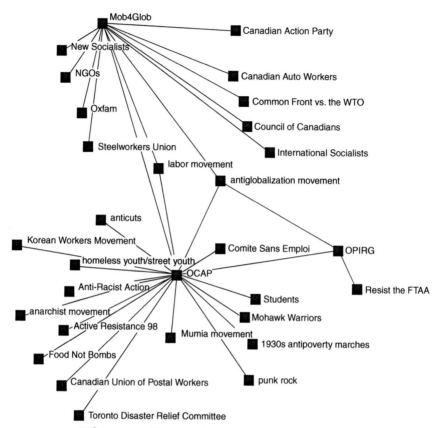

FIGURE 5.2. Influences on Organizations – Toronto.

student movement as influential, while activists from four organizations noted the influence of the labor movement, the movement against homelessness, and anarchist-influenced networks like Food Not Bombs, Earth First!, and Reclaim the Streets. These networks are all significant for having helped to build momentum for the Seattle protests.[1] Four organizations also identified the cultural-political movement of punk rock as a shared influence.[2] While the organizations in this study were different in many ways, these shared

[1] Food Not Bombs was first active in Boston in 1980 and has since had active, autonomous groups providing vegetarian food in public spaces in cities, primarily in the United States and Canada. Many groups are extremely short-lived, but as of April 2004, there were over 100 active groups in the United States and at least 5 in Canada. Earth First! was initiated as a network in 1979 and is organized primarily in the United States, Canada, and Europe. As their Web site reads "There are no Earth First! members, only Earth Firsters. Earth First! is not an organization, it's a movement" (Earth First! 2011). Reclaim the Streets, which I discussed in Chapter 2, is a similar network of autonomous groups. All three networks are extremely fluid and often act as entry points for new activists.

[2] This is not to suggest that this selection of organizations represents all direct action activists.

connections provided a basis for discussing and engaging in direct action. Given the importance of these influences on the Seattle demonstrations themselves, it is not surprising that many of the organizations in my study were able to identify with the Seattle protesters.

In both cities, the oldest organization in my sample (SLAM and OCAP) claimed the largest number of influences. This reflects their longer history in the political milieu, their longer average length of respondent participation, and their engagement with past coalition partners. These organizations had a clear sense of their relationships with past movements. Francesca Polletta (2002) found that respondents active in the 1960s had few social movements that inspired them and offered them preexisting models of organization. In contrast, I found that some of the activists I talked to referred to a plethora of movement influences. One SLAM member explained in 2003:

SLAM has always had an understanding of direct action. And I think it has to do with the founders; there were some anarchist, who also came from the student power movement which was a people of color only organization, or red diaper babies and radical people of color. We were coming out of a third world Marxist tradition that influences all sorts of young budding revolutionaries. The Young Lords, the Black Panthers, Latin American struggles, the Cuban struggle, the independence struggles of Puerto Rico. The independence struggles of Palestine. All of those things, and then the grassroots orientation of SNCC [Student Non-Violent Coordinating Committee] ... Everybody was like, "That's what we want, to be like SNCC was."

A pamphlet by More Gardens! Coalition similarly highlighted the historical importance of nonviolent civil disobedience by identifying with various social movements in U.S. history:

Non-violent civil disobedience has been used in many popular mobilizations in this country, including the civil rights and anti-nuclear movements. In the past couple of years, activists in New York City have revived this tactic as a tool for social change. A recent example of this kind of action was the voluntary arrest of thousands of people at City Hall to express their outrage at the brutal shooting of Amadou Diallo. (More Gardens!, undated)

When asked about influences of other movements on OCAP, one member explained:

I know a lot of people now are reading about what happened in the 60s and 70s, about the Black Power movement and how white people fit into the black power movement and what white people were doing at the time around anti-imperialist work. Because of OCAP and John Clarke a lot of people have read about the movements of the 1930s in Poor People's Movements.[3] And something that OCAP has ... is like, people who have come from movements that ... are involved in revolutionary movements in Mexico or Ethiopia and Kenya, Iran, or wherever else. And these people bring this sense of history too. They might have totally different politics from each other, and all these things or whatever, but they really are like serious and understand what it's going to take to build the sort of movements that can actually change the world or whatever. And from them we get a lot, a lot, a lot.

---

[3] Piven, Frances Fox and Richard Cloward. 1977. *Poor People's Movements: Why They Succeed and How They Fail.* New York: Pantheon Books.

Although certain role models, activist histories, and coalition partners were emphasized more by certain activists than they were by others, a shared respect for, say, the black power movement could facilitate identification and interaction between two organizations. Greater degrees of shared influences increased the likelihood of conversations about tactics among the three organizations. These conversations could then multiply the sources of information each organization had access to, facilitating deliberation in each one.

Direct action activists in New York were more interconnected than their Toronto equivalents. Activists from the all three organizations in New York cited five shared influences: anarchism, the student movement, Earth First!, Reclaim the Streets, and the movement around homelessness. In contrast, Toronto direct action organizations had only two cited shared influences – anarchists and the environmental movement – and even these were only acknowledged by three of the sixteen respondents. Despite operating in political networks that were centralized around a small number of actors, there was little overlap in influences in Toronto. The only influence that was identified by more than five of the Toronto respondents was the labor movement; however, even here, OPIRG activists did not see the labor movement as having influenced their organization.

Mapping these connections, we can see how direct action activists in New York City had a higher level of interconnectedness than did their Toronto counterparts. In Toronto, even though OPIRG and Mob4Glob both cite OCAP as an influence, there are few other shared influences among the three organizations (see Table 5.1).

The higher level of interconnectedness between New York organizations suggests that these organizations would be more able to deliberate about the Seattle tactics. In contrast, and despite OCAP's dominant influence on direct action tactics, the low degree of interconnectedness among Toronto organizations meant that they faced greater barriers to deliberation and diffusion unless OCAP or another dominant organization certified a particular tactic as useful. Neither OCAP nor OPIRG activists cited Mob4Glob – the organization that could have had the most impact on the reception of the Seattle tactics – as an influence.

THE IMPACT OF SEATTLE ON PROTEST IN NEW YORK CITY AND TORONTO

Why were New Yorkers more willing and able than Torontonians to experiment with the Seattle tactics? In part, the answer can be found in the structure and operation of national and local regimes; however, there are some surprises. Canadian activists were more experienced in fighting neoliberalism before Seattle than their U.S. counterparts. One might imagine that they would be eager adopters of the Seattle tactics. Although this may hold true at the national level, the histories of struggle at the local level meant that Toronto protest networks were centralized around a few key actors in the labor movement, OCAP, or NGOs. This centralization made these actors particularly influential.

TABLE 5.1. *Most Common Influences on Selected Organizations*

	# Organizations Influenced /6	NY /3 Orgs, / 15 Respondents	TO /3 Orgs, / 15 Respondents
Anarchists	6	3 orgs, 7 resp.	3 orgs, 3 resp.
Environmental movement	5	2 orgs, 4 resp.	3 orgs, 3 resp.
Student movement	5	3 orgs, 5 resp.	2 orgs, 3 resp.
Food Not Bombs	4	2 orgs, 4 resp.	2 orgs, 4 resp.
Earth First!	4	3 orgs, 8 resp.	1 org, 1 resp.
Reclaim the Streets	4	3 orgs, 7 resp.	1 org, 1 resp.
Homelessness movement	4	3 orgs, 5 resp.	1 org, 3 resp.
Labor movement	4	2 orgs, 3 resp.	2 orgs, 7 resp.
Punk rock	4	3 orgs, 5 resp.	1 org, 2 resp.

When the Seattle protests happened, these organizations already dominated the protest networks in Toronto. Because they disagreed about tactics and strategy, collaboration was neither easy nor frequent. In contrast, direct action protest networks in New York were fragmented. Within these fragmented networks, direct action activists operated within a tiny niche. Although they had few resources, they were more interconnected than their Toronto counterparts, and therefore, they were more able to discuss tactics and strategy and could thus more easily consider incorporating the Seattle tactics.

Historical differences of regime and political economy influence the ways political actors communicate and collaborate. Following Granovetter's (1973) study on the strength of weak ties, we find that clusters of strong ties connected to larger networks by weak ties provide the most fertile ground for diffusion. In this case, the fragmentation of left-wing political networks in New York meant weak ties between groups divided by issue, neighborhood, race, and class allowed for deliberation among an isolated cluster of direct action activists and facilitated reception of the Seattle tactics – at least to their own organizations. In Toronto, inherited patterns of struggle against neoliberalism and relatively well-resourced organizations limited the influence of the Seattle tactics. Centralized political networks dominated by a small number of organizations and a lack of interconnectedness between organizations interested in direct action prevented the Seattle tactics from being adopted locally. A strong history of successful organizing does not necessarily prepare movements to consider and incorporate innovations. Diffusion depends partly on the way national and local political and economic histories influence interactions at the local level. Have these histories facilitated relationships that would allow relatively diverse, relatively egalitarian, and reflexive conversations to ensue? If deliberation is possible, integration of new tactics becomes more likely – provided that potential adopters see themselves as similar to earlier users and that the tactics are considered useful and appealing. This partly depends on the culture and actions of local opinion leaders.

6

Opinion Leaders

After the Seattle protests, antiglobalization organizations sprouted up around North America. In New York, activists returning from the Seattle protests launched a local Direct Action Network.[1] In Toronto, activists transformed an existing coalition into the Mobilization for Global Justice. These coalitions were the local representatives of the wave of protest associated with the global justice movement. Both hoped to bring together local manifestations of the labor, youth, student, NGO, socialist, anarchist, and environmental movements that participated in Seattle to challenge neoliberal globalization.[2]

These coalitions were the local opinion leaders for the antiglobalization movement. By definition, opinion leaders play a key role in deciding whether an innovation is welcomed into a local context. According to Rogers, opinion leadership denotes the degree to which an individual or group is able, with relative frequency, to informally influence others' attitudes or overt behavior in a desired way (Rogers 2003, 300). Opinion leaders gain their perceived competency by providing an avenue for new ideas to enter their system. Organizations that operate as opinion leaders tend to have greater exposure to external linkages than other organizations (Lazarsfeld et al. 1944; Burt 1999 in Rogers 2003, 316–17). As Rogers (2003) says, the external linkages may be provided via mass media channels, by the member's cosmopoliteness, or by the member's greater contacts (317).

When a coalition becomes an opinion leader, it can be a particularly effective link in the diffusion process. A coalition connects diverse groups who may not otherwise work together while allowing autonomy in their activities. Coalitions can spread interpretive frames, organizational structures, political

---

[1] The Direct Action Network was the name of the organizing body that coordinated the direct action at the Seattle protests. It subsequently became a network of autonomous local groups with shared hallmarks in about a dozen cities, primarily in the United States, that coordinated resources and information through bimonthly conference calls.

[2] Other groups with the name Mobilization for Global Justice existed in Vancouver, Halifax, and Washington DC; all were autonomous. When asked, Mob4Glob respondents argued that the name was chosen because it was "a good name."

analysis, and tactics broadly. They can increase the breadth of a mobilization, encourage alliances, and coordinate resources, making campaigns more effective (Meyer and Whittier 1994, 290).

However, if the members of an opinion leader coalition are averse to experimentation and risk, their collaboration may hinder rather than facilitate the spread of new ideas. As Rogers notes: "If opinion leaders are to be recognized by their peers as competent and trustworthy experts about innovations, the opinion leaders should adopt the new ideas before their followers" (Rogers 1995, 294). But he warns: "Opinion leaders are not necessarily innovative. Their level of innovativeness depends on the system norms. When a social system's norms favor change, opinion leaders are more innovative, but when the norms do not favor change, opinion leaders are not especially innovative" (Rogers 2003, 318).

The innovativeness of an opinion leader is not only dependent on system norms; it is dependent on the strategic capacity of the coalition itself. As I mentioned in Chapter 1, Marshall Ganz argues, the strategic capacity of an organization is greater if "a leadership team includes insiders and outsiders, strong and weak network ties, and access to diverse, yet salient, repertoires of collective action" (Ganz 2000, 1005). The coalition most likely to deliberate about a range of innovations would have "weak" ties linking clusters of ethnic communities, subcultures, organizations, and habitual collaborators. Weak ties that bridge gaps in culture, community, and issue are important channels for allowing diffusion to spread past initial receivers. Mark Granovetter explains: "Social systems lacking in weak ties will be fragmented and incoherent. New ideas will spread slowly, scientific endeavors will be handicapped, and subgroups separated by race, ethnicity, geography, or other characteristics will have difficulty reaching a modus vivendi" (Granovetter 1983, 202). When a social movement field is fragmented, innovations will have difficulty moving between clusters of activists, communities, and movements. Political organizations with few weak ties will be deprived of information from distant parts of the social system and will be confined to the news and views of their close friends (ibid., 202). As I noted in Chapter 5, this fragmentation may also protect the deliberation essential for adaptation and experimentation (Ganz 2000, 1005).

LOCALIZING THE MOVEMENT

Mob4Glob and DAN-NYC's explicit purpose was to participate in and facilitate the new movement. They localized the tactics and politics of summit protests in five ways. Between the time of the Seattle protests and 2002, they helped mobilize locals in Toronto and New York City to participate in protests against global summits of international trade bodies like the IMF, World Bank, the Group of 8 (G8), the World Economic Forum (WEF), the Organization of American States (OAS), and the World Trade Organization (Conway 2003). They coordinated transportation and support for local activists traveling to summit protests in other cities. They provided an arena to discuss the tactics made popular by the summit protests and to evaluate their usefulness. I discuss this more in the next chapter. They also organized tactical and political trainings in preparation for these actions. Finally, they initiated local experiments with the Seattle tactics. I turn to these last two ways they localized the tactics now.

OPINION LEADERS, TRAININGS AND LOCAL EXPERIMENTS

Mob4Glob Toronto and DAN-NYC both promoted workshops that trained local activists in the Seattle tactics. Although these trainings varied, they generally involved participatory role-play activities intended to give participants direct experience with the tactics. In April 2000, activists in both Toronto and New York hosted trainings to prepare participants for the "A16" protests against the IMF and World Bank in Washington DC. In Toronto, the training was organized by a short-lived affinity group called Resist!, some of whose members also participated in Mob4Glob. The trainings included workshops on "consensus decision-making, affinity group structures and A16 info, a discussion on property damage, banner making, legal issues, non-violent resistance and blockading tactics." The e-mail announcing the training closed with the words: "Because reform/lobbying just doesn't get the goods!" (OPIRG, 2000). Other Toronto organizations affiliated with Mob4Glob also held trainings. One Mob4Glob member explained that, even though their organization didn't put on trainings themselves, they supported others who did: "We just kept funneling people to Toronto Action for Social Change and I know that they set up a number of direct action trainings over the course of those years between A16 [April 16, 2000] and the Quebec demos [April 2001]."

Mob4Glob was involved in two trainings in Toronto a year after Seattle. The first was part of the buildup for protests against the FTAA in Quebec City. Although the training wasn't organized by Mob4Glob itself, it was organized by "a bunch of 'activists on payroll'" from the Council of Canadians, Polaris Institute, Common Front on the WTO, and the Canadian Labour Council. All of these organizers were also in Mob4Glob. Hundreds of participants attended the training, which included sessions on antioppression, arrests, blockading, self-defense, and media skills. Trainers from Alberta's Co-Motion ran the workshops. One organizer explained that:

The object [of the training] was to provide some basic training but also to try to just get people in the room, with an eye to getting some trade unionists actually in the room, in the lead-up to Quebec City and create some intermingling there. Which was successful, we had about 20 reps from the Canadian Auto Workers came out, some people from Canadian Union of Public Employees, some Steelworkers came out, it was quite good in that sense. I think there were about 400 people through the whole weekend.

When asked whether those union activists used the tactics after the training, one Mob4Glob member explained that, in some cases, the trainings were simply a way of reminding experienced activists that they could engage in direct action again:

It was good and an opportunity to confront the trade union bureaucracy who didn't really want to touch such things. But it was good, it was very good and some of those big organizations I know still have ripple effects from what happened. When you look for example, back to Washington [April 16 2000], that was the first time that we were trying to get some of those big organizations on-side. As it progressed, more and more and more of them, those organizations started feeling serious rank and file pressure, to be more active and mobilize more significantly. It's just the way these movements build.

In May 2002, Mob4Glob members organized another training entitled "Movements: Direct Action Training: Building Creative Cultures of Resistance." Although e-mailed announcements didn't list them as organizers, funds raised at the event were explicitly intended for Mob4Glob. The e-mail announcement hinted at past conflict between anarchist and socialist participants and at dissatisfaction with earlier trainings. "Anarchists especially are invited, in the hopes of strengthening intra-movement solidarity, and other such buzz-terms. This will not be a typical 'don't swear at cops, here's how you do a puppy-pile' lecture weekend." The announcement went on to argue that solidarity had become both more possible and more necessary in the post-9/11 environment.

Intended to prepare activists for the 2002 Calgary and Ottawa-based protests against the G8 being planned for the coming summer, the skills workshops included:

Anti-oppression, Culture jamming, Medical, Legal, Communication, Art and revolution, Radical Cheerleading, De-escalation and creative escalation, Conflict resolution, Activism 101, Aftercare, Media, Guerrilla theatre, Consensus process and facilitation, Transforming fear, anger, grief and frustration into creative action, Grounding and Centering, Ritual, magic, and militant action, Post Traumatic/Critical Incident stress, Be an everyday urban Guerrilla (Captain Vegetable, 2002).

Despite obvious references to the Seattle tactics (radical cheerleading and puppetry), in the 2002 trainings, blockading, black bloc, and affinity group organizing are absent.[3] This suggests that the cluster of tactics had disintegrated over the 2000–2002 period.

In New York City, DAN helped to organize two large and many smaller direct-action trainings. The large events took place in March 2000 and July 2000. The event on March 3–5, 2000, was organized by the Education Working Group of DAN, and by Students for Solidarity and Empowerment, a local student group that emerged in the wake of the Seattle protests (Kauffman 2000c). The event included workshops in community organization, media, blockading, legal support, and outreach, using trainers from the California-based Ruckus Society. The event's sixty spots were quickly filled. The spring of 2000 also saw DAN hosting many smaller workshops at their meetings and in other spaces.

---

[3] Radical cheerleading was an innovation that began in the late 1990s in which activists would chant using traditional cheerleading props, dance routines, and costumes.

DAN's Education Working Group telephoned and sent letters to dozens of organizations in New York to offer training in direct-action tactics. By April 9, 2000, more than 300 people had been trained in Seattle-style jail solidarity techniques (DAN minutes, April 9, 2000). DAN-NYC activists also worked on trainings in Washington for the April 16–17th, 2000 protests against the World Bank and the IMF. With daily workshops offered during the week leading up to the DC protests, these trainings were more extensive than those that had previously taken place in New York. In addition to sessions already mentioned, the workshops in Washington included creative movement for activists, antioppression communications, peacekeeping/traffic management, and magic for activists, climbing for activists, diversity healing, and activist singing.

More DAN-NYC activists organized workshops in July 2000 in preparation for protests against the Republican National Convention in Philadelphia. Organized by the DAN-NYC Working Group on Police and Prisons and the August 1st Direct Action Coalition, these two days included sessions in blockading, street theater, legal support, civil disobedience and nonviolence, jail solidarity, puppets, affinity groups, spokescouncils, meeting facilitation, and video documentation. Additional sessions included strategizing, pirate radio, radical labor organizing, direct democracy, and women's self-defense. A range of workshops organized for and by people of color was also on offer. These workshops provided explicit opportunities to transmit information – and sometimes to deliberate about – the Seattle tactics.

LOCAL EXPERIMENTS

If opinion leaders wanted the tactics to become fully localized, they needed to go beyond trainings and support local experiments using the tactics. Through these experiments, antiglobalization movement tactics could become further incorporated into the repertoire of local organizations.

DAN-NYC brought the Seattle tactics to immigrant rights protests and picket lines in New York City. However, with the exception of puppetry, Toronto's Mob4Glob never initiated local use of the Seattle tactics. According to one Mob4Glob activist, tactics at Mob4Glob demonstrations were "painfully formulaic. You march from Queen's Park to City Hall or vice versa. The major debates became 'do you take the street or do you not take the street.'" Another Mob4Glob activist explained, after Seattle, "It wasn't so much that the tactics changed on the ground here in Toronto, we primarily did our standard, broad based, relatively mild and simple demonstrations when we actually did them here." In contrast, local protests that DAN-NYC activists organized or participated in the years after Seattle included black bloc, blockading, puppetry, and (on occasion) the affinity group/spokescouncil model.

The differences in willingness of the coalitions to engage in local experiments arose from two sources. The first was the structure of the relationships between the local antiglobalization coalition and the local activist networks. The second had to do with the membership of the local coalitions themselves.

As discussed in the Chapter 5, political networks were much more central-ized in Toronto than they were in New York City. At the same time, direct-action organizations were much more interconnected in New York City than they were in Toronto. Active left-wing organizations working in Toronto tended to have ties to one of the dominant organizations in the city. This centralization meant that these organizations's response to the Seattle tactics influenced other organizations. For example, as we have noted, the Ontario Coalition Against Poverty had a high profile. Although collaboration between Mob4Glob and OCAP was limited, one Mob4Glob member noted that the coalition's local tactical decisions were influenced by OCAP. In the central-ized Toronto context, OCAP's negative codification of the Seattle tactics quickly spread to Mob4Glob. When I asked one Mob4Glob participant why Mob4Glob didn't use blockading tactics, he replied:

I think the blockading had a bad rap in Toronto because of OCAP. Not because OCAP ever did it, but they had said, "no way do you ever lie down, you stand up and fight." ... Now there weren't many people from OCAP in anti-globalization stuff, at least through Mob4Glob, but some of the legends around OCAP seeped into Mob4Glob and some people who had been involved in both coalitions often used OCAP as an example to try to undermine things like blockades or civil disobedience.

In contrast, New York's political networks were fragmented by race, class, neighborhood, and issue, but its cluster of direct-action organizations was more interconnected. When DAN formed, its strong ties were mainly with white, young, and radical direct-action activists and organizations whose influence was mutual. In this context, NYC-DAN's activists had relatively few ties to other communities. This meant that, from its inception, DAN operated primarily within an isolated cluster of direct-action organizations and was more able to experiment with the Seattle tactics.

The membership of the global justice movement coalition also influenced the possibility of local experiments. Mob4Glob-Toronto emerged from the WTO Action Committee in the summer of 1999. It was formed by activists from organizations including Oxfam Canada, the International Socialists, the Council of Canadians, and Canadian Pensioners Concerned. After the Seattle protests, other members joined. Many of these new members also came from national organizations. Mob4Glob structured itself as a formal coalition whose goal was to coordinate logistics for groups protesting global financial institutions "so there wasn't duplication." New participants included people involved with the Canadian Action Party, the Canadian Auto Workers, the Canadian Federation of Students, the Canadian Union of Public Employees, Greenpeace, the Ontario Coalition Against Poverty, the Ontario Public Interest Research Group, the Sierra Club, and others. These groups were among the most visible social movement organizations in the city and, indeed, the coun-try. As one participant explained:

The MobGlobs or Mob4Globs, depending on who you were talking to around the country, were all quite similar in both design and function. In fact, the organizations that were onside [were similar] ... In every one of the cities for example, there was a Council of Canadians chapter that was part of spearheading the activity around anti-globalization stuff.

Mob4Glob was also open to individuals, who increased in numbers after the 2001 FTAA protests in Quebec City. As one participant explains, "Mob4Glob is a coalition in the truest sense. And when it became more of a coalition of individuals we had a lot of flexibility." It benefited from what Ganz (2000) calls that combination of "weak and strong ties" because it bridged gaps between clusters of participants with ongoing institutional and social connections, but those clusters were operating within a relatively centralized environment.

In New York City, some of DAN-NYC's initial members had been at the protests in Seattle. Many others had previously been involved with Reclaim the Streets – a loosely organized anticonsumerist, anticar environmental group based out of the rapidly gentrifying Lower East Side. Most of its founding members were white and middle class. Many were students. When DAN's first meeting was announced by e-mail, it was circulated on the Lower East Side Collective (LESC) and Reclaim the Streets-NYC lists and then forwarded to anarchist, student, and radical environmental and labor lists. Flyers were posted in radical bookshops and cafes (primarily in Lower Manhattan) and on university campuses. As a result, the founding membership was located within a particular cluster of small, local organizations with a particular political culture. Although they attempted a structured outreach program and frequently managed to attract attendees from other communities, DAN remained bound by the demographics and political subculture of its founding participants. Some of these activists were involved with other organizations; but only sometimes did they attend as representatives of those groups. The organizations that participated regularly in meetings "as organizations" were small and had few resources.[4]

The challenge of attempting to create a broad coalition of New York City organizations sparked a debate at DAN-NYC's very first meeting. Having recently returned from Seattle, organizers wanted to implement the spokescouncil model of organizing. In this model, decisions would be made by different organizations' "spoke"; however, unaffiliated activists argued that such an approach would exclude them. In 2003, one DAN activist

---

[4] DAN-NYC participants included people from ABC No Rio, Bard Student-Labor Coalition, Committees of Correspondence, Committee in Solidarity with the People of El Salvador, East Village Greens, Food Not Bombs, the Industrial Workers of the World (IWW), Jobs With Justice, More Gardens! Coalition, New Jersey Independent Alliance, New Paltz Greens, Rainforest Relief, Reclaim the Streets NYC, Students for Solidarity and Empowerment, Women's International League for Peace and Freedom (WILPF), Young Communist League (YCL), and other organizations.

explained how the outcome of this debate moved DAN away from its initial aspirations of being a diverse network and instead made it a collection of mostly unaffiliated individuals representing a much narrower section of the social movement field.

While it was naïve to think that a bunch of white kids in New York City were going to create a network of New York City groups, I still think we could have been a network of sorts and I think that it would have been a very different experience for the next few years if we'd had a network of groups rather than, essentially an organization. And at that first meeting, we wanted it to be a spokescouncil of groups and of course there were some people there who didn't feel like they wanted people who didn't have groups to feel alienated and in retrospect I wish I had argued a little more vehemently that those people who couldn't manage to organize in small groups probably shouldn't be organizing in a large group. But we went forward and created an organization where individuals could come and participate, and that it was really an organization of working groups.

Because many DAN participants did not represent organizations, the intended coalition of groups quickly became an organization in its own right. In Granovetter's (1973) and Ganz's (2000) terms, strong ties quickly dominated the group. DAN meeting minutes reflect this transformation. In early 2000, a participant would be identified as "Jill from the East Village Green Party." A year later the identification for the same person would likely be identified as "Jill from the Action Working Group." The shift away from a coalition model and DAN members' limited ties to other communities discouraged organizations who wanted to make use of the group's networking ability. These factors also limited the possibility of deliberation amongst diverse participants. Consequently, the Seattle tactics' local spread beyond a cluster of like-minded organizations was also limited.[5]

After DAN evolved into an organization, some weak ties were established and maintained through the development of issue-specific working groups. These included groups working on labor solidarity, and opposing police and prisons, and genetic modification. Ties to other organizations working on similar issues were fostered through these smaller groups. They created links to organizations that were otherwise uninvolved with DAN and created an additional site for deliberation and experimentation. For example, DAN activists previously involved in Union Summer (a summer training program organized by the trade unions) formed the DAN Labor Working Group and provided a bridge to the labor movement. Many of these activists had ties to labor unions including the Service Employees International Union, the United Auto Workers, and the Industrial Workers of the World. A similar process took

---

[5] DAN-NYC did have contacts with other Direct Action Network groups in Chicago, Los Angeles, Dallas, the Bay Area, Vancouver, and other cities. They communicated every two weeks on continental conference calls and were able to coordinate decisions to mobilize for particular actions like the April 16, 2000, IMF World Bank protests in Washington and the April 2001 protests against the FTAA in Quebec City.

place amongst DAN activists working against police brutality. The Police and Prisons Working Group became a space where deliberation with antipolice brutality movement activists about similarities and differences between the two movements, their tactics, and their strategies could occur, with many of these activists becoming involved in Critical Resistance, a national organization opposing the expansion of the prison industrial complex.

Overall, however the organizational membership in these global justice coalitions influenced local experiments with the Seattle tactics through their culture and structure. The type of organizations participating in the two coalitions differed in meaningful ways. As I've noted, the organizational participants in DAN-NYC were largely small, volunteer run, local organizations. In contrast, more of the organizations participating in Toronto's Mobilization for Global Justice were formal in character. Rogers (2003) defines *formalization* as the degree to which an organization emphasizes its rules and procedures. Research has shown that a high level of formalization within an organization may limit its willingness to experiment with locally new tactics. However, formal organizations are more likely to accumulate the economic and social resources necessary for long-term campaigns through fund raising, paid staff, and the building of skills of members or constituents (Ansell 1997; Staggenborg 1988). Susceptible to co-option, such organizations may become more cautious in order to protect their resources and influence. This may lead to increasingly moderate tactics.

Members of Mob4Glob Toronto were much more likely to be part of established formal organizations than were those in DAN-NYC. Correspondingly, they were less interested in deliberating about how the Seattle tactics might be used locally. According to one member, "The most experienced people in Mob4Glob were activists on a payroll ... so these people had been to Seattle and these were the key organizational people who helped form a vision of Mob4Glob up until [the protests in] Quebec [in] 2001." Some participants argued that these organizations may have limited the coalition's receptivity to new tactics. As one Mob4Glob participant explained, "One thing that does happen is sometimes those big organizations water down your tactics seriously, which is inevitable but at the same time you get larger numbers out."

Another member of Mob4Glob explained that tactical decisions were influenced by concerns around access to resources from the labor movement:

What sort of tactics do we want to use and [that] would be useful? And that [question] creates tension inside an organization a little bit.... We should get labor movement support, but at what cost do these things come at? And I would say that the labor movement never put any [pressure], "No we won't give you money," but you know this stuff well enough, if you go too far out on a limb, you lose potential sources of funding so the question is what is the principled line.

Although Mob4Glob had a more diverse membership than DAN-NYC, the influence of more formal and well-resourced members limited its willingness to discuss the Seattle tactics and to use them locally.

CONCLUSION

Local antiglobalization coalitions in Toronto and New York played an important role as opinion leaders. They organized the meetings and experiments that helped to bring the Seattle tactics into their communities. However, there were differences in each coalition's willingness and capacity to play this role. These differences influenced the extent to which the Seattle tactics were localized in the two cities. In the summer of 2004, New York activists organizing against the Republican National Convention used affinity groups and spokescouncils, organized samba classes, built puppets, and developed an infrastructure that looked a lot like the one used in Seattle. When I told this to one Toronto activist, he raised his eyebrows in surprise: "They're still doing it??" By then, the Seattle tactics had almost entirely disappeared from Toronto. Even when Toronto activists organized protests against the G20 summit in 2010, although a black bloc formed, radical cheerleaders chanted, and a few puppets were seen, affinity groups, jail solidarity, spokescouncils, and blockading weren't absent.

Local opinion leaders like Mob4Glob and DAN-NYC influenced deliberation about the Seattle tactics in Toronto and New York. Because Mob4Glob was dominated by a number of formal risk-averse organizations operating within a more centralized and polarized local context, deliberation about risky direct-action tactics was limited. Without much discussion, the Seattle tactics were deemed inappropriate for the local context. This dismissal was then easily broadcast through coalition members' ties throughout the local arena. In contrast, DAN-NYC's member organizations were smaller, poorer, and more willing and able to take tactical risks. In some ways, they had less to lose. As a result, their deliberations certified some of the Seattle tactics as appropriate for local use. However, the fragmentation of New York City's political networks meant that this certification had limited effects on the city's larger repertoire. Although structural context and membership did not determine the character of local discussions, they did influence each coalition's decision-making and deliberative processes. These processes are the visible traces of the struggles over tactics, strategy and identity. I turn to them now.

7

Talking about a Revolution

A: So, did you hear about what the activists in Seattle did?

B: They shut down the friggin' WTO meetings. Totally!

C: Wow! How did they do it?

A: Well, some of them just linked arms and wouldn't let the delegates into the hotels. They weren't violent or anything. They just blocked their way.

C: That's totally cool.

D: So, what are we going to do about the way the university is ignoring our demands for an anti-sweatshop policy?

E: God, I don't know.

F: We need to let them know that there is no way that they can get away with this anymore.

E: But how?

D: Well, we tried going to Senate and complaining. We tried writing letters. We tried to get a meeting with the President. What next?

F: What we need is something creative. Something that will make the media pay attention, and something that will be fun. Let's blockade the President's office with giant puppets and visuals that show how the exploitation is happening. They won't be able to get in or out, and it will look amazing. They'd have to deal with us. Those kids in Seattle did it. They just peacefully blockaded with puppets and wouldn't let business as usual carry on. We can do the same; we'd get tons of attention, and we'd get a meeting for sure.

D: I love it!

How activists discuss a new tactic will influence whether they will seriously consider using it. As I have argued in earlier chapters, successful diffusion is facilitated when activists have shared opportunities to reflect upon, evaluate, and adapt a tactic. Incorporation of innovations is most likely when discussion amongst potential receivers is deliberative. Such discussions are characterized by equal opportunities to hear a diversity of viewpoints, equal opportunities to express one's own perspective and to influence collective decision making. For some theorists, deliberation arises to the extent that participants are encouraged to be reflexive, to question both the agenda and the procedure of discussion (Cohen 1989; Dryzek 1990; Fishkin 1991; Guttman and Thompson 1996). In such conversations, deliberators do this by examining alternatives through evaluation, argument, and storytelling. Much of the time however, deliberation does not happen. Instead, discussions become polarized, dominated by particular participants or become ensnared by circular reasoning.

Activists have long understood the value of deliberative discussion. Activist and author Starhawk explains how, in order to develop good strategies in a successful movement, "we'd look for dialogue among as wide a spectrum of groups as possible, with no single organization or group preempting the turf. We'd actively seek a diversity of race, class and gender as well as diversity of political philosophies. We'd understand that no one group or tactic gets to define the movement" (2001). When such deliberation takes place, research has shown that participants become more innovative and open to new ideas, feel more confident and knowledgeable, and make more efficient and effective decisions (Amabile 1996; Brown and Eisenhardt 1997; Hackman 1990; Hutchins 1991; McLeod 1992; Nemeth and Staw 1989; Weil 1994). Through deliberation, an idea can be investigated, dislocated from its original context, and adapted to the new context if and when it is considered attractive or useful. As a heuristic process, deliberation facilitates the transfer of foreign symbols and forms of action by allowing an idea to be "dis-located" and then "re-located" in a completely different context. In this way, it makes locally new practices conceivable (Chabot and Duyvendak 2002; Ganz 2000, 1012). Awareness of deliberation's value is central to certain types of social movements. For both ideological and strategic reasons, activists sometimes work to create decision-making processes that maximize inclusive, diverse, and reflexive participation in their campaigns and organizations (Polletta 2002). In this way, both Toronto's Mobilization for Global Justice and New York's Direct Action Network made decisions using consensus decision making, an approach developed in part to maximize participation and allow for the expression of diverse perspectives. In such discussions, the facilitator becomes a very influential participant. The goal of a good facilitator in consensus process is to assist the group in its process of coming to consensus and to identify differences of power or opinion without imposing their own agenda. A good facilitator can maximize the strategic capacity of the group by helping it explore new ideas openly and reflexively. However, by managing the conversation and the agenda, the facilitator may intentionally or unintentionally direct the group toward certain ideas while ignoring others (Rutherford 2003). If a group is able to be reflexive during their discussions, the facilitator is more likely to remain accountable; however, if the facilitator is part of a clique that controls decision making in the group, if the group is polarized by an intense debate that becomes the sole focal point, or if outside pressures push the group to act quickly, the facilitator may become less accountable to the group and have disproportionate control over a group's decisions.

Activists in both Mob4Glob and DAN-NYC expressed ongoing concerns about hierarchy, resources, cliquishness, and control. In DAN, concerns focused on the power of cliques and on male domination. In Mob4Glob, participants worried that activists who were "on the payroll" or who were representatives of large, well-resourced organizations had undue influence. In both DAN and Mob4Glob, activists made sporadic attempts to limit such internal inequality. These attempts included rotating the facilitator position, training new facilitators, having multiple facilitators, and – in DAN during the second half of 2000 – having a person tasked with paying attention to gender inequalities attend each meeting. When these mechanisms were effective, the meetings were more likely to yield equal, reflexive deliberation.

However, deliberation doesn't only happen at formal, face-to-face meetings. As Lance Bennett points out, "An inseparable mix of virtual and face-to-face communication defines many activist networks; and contacts in these networks may range far from activists' immediate social circles" (2003, 11). Deliberation might occur at atleast four different types of sites, each of which can influence a local organization's reception of a new tactic. First, there are face-to-face discussions with other members at formal organizational meetings. Second, there are online discussions on organizational listservs among members of an organization. Third, there are face-to-face discussions with other members outside of formal organizational meetings. Finally, there are online discussions with people outside of one's organization, city, and even country. These may occur on listservs, bulletin boards, or Web sites. Each site influences the conversations taking place in the other sites, although such influence is difficult to measure or track; and each may influence the incorporation of a new tactic into an organization.

Systematically evaluating the existence and quality of deliberation is difficult to do, especially post hoc. Analyzing online discussions is often easiest because the text is sometimes archived. Evaluating the importance of face-to-face meetings or informal discussions is more difficult. In the absence of video documentation of discussions or transcripts of conversations, I've relied on my own journal entries and memories. I've supplemented these with minutes of meetings, which provide some direct knowledge of discussions about tactics. Finally, I draw upon my interview transcripts and secondary sources (Graeber 2009, Rutherford 2003). In the interviews, I asked activists about their use of, or attitude to, the Seattle tactics. They referred to discussions about tactics that had taken place inside and outside meetings and, more often, to discussions about ideology, identity, and strategy that supported or critiqued particular tactics. These included debates around violence and nonviolence, the appropriate locus for action, and organizers' relationships to participants and potential recruits.

When these discussions allowed activists to dislocate the Seattle tactics from their original context and to consider them more abstractly, it became possible to certify them as potentially useful and adapt the tactics for new locations. When these discussions led to a tactic's positive evaluation, they facilitated its adaptation by local activists who adjusted it to local needs, identities, and contexts. Of course, such processes partly depend upon the existence of local entrepreneurs willing to consider and promote the tactic. Such promoters would frame the meaning of a tactic or strategy carefully to make it more attractive to local users. In an ideal sequence, promoters frame the transmitting organization to highlight similarities between the potential adopter and the original user. This involves strengthening the cognitive relationship between "us" and "them." From there, a good promoter may intentionally or unintentionally change the meaning of a tactic by keeping past associations vague or ambiguous. This allows potential users to more easily project new meanings onto the tactic. If this process is successful, potential users might adapt the tactic and "make it their own."

To see how a tactic can be rearticulated and incorporated, it's useful to consider how – in the year leading up to Seattle – OCAP activists adapted the RTS street party tactic in order to use it in the context of antipoverty organizing. The street party tactic emerged in the United Kingdom during the mid-1990s and spread through listservs and Web sites affiliated with the People's Global Action network. It was influenced by the Situationist commitment to disrupting the patterns and assumptions of everyday life by using music, theater, and surprise (Debord 2004). Toronto activists learned of the tactic through online discussion and, more importantly, by participating in Reclaim the Streets protests, which first took place in Toronto on May 16, 1998. Organized by activists linked to OCAP members by friendship networks, the event was part of the global day of action known as the "Global Street Party" held to protest the World Trade Organization then meeting in Geneva.

The recoding and adapting of the RTS tactic may have become possible because of the police response. Although Toronto's first Reclaim the Streets was intended to be festive and nonconfrontational, replete with music, dancing, and art, the event became heated after police arrested three protesters in an effort to clear the streets. This confrontation may have inadvertently facilitated the tactic's incorporation by OCAP members who could now more easily frame it as militant and in keeping with its tactical identity. OCAP altered the tactic by using it against a direct target instead of reiterating the more prefigurative vision favored by Reclaim the Streets. One OCAP member explained:

Yeah, we've done that [had a street party]. It took place at Gerrard and Ontario in 1998. But obviously it had an OCAP spin. It's not like a street party in the financial district or in some distant highway. It was a street party on a set of streets where homeowners were banding together in associations that were lobbying politicians and the police and acting in combination to worsen the conditions for people whose conditions were already really bad. It was a street party that was in the face of the homeowners and with very public solidarity.

One OCAP member explained that, even though the OCAP street party was tactically similar to the Reclaim the Streets action in its use of music for disruption.

It was an appropriate tactic for OCAP because it conformed to the group's sense of who they were, who they represented, and who they were against.

Yes, we used the tactic, but it was more like a community celebration of resistance. It was poor communities specifically because it was Cabbagetown and Regent Park as opposed to Bloor and Brunswick [a neighborhood associated with the University of Toronto]. We had a load of food and stuff. Of course the food itself was, we present it as a tactic of solidarity, because I've heard it said that nothing scares the establishment more than an angry crowd of poor people with full stomachs. So when OCAP does that, it's just a necessity, people have to eat, it's not negotiable.

Activists localized the street party tactic in part by combining it with existing tactics. By 1998, OCAP was becoming well-known for doing public "feeds" that gathered poor and homeless people in highly visible locations. Often staged at the homes of local opponents, these actions were meant to be intentionally embarrassing.[1] Around this time, labor unions and the media had begun criticizing the organization for doing "home visits." Occasionally, such visits would bring more than a hundred homeless and poor people to the homes of local elites. OCAP did not cease home visits, rather, by combining them with the street party tactic and the public feed, they were able to adapt them and make the street party consistent with their ongoing efforts to construct an identity and strategy befitting a militant poor people's organization. Deliberation both inside and outside of meetings allowed them to adapt a locally new tactic and make it their own. To get a sense of the extent to which this incorporation has endured, one needs only to consider the buttons OCAP members wore during the fall of 2008, which read "Reclaim the Streets ... of the Downtown East End."

CHALLENGES TO DELIBERATION

Despite evidence suggesting that conversations that are relatively reflexive, egalitarian, and diverse allow for the introduction of new tactics and are potentially useful for building more effective strategy, such discussions are far from inevitable. Deliberation is often blocked because the organization of a particular political economy produces inequalities around resources and relationships that correspond to race, class, and gender. These inequalities may facilitate the development of a particular identity or strategy. In turn, these may make certain relationships and conversations inevitable, while making others impossible. This may mean that certain activists will want to introduce a new tactic regardless of the context. Alternately, they will want to defend the status quo because larger systemic inequalities limit trust, knowledge, and collaboration across boundaries. Deliberation can also be blocked by competition or animosity among movement organizations or

---

[1] OCAP's use of "feeds" increased after contact with the Mohawks from Tyendinaga increased. The Mohawks had long fed people at community mobilizations.

other groups. Such divisions can be activated by configurations of state and economic power or by the repressive activities of the police and courts. Such tensions exacerbate anxiety about time, fears of infiltration and repression, competition for power, and cultural divisions. Taken together, these anxieties limit opportunities to engage in open discussion. If no such discussion happens, activists are likely to either ignore or quickly reject locally new tactics.

Occasionally when discussions do occur, they become polarized between two or more rival positions. Such polarization can block the localization of tactics by limiting the reflexivity, diversity, and equality among those considering the new tactic. When this happens, organizations may become more susceptible to what has been called *tactical fetishism*. This occurs when potential adopters respond to locally new innovations so enthusiastically that they fail to adopt them to the local context. Without adaptation, adoptions tend to be less sustainable (Rogers 2003, 429). Describing the diffusion of Gandhian nonviolence, Chabot and Duyvendak (2002) call this dilemma "oversimilarity." Whether ignoring, rejecting or mimicking, without deliberation, the sustained and sustainable incorporation of locally new tactics becomes much more difficult. L. A. Kauffman (2000c) describes the tactical fetishism that surrounded blockading during the post-Seattle demonstrations in Washington, DC: "What wasn't discussed, in big meetings or small, was why exactly we were doing a blockade, and doing it the same way as in Seattle? The actions were powerful, but it felt like a slogan – shut it down – had dictated our strategy, and defined our success.... Can we try something new?"

Without discussing Seattle tactics deliberatively, it became impossible to adapt them for a new context. Deliberation about the Seattle tactics in Toronto and New York was rare; however, it did happen, at least initially.

TALKING ABOUT TALKING

Formally, all of the organizations in this study shared an emphasis on participatory democracy and embraced deliberation at least some of the time; however, some of them were more able than others to turn their formal commitment to "democratic process" into reality. OPIRG, SLAM, and OCAP each had some sort of board of directors or an elected executive and paid staff. OPIRG Toronto is funded by University of Toronto student fees. Each student is automatically a member of the organization. Community members interested in working on social justice issues can also become members. Most "members" are not actively engaged. Within this number, smaller clusters of people are actively engaged in OPIRG through working groups. In a given year, a few hundred people may be involved in these working groups; however they rarely meet as a whole group. During the period under review, OPIRG Toronto was comprised of a board of directors that held open, monthly meetings, two paid staff, and working groups on various issues. Even though the organization emphasized participatory democracy and consensus decision making, ordinary participants had few opportunities to or reasons for discussing tactical questions in formal meetings. Administrative decisions often dominated these board meetings. The only time that multiple working groups of OPIRG activists discussed tactics or strategy together was at the annual general meeting. However, because such events were often overwhelmed by agenda items, the discussion's reflexivity and openness often remained limited. Deliberation was more likely at the working group level where intense strategic and tactical discussions were frequent.

Like OPIRG, SLAM contended with the constantly shifting membership of a student organization. Between 1996 and 2004, SLAM was elected for student government eight times by Hunter College students. At times therefore, the organization was occupied with the business of student government and less concerned with discussions of direct action strategy. As I've noted, while SLAM separated its own decision making from the more ideologically diverse and differently oriented University Student Government Executive (USG). The USG had open meetings, whereas SLAM only included people as members if they shared the same antioppression analysis and goals. This approach coincided with the group's desire to be a women-of-color-led organization. In almost all circumstances, SLAM used modified consensus decision making. In theory, this meant that questions could be resolved through recourse to a majority vote. In practice, it meant consensus. As time passed, the group felt more comfortable using majority rule for logistical questions, and consensus continued to be used for making programmatic and political decisions. The organization valued and made time for deliberative discussions about tactics and strategy. Such discussions were made possible in part through ongoing internal political education.

Then, as now, OCAP's main decision making was done at biweekly general membership meetings. These meetings took two hours and were held in libraries and community centers. Although their size varied during the period, most meetings included twenty to fifty participants. OCAP meetings have formal agendas, but minutes weren't recorded. Decisions were made by simple majority vote. Unanimity was frequent. Each year, the staff and executive of the organization were elected by the membership. The founder of the organization was consistently elected as a staff person, and the other positions shifted regularly. The executive and staff met every other week at executive meetings to discuss how to implement decisions made by the general membership. Tactics and strategy were discussed at both general membership meetings and at executive meetings. These discussions often considered the "tone" and "goal'" of upcoming actions.

During this period, More Gardens! held meetings weekly in a leading member's apartment, where attendees could also enjoy a potluck dinner. These meetings were long and relatively informal, with only a small proportion of the active community gardeners participating. Although participation in these discussions was not always as diverse or authoritative as it might have been in larger, more formal meetings, tactics and strategy were often discussed.

As I discussed in Chapter 6, both antiglobalization coalitions held large, formal, and diverse meetings. Taking place weekly during periods of high mobilization, and with working group meetings and online discussions taking place between general meetings, meetings were lengthy and – during periods of high mobilization – large. Sometimes, they attracted upward of 100 people. Decisions were made by formal consensus and, in SLAM, DAN, and Mob4Glob, there were formal attempts to incorporate underrepresented voices in decision making. Because of the large size of their meetings, activists in DAN, and to a lesser extent Mob4Glob, were particularly concerned about decision making and often trained participants formally in meeting procedure. However, Stephanie Rutherford (2003) reported in her dissertation at least one Mob4Glob activist felt that consensus was more of an ideal than a reality:

There's an ASPIRATION, kind of, that people want to use consensus until they figure out that consensus might not work for their particular project and then they switch. So I don't even know if we have any goal or ideal that we are trying to achieve. We don't really talk about it. We say we operate on consensus. What does that mean? It means we TWINKLE.[2]

Another member concurred, arguing that – despite aspirations of consensus decision making – Mob4Glob meetings had ceased being deliberative or open by 2001: "I think there's a lot of disrespect … umm a lot of manipulation, a lot of backbiting, a lot of gossip, a lot of, umm, of undermining some people's projects, umm, not a lot of support, not a lot of solidarity, umm, and a complete ignoring or process and reflection and the importance of group dynamics" (in Rutherford 2003, 37).

Regardless of their decision-making process, none of these organizations made tactics a frequent topic of conversation. As with other organizations, social movement organizations quickly established routine ways of operating. It is only at certain moments that such routines were questioned. There were five types of moments when tactics tend to be discussed. The first type of moment was when new organizations formed and established their norms, statements of unity, or purpose. An example of this was when the Direct Action Network discussed whether to endorse the hallmarks of People's Global Action, which supported "confrontational direct action." The second type of moment occurred when a related movement or organization used a new tactic, and the results were either dramatically successful or disastrous. For example, when immigrant rights activists in Australia pulled down fences surrounding a local detention center and enabled detainees to escape, immigrant rights activists in New York discussed whether such a tactic would work in the U.S. context. For groups already in possession of strong tactical identities, such discussions might involve reinforcing or rearticulating existing positions. For example, in the wake of the Seattle demonstrations,

---

[2] *Twinkling* is the deaf sign for applause. It is used to signify consent within the meeting. It was widespread within the anti-globalization movement, and continues to be used in the Occupy movement.

groups like the War Resisters League rearticulated their commitment to the strategy and identity of nonviolence. In such discussions, groups related to the Seattle demonstrations by identifying with the protesters, framing their actions as "like" or "unlike" their own, and subsequently declaring them to be "appropriate and important" or "inappropriate and misguided." Because such discussions largely involved sharing information and rarely involved attempts to adopt tactics as a group, they tended to be exploratory and nonconfrontational.

A third moment in which tactics are discussed arose when an upcoming action requires that decisions be made about tone and goal. An example of this type of discussion can be found when activists preparing for the April 2000 Washington, DC protests against the IMF and World Bank considered the question of property destruction. A fourth moment would be when a protest by another organization needed to be endorsed, as when Mob4Glob needed to decide whether or not to endorse the October 2001 protests against the Ontario government in the post 9/11 context when the mobilization welcomed a "diversity of tactics," refusing to condemn particular tactics

The fifth type of conversation about tactics did not consider the tactics directly. Instead, these discussions considered movement strategy and identity. Through their consideration of "who we are" and "how we achieve our goals," these discussions articulated and rearticulated boundaries that either facilitated or constrained a particular tactic's use.

These different discussions do not come out of thin air. They take place within what Steinberg (1999a) calls a *discursive field*. This field contains the genres that collective actors draw upon to construct and analyze particular actions. According to Erickson (1999), genre is a patterning of communication created by a combination of the individual (cognitive), social, and technical forces implicit in a recurring communicative situation. A genre structures communication among participants by creating shared expectations about the form and content of the interaction. Genres are historically and contextually dependent and involve people in particular fields talking in particular ways. In the field of direct action activists, talk about tactics occurs in particular ways. These discussions often involve evaluations of success (both long- and short-term discussions of values) as well as stories of worthiness (what honorable activists do), stories of fighting powerful opponents (how the underdog wins against a powerful enemy), and stories of mobilization (how the people rose up and joined us), among others.

Within such discussions, the meaning of key terms is often contested. The way that an activist uses a particular term (e.g., *diversity of tactics*) is partly dependent on that activist's past and present relationships. If an activist only has a few ties to other organizations and all those organizations were pacifist, the meaning of diversity of tactics may be a particular one. In contrast, if an activist has a larger number of weak ties to a larger range of influences, he or she is more likely to have access to a divergent set of meanings. According to Steinberg, "there is an ongoing struggle between actors trying to invest discourses with their preferred meanings, given their life experiences, situations, and their power to exert control over the meanings provided by words" (Steinberg 1999a, 744–5). By looking at the widespread post-Seattle debates about property destruction and violence, race, class, and summit hopping, it becomes possible to identify important moments in these struggles and to see how they facilitated or blocked adaptation. It also becomes possible to identify moments in which debates became polarized, deliberation ceased, and diffusion was blocked.

In the following chapters, I examine discussions about property destruction and race and class identity within the antiglobalization movement and consider how these debates influenced reception of the Seattle tactics. First however, I want to look at the debate that counterpoised summit hopping to local organizing. After outlining the evolution of the online debate between 1999 and 2002, I will look more closely at how this debate unfolded in Toronto and New York. In this way, I will show how activists interpreted and responded to one aspect of the antiglobalization movement the summit protest, and how the form and content of their conversations influenced the localization of the Seattle tactics.

TALKING ABOUT SUMMIT HOPPING

The protests in Seattle dramatically increased popular interest in mass direct action in North America. For many newly mobilized activists, the obvious next step was to plan for the next "Seattle-like" summit of an international financial institution. Consequently, many began to mobilize for the April 2000 protests against the IMF and World Bank meetings in Washington DC. After those protests, activists who identified with the global justice movement (and some others) began to mobilize for summits or conferences in Windsor and Philadelphia. These summits provided activists with an opportunity to confront institutions and were exciting spaces to converge and feel powerful. They attracted a great deal of media attention and provided a shared target for activists working on a range of different issues. This was not the only choice for those inspired by the Seattle protests. Other activists – and especially those already mobilized around local issues – interpreted Seattle as encouragement for their own community organizing campaigns, lobbying activities, and fund raising.

As police forces became more adept at repressing summit protests in 2000 and 2001, activists' abilities to disrupt summit meetings declined. Consequently, the strategy of targeting these meetings – summit hopping – faced more criticism both online and offline. After protests against the conventions of the Republican and Democratic parties in August 2000, activists expressed concern that such mobilizations took too much energy, resulted in too many arrests and legal battles, and yielded gains that were too limited. Others worried that the events privileged young activists with the time and money to travel from protest to protest. Still, there was ongoing enthusiasm. The debate about summit hopping's utility and appropriateness became intense. Traveling to Europe during the summer of 2001, one Toronto activist developed a Web site to discuss the pros and cons of summit hopping. The site was prefaced with the following introduction:

While summit hopping is definitely a reality based on privilege it is a growing trend that is strengthening the resistance against capitalist globalization. As long as our organizing is not primarily focused on these symbolic meetings, and we continue to meet and discuss these things, there can be some real benefits to organizing around massive days of action. (Ridefree 2001)

After massive police violence against protesters took place at the June 2001 G8 summit in Genoa, criticism of the strategy increased both online and offline. The different critiques were brought together in a piece entitled "What Moves Us," written by PGA-affiliated Dutch activist Marco. Marco outlined the critiques of summit hopping in the following way:

1. Summit protests were geared mainly at creating a spectacle (and not at creating alternatives).
2. The international mobilizations were gaining a disproportionately large influence/role within the movement.
3. Summit hopping is only possible for relatively rich, white Westerners.
4. Summit hopping will lead to (has led to) an escalation of violence.
5. Summit hopping will become (has become) predictable, and therefore would lose any threat to nation states.
6. Summit hopping does nothing to create an alternative to capitalism.
7. Summit hopping could be (is being used) by authoritarian "anticapitalists" and by "various big shots for their own ends." (Marco 2001)

Marco's comments were reposted on the "Summit Hopping" Web site, where they prompted a discussion involving activists from Israel, Canada, Germany, Brazil, and the Netherlands. Each participant brought issues and experiences from their own local context into dialogue with the more abstract strategic questions raised in Marco's contribution. Regina from Germany posted a lengthy rebuttal, arguing that, from her perspective in Germany, summit hopping had led to some good public discussion about globalization. She continued:

I agree that there should be other strategies to fight globalization, but at the moment I think "summit-hopping" strengthens the international protest networks in an indispensable way. It's one thing if you read that there are a lot of people who don't agree, but it is far more important to experience that a lot of people are strongly opposed against our economic systems, it is important to experience that, to have real contact with the people, to have the possibility to talk with people from other countries directly. We shouldn't underestimate the importance of this experience – no internet can replace that.

A contributor from Israel countered Marco's critique by supporting and extending Regina's argument. Unlike Regina, this activist commented on each argument in Marco's post: "Marco expressed his disappointment that there was no serious discussion of summit hopping – 'Partly due to the pressures of the approaching 'summer of resistance', the discussion around summit hopping faded away after just a few months.'"

The activist from Israel responded:

It faded away as the criticism was exposed very fast to be not sound. It [the criticism] started a bit earlier by the van der illegal [No One Is Illegal organization] who called for people to withdraw from the international struggle against WTO because [a] few of the right [wing] joined it too. In most countries the contradiction of summit hopping with local activity was found very fast to be absurd [sic].... How to use and integrate the best international days and summit hopping with the local and daily work is a never ending discussion.

In response, to Marco's comment that "It has become clear over the last few months that summit hopping is literally a DEAD end strategy," the poster from Israel replied, "They say that even a broken clock shows the correct time once a day.... So, may be the above claim will be true one day." The argument continues, with this poster arguing that the movement necessarily engages in both types of organizing.

As the discussion continued, participants increasingly incorporated previous postings into their responses. This seemed to express the consideration (or, at the very least, awareness) of other opinions. Often, participants would introduce their dissenting opinion with some sort of common ground: "I agree on x, y, but not on z." For example, Marco included the following excerpt from a post from a Canadian before he responded:

hey Marco ... liked what ya wrote ... i pretty much see it the same way ... i'm definitely into putting more focus around local anti-capitalist organizing ... but I'm not sure that I think we should entirely quit organizing around summits. I've seen a bunch of good things come out of them too ... and I think maybe something we need to build on is how to effectively take the benefits out of these big days of action and (like tons of new folks coming together) solidify them.

Marco then argued that the emphasis should be on building decentralized networks of locally oriented activists: "Instead of putting so much emphasis on summits and summit hopping I think we should put the emphasis on building decentralized networks of anarchist-minded collectives and organizations. Secondly we should bring 'evil capitalism' back to level which folks around us can visualize it in their own lives. Thirdly we should create alternatives to capitalism besides the political organizations of resistance."

This online debate continued for a few months during the summer of 2001. Participants posted comments twice and sometimes three times. The debate was conducted in English, despite the fact that only a fraction of the participants shared English as a first language. At the end of the period, Marco posted a note acknowledging the ongoing dialogue:

Dear people, First of all thanks to Regina, Ilan, Brian and Jeroen to take time and discuss the stophop-critique which in fact is shared by a large part of the Dutch direct democracy network (basisdemocratisch netwerk). The critique does NOT as often said arguing that all protesting around summits is wrong. That is really an oversimplification which does NOT do just to the points of critique. It does however criticize the dominating place such protests have within the international movement as well does it criticize the (predictable) way these protests take place. I hope more people will join in the discussion and will be able to reflect on the effect of our internationally co-ordinated actions. And Regina, it also takes me a long time to find the right words since English is not my language either. It shows you do think it is an important discussion and that I am really happy about.

Although operating with a different speed and pacing than a face-to-face discussion, this online discussion appeared to involve relatively diverse participants with differing opinions engaging in reflexive, egalitarian discussion. People supplemented more abstract arguments by recounting stories about personal and collective experiences in their own countries and cities. Sometimes, it seemed that such online debates were able to be more open and reflexive because they weren't tied to the decisions of an organization. Indeed, they were debates at the level of the "movement" rather than at the level of the organization. This should not be taken to imply that they had no impact; such online debates about summit hopping influenced local discussions by providing frames, arguments, examples, and stories that were used in concurrent, face-to-face debates.

The Local Debate – Toronto. In Toronto, criticisms of summit hopping first emerged among OCAP activists. Key OCAP members attended presentations given by activists returning from Seattle, intrigued by the success. Indeed, some OCAP activists became involved in mobilizing for the April 2000 protests against the IMF and World Bank in Washington DC and against the Organization of American States in Windsor, Ontario (June 2000). However, after incurring multiple arrests and injuries at protests against the provincial government on June 15, 2000, Toronto opponents of summit hopping emphasized that "organizers should be fighting where they lived." The articulation of the divide between "local organizer" and "summit hopper" hardened between 2001 and 2003. In 2003, one OCAP organizer distanced himself from summit hopping in the following way:

I was very suspicious of the anti-globalization [movement]; still to this day I'm still very suspicious. It seemed like it was too trendy to me. It was this mass of hysteria about it that made me rebel against it. I was just like, "I can't go to Seattle, and I don't want to go to Seattle. I live here, therefore I should fight here. I'm not going to go to Seattle and then go somewhere else, and go somewhere else." It seemed too easy in a way to get caught up in the moment. Almost like make love to a beautiful woman and get drunk and do drugs and go to the protest and live that sort of bohemian lifestyle and it's just like, I had a full slate of casework at OCAP and couldn't just take off and go.

Recounting their conversion from global justice activists to local organizer, another OCAP member explained how OCAP activists who organized for antiglobalization protests in Windsor in June 2000 had similarly distanced themselves from those mobilizing for the protests against the FTAA in April 2001.

I was convinced that it was not serious activism. So I didn't go [to Quebec City]. People were not feeling that this was the sort of movement that needed to be built. We needed to build something very different.... The flaw looking back on it was, we were just like, "these kids are on the wrong page, they need to come to the right page." It wasn't looked at as though like, "we went through this process, we learned our shit, but we have to help steer this so other people learn their shit too." It was like a "no, we don't need you."

Another OCAP activist described how many Toronto activists moved from summit protests to local organizing after encountering repression during the summer of 2000: "The anti-globalization phenomenon, the people born out of that movement and the transition into a search for community based and local organizing is a long hard road." Portraying the transition from global to local in a manner that counterposed the two foci activated a particular boundary between the identities and strategies. Another OCAP activist described a similar transition:

But a lot of the people who went and did that (anti-globalization) and went back and said 'It politicized me, now I'm going to go back and build these community organizations and do this serious work," and who are committed. That happened at OCAP too. A lot of people who did join OCAP now would have been anti-globalization movement people. We don't see them as that, they don't see themselves as that, but that was the way that people thought about these things. There was anti-globalization and it was connected to that way of thinking. And Seattle created that stepping stone for those people.

As local activists redefined their identity and strategy in relation to the Seattle protesters, the critique of summit hopping began to be taken up by other Toronto-based activists. A Mob4Glob activist argued that after the protests in Quebec City in April 2001, "it was a concern that the [antiglobalization] movement couldn't sustain itself if they keep just having these big protests. You just organize people on buses to go somewhere else. The issue was also that this type of organizing just didn't resonate with lived experience of the vast majority of people."

What needed to happen next, he continued, was to "use the same types of organizing, the same types of tactics but just ... into the spaces in which people spend most of their lives. So this was some of the thinking behind the critique of summit hopping and the move towards going local."

As with some of the online debates, the divisions between those who prioritized local organizing and those who prioritized summit protests became extremely polarized in Toronto. This led many Toronto activists to commit to either a "global" or a "local" position. It was an outcome that helped to block the localization of the Seattle tactics. Mob4Glob meetings and listservs became central fora for this debate. Tied to historical competition between activists affiliated with the International Socialists who favored mass protests but shied away from direct action, and activists identified with OCAP and the New Socialist Group, who prioritized locally oriented direct action, things came to a head in the spring of 2002.

At that point, debate centered around priorities in the post-9/11 context and, in particular, around the appropriate responses to the June 2002 G8 summit planned for Kananaskis, near Calgary. Would Mob4Glob focus on local organizing bring people to protest the G8 in nearby Ottawa or mobilize people to travel to Kananaskis? Tensions between these three positions ran so high that, shortly before the Ottawa protest, the group operated with parallel communications committees, e-mail lists, logistics committees, and education committees (Rutherford 2003). In this context, communication between the different positions effectively broke down. One Mob4Glob activist explained the debate:

And that was a very nasty debate inside Mob4Glob. Extreme polarization, lots of plotting and maneuvering behind the scenes and both sides were equally guilty in that sort of thing. It was again the line-up there was the IS [International Socialists] being the leaders of the "fly to Alberta" side and the NSG [New Socialist Group] and the OCAP people being the organized force for the regional protests. A lot of people in between said this is ridiculous, let's not do either, let's just have something in Toronto instead and let's get away from this sectarian split. That's how they interpreted it. So there was also a Toronto action as well. And so a key strategic issue that caused a lot of friction and splits inside Mob4Glob was this issue of summit hopping, organizing locally, and I don't think we ever really theorized those issues or debated them adequately.

Polarization of the debate between summit hopping and local organizing signaled the collapse of Mob4Glob and, with it, the loss of a central opportunity for deliberation. Without an antiglobalization coalition to certify the Seattle tactics as useful and appropriate, their incorporation became much less likely in Toronto. Those doing direct action locally or regionally in Toronto rejected the Seattle tactics because they perceived them to be tied to "global" summit protests and because those working on the summits were perceived as not "serious." Too much energy had been absorbed into defending the different positions.

The Local Discussion – New York City. Like Toronto, the critique of summit hopping in New York came first from organizers and activists already engaged in local struggles. Some were frustrated that so much energy was being given to campaigns taking place outside the city when so many local issues – particularly police brutality, homelessness, and community gardening – needed attention and resources. Despite this frustration, some local organizations attempted to reach out to the summit hoppers and engage with them locally, although they coupled their outreach with a critique of summit hopping. One More Gardens! activist explained:

DAN was meeting at that time, so there was a lot of connectivities with other groups and lots of energy. And I think Seattle had happened a little before and everybody was really excited about the actions ... and so I had to convince a lot of people, "Look,

Esperanza is an encampment right in your back yard. You don't have to go six hours to DC or eight hours to Canada or whatever else is going on. Come help people locally and that's the best reward."

Whereas in Toronto, there was a critique of summit hopping as middle class, in New York, the critique of summit hopping was partly framed as a critique of the whiteness of the antiglobalization movement. Over time, this led some activists to change their focus and to inadvertently localize the Seattle tactics. Unlike in Toronto, the shift from global to local didn't correspond to a rejection of either the Seattle tactics or the global justice identity. Instead, a bridge was built. A large proportion of DAN activists who were very new to politics shifted their focus from summit protests to local organizing after the August 2000 Republican National Convention. This transition was facilitated by SLAM and More Gardens! activists who made a point of articulating the connections between local and global, welcoming direct action tactics into the local context, and joining the summit protests themselves (Subways 2010). One DAN activist explains how the critique advanced by more experienced local activists led some summit hoppers to shift tactics and to gradually become local organizers:

Because one of the themes throughout [the period] was people were asking; "Why don't you do real organizing?" "Why don't you work in your communities?" And both of those things are I think that are really easy to say, and not so easy to figure out. DAN in New York was a largely white group of people who were not from New York City so questions of "our community" and questions of organizing were complex.... What felt like a strength that we had (i.e. direct action); we were trying to figure out how to use that to support organizing that was actually going on locally. And I think that was a really good idea and it was a good thing for us to be talking about.... And part of what that meant was having conversations with groups who were doing different kinds of organizing locally. Who were not doing direct action stuff. And then eventually I think led to, people who had previously just identified as direct action activists, people who were sort of born through Seattle, stopped identifying that way. We began acknowledging something that was a tactic as a tactic instead of as a political identity.

During this transition, some antiglobalization activists began to discuss how direct action tactics used at summit protests might be adapted and incorporated into local organizing. One activist explained how the DAN Labour Working Group successfully used the Seattle tactics in local labor organizing: "I feel that one good thing that we did was ... we showed how we could use direct action to support actual [local] campaigns that people were in." Another DAN organizer explained how that organization brought the Seattle tactics to the local immigrant rights movement: "In Mayday 2000, DAN threw its weight behind a local immigrant rights amnesty march and provided some really good theatre and puppets and stuff that added to the march." DAN also brought the Seattle tactics to local struggles around community gardens through such experiments, the Seattle tactics were able to influence the repertoire of a number of New York City organizations.

GLOBAL SUMMIT HOPPERS, LOCAL ORGANIZERS

Unlike in Toronto, the debate around summit hopping in New York City did not become polarized. Even though global justice movement activists in Toronto became involved in local struggles, they did so in a centralized and polarized context where local and global were diametrically opposed. In contrast, even though many DAN-NYC activists gradually became more focused on local issues, they continued to use the Seattle tactics and identify as antiglobalization activists (albeit sometimes self-consciously). Although local labor and immigrant rights groups remained wary, they welcomed the antiglobalization activists who supported their campaigns using puppets and blockades.

In the period immediately after Seattle, Toronto and New York activists deliberated about the Seattle tactics and debated the merits and drawbacks of summit hopping. When these discussions involved both local and global activists in relatively reflexive and egalitarian discussions, both online and offline, they built more strategic capacity in their organizations and were more able to reject, adapt, or encourage experimentation with new tactics. The possibilities of and barriers to deliberation arose from the structure and history of local interactions, but such dynamics do not simply influence diffusion in a single location. When deliberation or polarized debates take place outside of a local context, they can alter the incorporation of innovations elsewhere. I turn to an example of this in Chapter 8, where I look at activist debates around property destruction and the black bloc.

8

Talking about Smashing

In the months after Seattle, the most heated debate among direct action activists in the United States and Canada concerned the question of violence or – more accurately – the appropriateness of destroying property during mass protests. Initially, the issue almost divided the emerging movement; however, rhetorical strategies that emphasized solidarity managed to keep the conversation going – for a while at least. The division reemerged in Canada during organizing for protests against the FTAA in Quebec City in April 2001. Again some, leading activists attempted to de-escalate the division. Like the discussions about summit hopping considered in Chapter 7, these exchanges were simultaneously international, national, and local. They took place in both face-to-face and online contexts. The debate's focus and level of intensity influenced the spread of the black bloc tactic and the use of property destruction to new cities. Where the debate was most intense, but there were ongoing relationships between the positions, the black bloc tactic spread most effectively, and property destruction became more frequent. The online and face-to-face debates about property destruction were particularly intense in the lead-up to protests in Washington DC (2000) and Quebec City (2001). Property destruction and black bloc tactics were incorporated at both protests. The New York and Toronto organizers had observed these debates, and their perception of them led them to avoid such discussions. In the absence of such debates, activists in either city did not experiment much with either property destruction nor the black bloc tactics.

Debates about the black bloc were unlike debates about summit hopping or identity because of the risks involved in publicly arguing for property destruction. Clearly illegal, property destruction is outside of the North American protest repertoire. For an organization to publicly embrace it would be risky. The vast majority of activists were unlikely to deliberate publicly about whether their organization should engage in property destruction or join black bloc formations, making it more difficult for property destruction or black bloc tactics to diffuse. However, activists could and did talk more easily about whether activists who did engage in property destruction should be rebuffed, excluded, admitted, or considered a valuable part of the movement. Although such debates were not explicitly about the tactics that activists would use themselves (and thus didn't facilitate adaptation and incorporation in the way that discussions about puppetry or blockading might have), the debate did maintain the networks among activists with shared strategies and identities. In this way, they facilitated the future possibility of experimenting with and incorporating property destruction and black bloc tactics in Toronto and New York City.

THE DEBATE BEFORE SEATTLE

Many activists became interested in black bloc and property destruction as a rejection of apparently predictable and ineffective protest tactics. In the ten years prior to Seattle, most activists in the United States and Canada – and even those who engaged in civil disobedience – would publicly condemn most forms of property destruction and distance themselves from those who used such tactics. Since the civil rights movement, most activists have drawn on the civil rights movement's repertoire – a civil disobedience rooted in Gandhian nonviolence.[1] In the 1980s and 1990s, these tactics became routinized within sections of the antinuclear, environmental, and feminist movements. Leading up to the Seattle protests, veterans of these movements held training workshops so that new activists would learn this approach. However, with the rise of a new wave of direct action tied to the animal rights, radical environmental, and police brutality movements during the mid-1990s, some activists had begun to argue that the existing strategy overemphasized moral suffering and symbolic opposition.[2] Some argued that protest had become predictable and, as such, had become ineffective for making change. As a result, increasing numbers of activists in the period leading up to the Seattle protests began to express their desire to disrupt "business as usual." Two different but related strategies emerged. Inspired by the Reclaim the Streets and Art and Revolution networks, the first used street theater and puppetry to block streets, visually portray injustice, and present alternatives to the current system. The second stream was influenced by European antifascist, anarchist, radical environmentalist, and animal rights movements. Experimenting with black bloc tactics, these activists aimed to disrupt corporate targets and increase the "costs of doing business." For many of them, Native American scholar Ward Churchill's book *Pacifism as Pathology* (1998) was an important source of inspiration. According to Churchill, "Pacifism, the ideology of nonviolent political action, has become axiomatic and all but universal among more progressive elements

[1] Gandhian approaches can involve property destruction, but many activists in North America interpret the Gandhian tradition otherwise.

[2] There are many exceptions to this, but see Keck and Sikkink (1998) and Staggenborg (1988) on professionalization and routinization of protest.

of contemporary mainstream North America (29)." In his view, strict nonviolence was a product of privilege and limited thinking. In contrast, he argued,
a strategic movement needed to consider all alternatives. Networks committed
to both strategies were building strength in the Pacific Northwest before the
Seattle protests. Both helped to disrupt the summit and draw attention to the
relationships between institutional targets and environmental, economic, and
human rights concerns.

Before the protests, these different strategic strands hadn't consolidated
into a cluster of tactics; however, the Direct Action Network laid the groundwork for them to become affiliated by citing People's Global Action as inspiration. PGA hallmarks include:

- A confrontational attitude, since we do not think that lobbying can have
  a major impact in such biased and undemocratic organizations, in which
  transnational capital is the only real policy maker; and
- A call to direct action and civil disobedience, support for social movements' struggles, advocating forms of resistance which maximize respect
  for life and oppressed peoples' rights, as well as the construction of local
  alternatives to global capitalism. (People's Global Action 2001)

Because of their association with the Zapatistas and the landless peasant movement in Brazil, the PGA hallmarks provided a foundation of legitimacy for a
broad tactical repertoire. Nevertheless, organizers from Global Exchange,
Rainforest Action Network, the Ruckus Society, and others who formed the
Direct Action Network used the standard guidelines that rejected property
destruction. When this agreement was communicated more widely, activists
committed to property destruction argued that this agreement did not represent
the movement. Warning that they were going to use property destruction in
Seattle, they asked that the agreement be amended or canceled (Hurl 2005).

In the period immediately before the protests in Seattle, New York activists avoided destroying property, even during large militant protests. Nor
were there any black blocs in the city, although some New Yorkers had participated in a black bloc during the April 24, 1999, Millions 4 Mumia March
in Philadelphia. In Toronto, confrontation at protests and picket lines was
routine for organizations like OCAP. Nevertheless, property destruction
remained unusual – even for militants engaged in large protests like the days
of action or those that coincided with the anarchist conference of 1998. In
the wake of the Seattle protests, this constraint was called into question in
both cities.

NOVEMBER 30, 1999–APRIL 17, 2000: STORYTELLING
ABOUT THE BLACK BLOC

When the first brick broke through the first window of the first Starbucks,
the debate about property destruction erupted. Lori Wallach from the NGO
Public Citizen told her version of the scene in Seattle:

These anarchist folks marched in there and started smashing things. And our people actually picked up the anarchists. Because we had with us longshoremen and
steelworkers who, by their sheer bulk, were three or four times larger. So we had
them ... a Teamster, just pick up an anarchist. We'd walk him over to the cops
and say, "this boy just broke a window. He doesn't belong with us. We hate the
WTO, so does he, maybe, but we don't break things. Please arrest him." (In Davis
2002, 177)

An organizer with Global Exchange, Medea Benjamin told the media that she
believed such protesters should be arrested or, at least, should not be protected
by the collective legal strategy (something for which she later apologized).
Clarifying her position, she indicated that her concern was about "losing the
message" of the protests. In her story, she makes clear identity claims about
the nature of the movement. For Benjamin, *we* were collective and democratic,
and *they* were small and unrepresentative.

The nonviolent part of the WTO protest was the culmination of a complex process of
coalition building by organizations that did not initially know or trust each other....
We finally agreed, through a collective and democratic process, that the banner that
united the scores of organizations and thousands of individuals was a strict commitment to nonviolence, defined to include no property destruction. After that collaborative and democratic process, a small number of protesters who had boycotted
those meetings took it upon themselves to break that solidarity.... We think it was
totally unfair for a small, unrepresentative group to use a massive, peaceful protest
as a venue for destructive actions that went against the wishes of the vast majority
of protesters. We are far less concerned about the glass that they broke than about
the sense of collective unity that they attempted – but failed – to shatter (Quoted in
Dunbar-Ortiz 2000).[3]

This condemnation created a backlash across the continent. Activists on each
side of the debate argued about the sequence of events in Seattle, the identity and legitimacy of those who engaged in or interrupted property destruction, the impact and interpretation of property destruction by marginalized
groups, and justifications of the attacks on corporate targets. The majority of
voices condemned property destruction, but some heralded it as an appropriate escalation that drew attention to multinational corporations as purveyors
of violence and inequality.[4] One of the most widely circulated contributions
to the debate was a communiqué penned by the ACME Collective, which
had participated in the Seattle black bloc. It linked the black bloc to property
destruction by telling a story of solidarity and success:

The black bloc was a loosely organized cluster of affinity groups and individuals who
roamed around downtown, pulled this way by a vulnerable and significant storefront

---

[3] See ZNet Vision and Strategy Pages, http://www.zmag.org/stratvision.htm, and others for
   discussions of strategy.
[4] For activist and academic contributions to the debate see writings by Michael Albert 1999,
   Medea Benjamin 2000, George Lakey 2002, Brian Dominick 1999, L. A. Kauffman 2002;
   Geov Parrish 2002; and Starhawk 2002.

and that way by the sight of a police formation. Unlike the vast majority of activists who were pepper-sprayed, tear-gassed and shot at with rubber bullets on several occasions, most of our section of the black bloc escaped serious injury by remaining constantly in motion and avoiding engagement with the police. We buddied up, kept tight and watched each others' backs. Those attacked by federal thugs were un-arrested by quick-thinking and organized members of the black bloc. The sense of solidarity was awe-inspiring.

Framing contests about the movement's strategy and identity revealed starkly different visions of the global justice movement. The black bloc statement described *we* as being unlike two different *they's*. According to ACME (1999), black bloc activists were unlike the "peace police ... so called 'non-violent' activists who physically attacked individuals who targeted corporate property" whom they critiqued for being ineffective and unprincipled. Reframing the accusation that those engaging in property destruction were agents provocateurs, ACME suggested that activists seeking to control protester behavior may themselves have been undercover police. Responding to accusations that the back bloc consisted primarily of privileged youth who lacked awareness that their tactics may cause harm to people of color and poor people, the communiqué used Ward Churchill's argument to infer that those opposed to the black bloc were elitist and racist, countering that the black bloc was in fact antiracist and populist: "Window-smashing has engaged and inspired many of the most oppressed members of Seattle's community more than any giant puppets or sea turtle costumes ever could (not to disparage the effectiveness of those tools in other communities)" (1999).

The mainstream media amplified and simplified the debate into one about "good" nonviolent protestors versus "bad" violent ones. Despite the relatively small size of the black bloc in Seattle, disproportionate amounts of coverage quickly identified the tactic with the protests' successes and limits. This coverage communicated a simplified "violence vs. nonviolence" debate to many new activists.

In the week following the protests, various intellectuals and organizers attempted to reframe the debate online. Many expressed concern about the effects that such polarization might have on the strength and sustainability of the movement. Some of these "movement entrepreneurs" managed to facilitate some agreement between the two positions. On the left-wing *Z Magazine's* online discussion boards, a whole file of commentary about property destruction developed. Most contributions were posted in the week after the protests. Many tried to propose a strategy for the movement in an abstract way (Hurl 2005). Others were less decisive. One of the most widely read articles was posted by movement intellectual Michael Albert (1999) entitled "Nonviolence, Trashing and Movement Strategy." For Albert:

What modestly (as compared to "seriously") impaired the movement's ability to get on with growing and struggling was a very real division over tactics and that that division in this case was handled poorly largely due to a lack of mechanisms for dealing with disagreement. I think a priority task ought to be to develop and agree on such mechanisms, so that we don't suffer such problems again in the future, or even see them get worse.

Albert's piece reframed the discussion by arguing that the real violence was from the state. Asking what strategy best builds the movement, he suggested that the "trashers" support those most vulnerable at protests. It was in the midst of these debates that global justice coalitions like DAN-NYC and Mob4Glob held their first meetings.

DAN-NYC included both committed pacifists and black bloc enthusiasts. Because the Direct Action Network in Seattle had condemned property destruction, one might assume that its spin-off groups would follow suit; however, DAN-NYC's position was influenced as much by the position of its Seattle predecessor as it was by backlash against that position at the national and international level. One activist explained: "I think that immediately after Seattle there was a lot of concern about supporting the more militant aspects of the movement even if they weren't necessarily more effective. They were supported to show that you were more in support of 'the people' than of the NGOs."

On February 20, 2000, DAN-NYC members discussed a proposal to spend at least an hour talking about the PGA guidelines (DAN-NYC minutes); however, some remained reluctant to engage in a debate that might divide the group unnecessarily. Although those with concerns and ideas for resolving the violence/nonviolence debate were encouraged to bring written proposals to the meeting, the discussion never happened.

By the beginning of March 2000, the topic had become tied to the upcoming Washington, DC protests against the IMF and World Bank taking place the following month. Forces strongly opposed to property destruction worked hard to ensure that it would not take place at the upcoming protests, whereas others suggested that its incorporation into demonstration plans could avoid tactical divisions. In Washington, a great deal of the debate hinged on whether to ask participants to commit to a code of nonviolence and a rejection of property destruction.

With Washington marking the first large U.S. protest against neoliberalism since the Seattle protests, the property destruction debate loomed large. Although Toronto activists were aware of its dynamics, they were geographically removed from the debate and didn't really engage with it. In contrast, DAN-NYC activists used the debate in Washington to develop their own organizational position on property destruction.

Activists in New York used the debate in Washington to make arguments and tell stories about who *we* are and who *they* are and to describe the relationships – past, present, and future – determining how *we* and *they* interact. Although this deliberation wasn't about a local protest, it deeply influenced the local attitude to black bloc and property destruction. By looking at e-mail exchanges between DAN-NYC participants and activists in Washington DC and between the New York activists themselves, it's possible to see how the debate within the larger movement became localized in both Washington and in New York City and influenced the way these activists related to those who destroyed property. Because DAN-NYC never discussed using property destruction as a collective strategy for a particular event, it never became incorporated into its overall repertoire; however, discussions about the boundaries of appropriate action allowed those within DAN-NYC's networks – including some affinity groups – to conduct autonomous experiments with property destruction without becoming isolated or targeted. Online and offline deliberation indirectly facilitated these limited experiments.

In March 2000, a small number of New York-based activists traveled to Washington, DC to help coordinate the upcoming demonstrations. When plans for the protests began to coalesce, a discussion about tactics ensued in DAN-NYC and activists decided against advocating a nonviolence code of conduct. This decision put DAN-NYC in opposition to many of the main organizers in DC.

One New Yorker began attending DC Mobilization for Global Justice meetings in Washington and participating in the action's organizing listserv. She then forwarded these e-mail exchanges to the DAN-NYC list, explaining "I just wanted to let you guys see some of the conversation in DC regarding what I call property destruction and what others call violence." She recounted that she was disturbed by the tone of the conversations, that activists were being prompted to enforce nonviolence guidelines, and that New York activists should be prepared "by knowing what some of the discourse is." The forwarded e-mails illustrated how movement identity and strategy boundaries were being discussed in order to argue for or against particular tactical choices.

In her first post to the NYC-DAN list on this topic, the activist included an e-mail from a Washington opponent of the black bloc who described the shared nonviolent identity/strategy of DC's Mobilization for Global Justice as one that differed from:

Black bloc anarchists or agents provocateurs or anyone who does not conform to the four guidelines. ... The guidelines for the Seattle demonstration were similar [to the proposed guidelines for A16], yet that did not prevent the "black bloc" people from violating them with impunity.... I think that a concrete proposal for holding accountable black bloc anarchists, or agents provocateurs, or anyone who does not adhere to the four guidelines, would be very useful in squelching rumors of violence and violence itself; and would help us shift the media discussion toward the real issues. It would also serve to blunt accusations that the MGJ tacitly condoned property destruction by not taking steps to prevent it.

In this post, the Washington opponent clearly articulates who he envisions *we* and *they* to be and uses personal stories about Seattle and its effect on the media to support arguments for his position. To make her case, the New Yorker in Washington responded with a different articulation of who *we* and *they* were. After introducing herself as a DAN-NYC media working group member, she stated:

I think it is important that we don't show the media that we think we can control what other groups or individuals do, if for no other reason than we really have no CONTROL of what others do. We must remember that we are working as part of a coalition of groups that include anarchists and other anti-authoritarian groups, many of which are against property destruction always and some who believe it's sometimes a warranted tactic.

The activist continued by asking "who are we to do that [control tactics]?" In conclusion, she stated: "We must respect political differences or we risk emulating the kind of thinking that we abhor in institutions like the IMF and World Bank."

The activist from Washington responded by highlighting the division between *we* (nonviolent protesters) and *they* (violent protesters) who take advantage of "non-violent protesters." He then again justified this division by emphasizing his experience in Seattle: "The ones I met in Seattle were violent, and I am just not interested in fist fights." He then recommended that *we* disassociate from violent protesters, use the police to help enforce guidelines, and publicize our cooperation in that regard. "I think there are some major benefits of doing this," he continued:

1. It blunts accusations that the MGJ (Mobilization for Global Justice) tacitly condones property destruction.
2. It strongly disassociated MGJ from violent protesters.
3. It asserts something that is already true, namely that the police already are responsible for responding to such acts of violence.
4. It makes clear that we expect and demand the cooperation of the police in enforcing the guidelines of our protest, and in protecting our constitutional rights.
5. Police have the training and ability to deal with violence, and we do not.
6. It enhances our credibility in the media, with the police, and ultimately with ordinary people who are becoming aware of the issues for the first time.

By placing a thicker boundary between protesters using different tactics than between protesters and police, this activist challenged the collective identity/strategy of New York protesters, many of whom had recently been involved in the movement against police brutality.

In response, the New Yorker in Washington told a story that highlighted New York struggles against police brutality, dynamics around race and racialized policing, and the implications of not understanding these dynamics. She thus placed the boundary between *we* who understood how race and power operate in the context of the state and economy and *they* who do not:

There is a fundamental political disagreement here about how we view the system of government we live under and its police force. Perhaps this is related to our different position in this society, perhaps not. One thing I can say for sure, hardly any people of color activists in NYC would want to work with an organization that would turn people over to the police.

She ended her e-mail with a gesture that was half reconciliation, half ultimatum,

I send this email in the spirit of struggle and because I seek to reach out to people involved in this movement. I am a Latina and one of not many people of color in this movement in NY. In my opinion, if more of the people involved in this struggle do not attempt to see how cultural and social historical differences affect people's politics and how they relate to the police and non-violence and try to come to some compromise that reflects that understanding, our movements will always be divided.

When the New Yorker in Washington forwarded this exchange to the DAN-NYC list, it exploded into discussion. Between March 30 and April 3, 2000 (two weeks before the protest), the online debate helped DAN-NYC construct a collective identity and associated strategy. In the end, the group decided not to condemn or isolate anyone who would engage in property destruction.

The week before the Washington demonstrations, DAN-NYC's Education Working Group co-hosted a "hypothetical revolutionary potluck discussion" on Property Destruction and Violence as Tactics. This allowed participants in the group to wrestle with the ideas more openly and without direct consequences. Because of its extensive online and offline discussion, DAN-NYC had largely come to agreement that those using property destruction would be supported by the time they loaded onto the buses to DC. Indeed, because of concerns that black bloc activists might be refused support, the cluster of organizations from New York organized its own legal team. In this way, external discussions about tactics inadvertently built a group identity that supported limited tactical experimentation with black bloc and property destruction by NYC-DAN.

In Toronto, the discussions about black bloc and property destruction that took place in Toronto during this period, took place outside of formal organizations. However, in the wake of arrests in Washington, Toronto activists mobilized a black bloc in solidarity (described in Chapter 10), which was quickly repressed by police. Here too, it seems the possibility of incorporating black bloc tactics had not been foreclosed.

RESOLUTION AT A16

In the end, an agreement was brokered between those who favored nonviolence guidelines and peacekeepers (the majority of the Mobilization for Global Justice-DC organizing body) and their critics (including the local Revolutionary Anti-Capitalist Bloc, who was publicly planning to act as a black bloc). Mob4Glob organizers agreed that they would not "marginalize" or condemn those engaging in property destruction. Meanwhile, the black bloc agreed to do solidarity actions supporting blockading protesters (Solstice 2000).

During the protests, both sides fulfilled their promises. The black bloc intentionally distracted police from blockades and kept property destruction away from more vulnerable participants. As a result, there was little animosity to the black bloc on the streets of DC, and the tactic began to be incorporated into Washington's protest repertoire. Brokerage between the two sides seemed to hold, at least temporarily. DAN-NYC activists were enthusiastic about the resolution and about its support for an inclusive tactical repertoire.

MAY 2000–AUGUST 2000

After A16, online and offline discussions about property destruction became less volatile. In DAN-NYC, the peripheral experience of the heated debates in Washington and Seattle meant that to raise the question meant risking being accused of "doing the police's work for them" by dividing the movement. The refusal to see property destruction as ethically wrong and to reject those who used it made DAN-NYC different from other Direct Action Networks. Unlike the founding group in Seattle, DAN-NYC did not explicitly commit itself to nonviolent action. The group's identity was tied to a more open tactical position, its connection to antiracism, and its ties to local struggles against police brutality, which was rooted in the interconnectedness discussed in Chapter 5. One member explains:

Before A16, for a lot of us in New York, there was an important connection between the DAN stuff happening and a lot of police brutality stuff coming to a head ... and being involved in the anti-globalization stuff and finding connections.... So what I was thinking before A16 was its crazy that I'm spending so much of my time doing this police violence stuff and in DAN we talk about that only explicitly as what happens to us when we get arrested.... I remember talking to all these black bloc kids at A16 and people being like "yeah, it's crazy" because people were so pissed about police violence in NY, and not on a stupid level, but really pissed and really not knowing what to do about it. Partly being really aware they weren't the people who were affected mostly by police violence in New York and not knowing how to act in the face of that.

This position did not mean that DAN-NYC organized property destruction and black blocs at demonstrations; but it did mean that ongoing relationships were fostered between movement participants with a range of tactical preferences. These relationships facilitated local experiments by autonomous clusters of activists at demonstrations organized or endorsed by DAN-NYC. During May, June, and July 2000, some New York activists experimented with black bloc formations. In part because of heavy policing, little property destruction took place at these demonstrations. Lacking the opportunity to deliberate and strategize in more depth about how the tactic might be adopted to the NYC context, these activists attempted to use black bloc tactics exactly as they had been used in Seattle at a protest on May 1, 2000. They were quickly arrested.[5]

---

[5] See Highleyman 2001, From Somewhere in the Mid-West 2001, and Young 2000 for discussions on how the black bloc is a tactic, not an identity.

In Toronto, there were fewer experiments with black bloc formations, and the tactic was never discussed at any open meetings of Mob4Glob, OPIRG, or OCAP. This is not to say that the tactic was rejected because of its confrontational connotations. OCAP activists had some familiarity with its use through their connections with Toronto's Anti-Racist Action. Nonetheless, OCAP never incorporated it into its own demonstrations. One organizer explains:

OCAP will be militant and use similar tactics of a black bloc but why you would label yourself as a black bloc? I think would just kind of be odd to people, it doesn't really make sense. It might have been a good political movement at a political time in a climate that we weren't in. ... It seemed like it was something that was inspiring to people when Seattle was happening and people were willing to go out and take this line or whatever but OCAP has always taken a militant line and we haven't had to dress up in black to do it.

Although OCAP admired movements that emphasized community defense. When asked whether OCAP would ever use a black bloc formation, one organizer explained:

The notion that people actually organizing to defend themselves might be something that's really quite viable and important. The only reservation that I have is that we would place a premium on broad social mobilization getting deeper and deeper into communities and bringing out more and more people as opposed to the notion of the elite units [like the black bloc].

Partly because of its association with "global" protests, OCAP was not interested in forming a black bloc. However, they were not going to condemn the tactic. In the wake of Seattle and condemnations of the black bloc, many OCAP activists identified with the militancy of the demonstrations; but they already had an existing repertoire and ongoing campaigns and in a context that sharply divided local from global, they were not interested in changing their approach.

As in New York, discussions about the Seattle tactics became more frequent in Toronto during mobilizations for large Seattle-type protests. Organizing for the Windsor protests against the Organization of American States in June 2000 (discussed in Chapter 10), an affinity group tied to OPIRG and OCAP called Resist! adopted a tactical identity partly in opposition to the less direct action orientation of Mob4Glob. Rather than emphasize the Seattle frames of black bloc or property destruction, OCAP's frame of self-defense was adopted. One activist explained that, when the organizers of the direct action protests first met in March 2000, "we decided in advance that we were going to take a position in favor of self-defense." One OPIRG activist described a tactical approach that supported militant tactics in the following way:

We were very, very adamantly diversity of tactics, it was very much about self defense and if the cops bring it, we'll dish it back and all that stuff. So that was where we were coming from and we were all agreed on that because that was one of the core things we all bonded on. We weren't just going to sit there and take a thrashing you know or wave a picket sign and call it a day, say a prayer and be on our way.

Despite the fact that it was a summit protest, Mob4Glob had only limited influence on this mobilization. The divisions between organizers more identified with OCAP and those advocating a more "mass/moderate" position began to grow.

On June 15th 2000, one week after the Windsor protests, OCAP held an antipoverty protest at the provincial government buildings. The demonstration built on a confrontation that took place six months earlier in Ottawa; however, it was also influenced by the militancy of the Seattle demonstrations. Activists came prepared with goggles, bandannas, shields, and mattresses to protect themselves from anticipated police violence. Despite these accoutrements, a lot of black-hooded sweatshirts, and the resulting battle with the police, none of the OCAP respondents I interviewed identified the formation as a black bloc. Indeed, they distanced themselves from the anti-globalization movement and the tactic, which they considered to be the purview of "middle class, white students."

After these protests were heavily repressed, there was a retreat from militant street action in Toronto. Although the self-defense frame continued to be used, the intensity of the arrests and violence in both Windsor and at the OCAP protests, led others to distance themselves from tactics they associated with repression. The opportunity for incorporating black bloc tactics into local protests had seemingly disappeared. After this point, discussions of the tactic was tied to mobilizations in other cities.

In the lead-up to the political conventions of the Republican (Philadelphia) and Democratic (Los Angeles) Parties in the summer of 2000, discussions about property destruction and violence in the United States became similarly tied to consideration of the movement's racial and class identity. Activists in New York and Toronto were aware of these debates. For the most part, they could participate in them or avoid them as they pleased. This was especially true for the debates taking place around the Democratic National Convention in Los Angeles. In that city, consensus emerged that, in order to make the protests accessible to people of color and poor people, protesters had to commit to not destroy property and not use physical or verbal violence toward police officers. These guidelines were promoted using an antiracist framework that argued that, in their absence, people of color, immigrants, poor people, and families would be unlikely to participate. On this basis, organizers worked to gain police permission for most of their protests. Although there was a major confrontation at the end of a Rage Against the Machine concert, during which police fired rubber bullets, there was only a small black bloc and little property destruction (Antibody et al., 2000, Van Deusen and Massot 2010, Von Blum 2006).

A few weeks earlier, in Philadelphia, when preparations were underway for demonstrations against the Republican National Convention, activist arguments about property destruction also hinged on the movement's race and class dynamics. Here, the conclusion was the opposite to what it had been in Los Angeles. Local activists argued that, if one was to be antiracist, one couldn't dismiss tactics that reflected people of color's rage against corporations and government even if these tactics included property destruction. These stories about who *we* are and who *they* are filled that summer's discussions about property destruction. Although some participants hoped for a prohibition of property destruction, many respondents rejected this position as one taken by privileged, white, middle-class activists and as one that would be divisive to the movement. Arguments in these discussions often referenced Churchill's Pacifism as Pathology. This is not to say that tactical debates were constrained in Philadelphia. As a center of Quakerism and as home to pacifist George Lakey's Training for Change, activist training sessions leading up to the demonstrations were full of deliberation around tactics and strategy and identity.

As part of the August 1st Direct Action Coalition, activists from DAN-NYC and SLAM were deeply engaged in planning for these protests. This planning never excluded confrontational tactics or property destruction. Indeed, one of SLAM's reasons for participating was to show that people of color could engage in militant tactics (Subways 2010). In the end, the protests involved a large black bloc. Organized along similar lines as Seattle, the event involved a range of tactics including puppetry and blockading. With police car windows smashed and with banks, government buildings, and corporations spray painted, the action also included property destruction; however, unlike the events in Seattle, organizers refused to condemn these tactics. In a zine written to commemorate the ten-year anniversary of the protests, Kai Lumumba Barrow from SLAM explained, there was ongoing respect for the black bloc, even after the arrests:

One of the things I dug about black bloc was the thing I think everybody dug about black bloc: their fearlessness. I dug that they were willing to move as if they had nothing to lose. The critique of that is that they were, I think, predominantly white. They functioned as if they were predominantly white. They functioned as if they had predominantly come from a middle-class background, but I could be stereotyping here, I don't know. But that kind of freedom to say, "I don't have shit to lose, and I'm going to do what I came to do, which is disrupt." I'm seeking a certain amount of freedom, and that's what the black bloc represented to me. They were purposeful and courageous. The other thing I dug about them was that they were tight. For the most part, I didn't hear leaks about who black bloc was. Another critique is that they were cool. And being cool brings a certain cult of celebrity. But I think they were cool because they were effective. In the Philly action, we would get somewhere and the shit had already been dealt with. We were like, "Damn, the black bloc beat us to it." To come into an environment with the purpose of disrupting this entire shit, similar to graffiti, saying, "This is no longer your space. I'm taking this space." And to come into that space after black bloc had been there was to come into a space that had been reclaimed. And I have respect for that. I still do. (In Subways 2010)

Over the course of the protests in Philadelphia, hundreds of activists – many from DAN-NYC and SLAM – were arrested. Some were picked up for blockading in the Seattle style, and others were simply surrounded. Once in jail, most of the protesters refused to cooperate, used jail solidarity tactics, and remained in custody for almost two weeks.

In the wake of these protests, and as a result of the significant police repression, DAN-NYC's e-mail list witnessed another flurry of discussion about the role of property destruction. One poster wrestled with the pros and cons of property destruction:

Like you, I too have been reflecting on property destruction. Primarily, I was concerned that property destruction is too much like activist jargon – not only ineffectual as a form of outreach because no one but involved activists understood its meaning, but also alienating because so few other people can comprehend it. I now suspect I arrived at this reaction due to the way the press hammered our August 1st demo, a frustrating experience that I think all of us in Philadelphia felt acutely. However, it is important to figure out whether the property destruction caused the bad press, or whether the response was caused by other factors and the property destruction was merely the most visible and easy target. Basically, I think we were hammered because the property destruction was the only real story. Our numbers weren't impressive. We didn't have great protest visuals like signs, puppets, or other sorts of publicity attracting gimmicks. Our lockdowns of major arteries were quickly and efficiently cleared. Stripped of all this important livery, the protest looked like naked destruction. Clearly, naked destruction is bad. But I think Seattle conclusively demonstrates that property destruction clothed with spectacular large scale, sophisticated activist strategies can produce very satisfying results. So, what good does property destruction do? How about this? Property destruction gives the movement … an edge that makes it impossible to ignore.

The conversation continued online and offline for the next few months. At the August 1st Direct Action Coalition postaction evaluation, few condemned the property destruction. Instead, activists reflected on how to adapt these tactics so that they might be more effective with respect to police repression and media coverage.

Despite the limited success in disrupting the RNC, both DAN-NYC and SLAM continued to discuss a broader and more transgressive set of tactics than had been previously considered feasible or appropriate. Nonetheless, both organizations conceded that property destruction was strategically ineffective in the more heavily policed New York context. This distinction between appropriate and inappropriate contexts allowed New York City direct action activists with different tactical preferences to endure relatively harmoniously.

Reflecting on the RNC protests ten years later, SLAM activists recognized that their connection to local communities of color had been weak. But they continued to endorse more militant tactics and argued that the strength of that moment arose from their use. For SLAM, militant direct action was central to building a strong diverse movement. Kazembe Balagun explained his position:

I think the lesson is that A) direct action is so central to the work of dismantling the state and capitalism; B) direct action, done correctly, can foster solidarity across racial and gender lines, and that's something we definitely learned; and C) we really need to maintain this sense of communication and national network, and be really innovative in terms of strategy. We consistently go back to Seattle, but the world has changed since Seattle, and the police state's learning curve has increased since Seattle. What are we going to do in terms of re-imagining our tactics? (In Subways 2010)

By the end of the summer of 2000, New York City activists in the three organizations studied here continued to discuss black bloc tactics and how they were useful in certain contexts. Unlike in Toronto, where the class and race identity of the black bloc was a central consideration in such discussions, in New York City, SLAM's emphasis on militancy, along with a distinctive relational context, allowed the conversations about the tactics to continue.

SEPTEMBER 2000–APRIL 2001, QUEBEC CITY

With no U.S. summit on the horizon, activist debates in the United States around property destruction became less heated over the fall and winter. However, the debates became more intense in Canada as preparations for protests against the Free Trade Area of the Americas (planned for April 2001 in Quebec City) began. The most intense debates about property destruction and its rejection took place in Montreal and Quebec City and between Operation SalAMI (a pacifist organization fighting neoliberalism), CLAC (a Montreal-based, anticapitalist coalition), and CASA (a Quebec City-based, summit "welcoming committee"). Months before, Operation SalAMI argued that "to achieve our objectives, a number of conditions will need to be adhered to, including that of a strategic, nonviolent discipline and dignified outrage in our mobilization" (Dwyer 2001). Operation SalAMI went on to list conditions for protest, including abstaining "from any physical or verbal violence, including insults, property damage, and wearing masks or hoods. On the other hand, CLAC and CASA argued that activists commit to "respect for a diversity of tactics," which meant that no one should be excluded for their tactical choices (Dwyer 2001). Despite fierce disagreement, Katherine Dwyer argued that, by the time of the summit, coordination among the different groups was possible. "All of the main groups held a press conference during the demonstration to proclaim their points of agreement. Nevertheless, Operation SalAMI decided to abstain from the direct actions, choosing instead to focus on organizing a teach-in and other educational forums" (ibid).

During this debate, activists used the phrase "respecting a diversity of tactics" with increasing frequency. Associated with CLAC organizer Jaggi Singh, the concept offered a way to minimize tactical divisions within the movement.

L. A. Kauffman explained the logic of "diversity of tactics" frame in the following way:

Some people took the phrase simply as a synonym for property destruction. But the idea behind it was more complex. It was a way for all wings of the movement to work together, without flattening out their differences in the name of some false "unity." Those who were going to engage in direct action of whatever kind would agree to make sure that their tactical choices did not endanger other people, especially those who wanted to engage in safe and legal forms of protest. Those who were organizing safe and legal forms of protest would agree not to publicly denounce others for their tactical choices, especially in the media (Kauffman in Shepard 2004).

At planning meetings for the protests, the debate around diversity of tactics became polarized. For its part, CLAC became especially interested in discussing the role of black bloc tactics, which had been the subject of local experiments during antipolice brutality demonstrations in March 2001 and at the G20 summit in Montreal in October 2000.

During this period, Toronto's Mob4Glob emphasized its logistical role and refused to engage in debates about violence or property destruction, which had divided organizations in Montreal. One participant explained why they avoided the discussion: "The debate of diversity of tactics that would come up and it would be sort of like, we're not taking a position on that because we've seen what went on in Montreal between CLAC and SalAMI and we're not going to go through that.... It [Mob4Glob] was largely a logistical organization."

Because of their awareness of and peripheral engagement with online debates and debates at the planning councils for the protests in Quebec City, Mob4Glob Toronto activists avoided talking about the tactics in the local context. This limited the likelihood that black bloc tactics and property destruction would become incorporated into the Toronto repertoire. Similarly, although DAN-NYC activists were aware of fierce debates taking place in Canada, they didn't engage with them locally. Representatives of both sides of the debate visited New York City from Quebec and Montreal. Although DAN-NYC agreed to work with both coalitions, the organization had much more ongoing contact with CLAC. Like DAN-NYC, CLAC had endorsed the People's Global Action hallmarks and promoted the diversity of tactics framework; emphasizing the inclusiveness of the frame. One DAN participant explained:

People just took diversity of tactics to mean violent tactics or confrontational tactics or property destruction tactics. Whereas I saw it as an interesting debate because the idea was, "this is a diverse movement, we need to always say this is a movement of movements we're not about creating a single movement, we are about representing the incredible richness and diversity of our planet."

DIVERSITY OF TACTICS AFTER QUEBEC CITY

The Quebec City protests against the FTAA were widely seen as successful. Because they were broad, militant, and widely supported by the local population, people's fears around the diversity-of-tactics frame seemed to abate. The police use of tear gas, security fences, and riot units seemed to build solidarity among participants with different tactical preferences. Indeed, many high-profile participants (including Council of Canadians Director Maude Barlow and Member of Parliament Svend Robinson) who had initially distanced themselves from aggressive tactics went on to express solidarity with black bloc activists who pulled down the fence, threw back tear gas canisters, and expressed the crowd's rage. As in Seattle, a significant number of labor and NGO activists abandoned a less confrontational march to gather with others at the security fence surrounding the summit site.

Reflecting on the protests in a piece entitled "Quebec City: Beyond Violence and Non-Violence," activist writer Starhawk (2001a) argued that "the debate around 'violence' and 'nonviolence' may itself be constricting our thinking." She continued: "My fear about 'diversity of tactics' was that it would open a space for people to do things that I thought were stupid and wrong. That, in fact, proved to be partly true – at least, people did do things I would never have agreed to. But what surprised me is that it didn't seem to matter in the way I thought it would."

She argued that, instead of arguing for nonviolence or for diversity of tactics, there should be a way of changing the terms of the debate to adopt "empowered direct action." She explained, "We'd start not with debates about tactics but with clarifying our intention. What would victory look like? ... In those initial discussions, we'd look for dialogue among as wide a spectrum of groups as possible, with no single organization or group preempting the turf." This widely read piece offered a way to broker discussion among the different positions in the debate.

Similarly, in his 2005 thesis, Chris Hurl quotes key activist David Solnit as saying that in the post-Quebec City context, diversity of tactics came to represent "the evolution of a new model of unity and expanded definitions of solidarity" (Solnit, 2004, in Hurl 2005, 43). Interviewing Jaggi Singh, Hurl notes that, for Singh, respecting a diversity of tactics "creates a context of solidarity whereby even though we have disagreements about what might be effective or appropriate in a given situation, we can disagree about them while maintaining a certain level of solidarity in the face of a very concerted effort by the State and by the police to marginalize political movements." Keeping the conversation going was seen as central to the survival of the wave of protest and the movement as a whole.

Nonetheless, even a phrase like "diversity of tactics" wasn't a solution it itself. Others argued that, after Quebec City, diversity of tactics became reified as a code word for more confrontational tactics. One DAN activist argued that diversity of tactics was a useful strategy that was being manipulated:

I mean the whole question of diversity of tactics to me is a misnomer. Because I think people when they are saying diversity of tactics, the small text is basically that we're not condemning property destruction and we're not condemning people's rights to defend themselves. But I really don't think that diversity of tactics is saying if somebody came in there with a gun that we'd be okay with it. We wouldn't and I think people need to be okay with saying that. We're talking about diversity of tactics, but right now in the United States it doesn't include armed warfare during our street protests, and if you can't say that you're asking for trouble. So I think people need to be a little more real and a little bit less worried about being cool. Otherwise we're stupid, given what we're faced with.

As time passed, the dynamics of this debate led many activists in New York and Toronto to become increasingly frustrated about a reluctance to think strategically when talking about property destruction and black bloc. This frustration increased after a protester was killed during protests against the G8 in Genoa, Italy. In this new moment, critics argued that advocates of diversity of tactics were dismissive of those who were not interested in confrontational protest. Advocates of diversity of tactics countered that nonviolence guidelines were exclusionary, privileged, and not concerned with success. In cities like Montreal and Washington DC where the debate had been extensive, black bloc tactics continued to be used. In cities like Toronto and New York where the debate had been peripheral and indirect, black bloc tactics and property destruction remained rare.

TALKING ABOUT SMASHING AFTER 9/11

The global justice movement went into a period of self-reflection when the World Trade Center (WTC) buildings were hit. In Canada and especially in the United States, the level of mobilization decreased. The range of organizations, issues, and tactics involved in street protest changed. I discuss this more fully in Chapter 11. But overall, in the United States, more activists criticized confrontational tactics as being inappropriate and unstrategic. Increasingly, diversity of tactics came under open attack. Activists condemning property destruction became more visible. Meanwhile, those defending it were accused of being unreasonable and exclusionary. Long-time nonviolence trainer George Lakey reported, "I'm hearing from various parts of North America a trend to use" diversity of tactics "to shut down debate and refuse to explore pros and cons of strategies and tactics!" (Lakey 2002b).

The new context made the protests in Seattle seem like a very different era. Identification with the Seattle black bloc became more difficult, and deliberation about and certification of property destruction became rarer. In the years immediately following the WTC attacks, few spaces existed in which real equal, reflexive, and diverse discussions about property destruction could or would take place.

NEW YORK CITY

After the September 11 attacks, tactical differences in New York were revisited, but divisions were never hotly contested. This was due in part to a simple lack of contact among different positions. As one DAN activist explains:

There was a lot of splintering in the New York City community along tactical lines as well because some people were very comfortable with the tactic of wearing all black and organizing in group on the street. Some people were very comfortable with using the word anarchist. Some people weren't. Some people wanted to be in an explicitly anarchist group and some people didn't. Some people were into coalition building, and others were not.

A few months later, tactics once again became a topic of conversation as preparations began for the protests against the World Economic Forum planned for the end of January 2002. It was the first time New York activists would host a summit protest in the post-Seattle period. Local media and police condemned protesters well in advance. Under the slogan "New York is not Seattle," the NYPD declared a "zero tolerance" policy toward violent protesters. Painting the entire movement as being comprised of such protests, the police hoped to frighten people off the streets and justify repressive measures (Fiori 2002). In this context, the vast majority of organizers agreed that – although there would be no condemnation of those using black bloc formations or property destruction or any official exclusion of those tactics – it would not be strategic to use more aggressive tactics. Nonetheless, black bloc activists were represented at the organizing spokescouncils, marched in the mass march, and held an independent "snake march" at which many were arrested. Animal rights activists also smashed a window during their march. Since that time, black bloc and property destruction remain very rare in New York City, even in large scale Seattle-like demonstrations like the protests against the Republican National Convention of 2004 or the Occupy Wall Street protests of 2011.

TORONTO

Following protests in Quebec City, Toronto's Mob4Glob was at its largest and most active. During this period, more OCAP-sympathizers became involved in the group. With no immediate Global Justice Movement protests on the horizon, a debate, tangentially about property destruction, ensued around Mob4Glob's participation in OCAP's fall 2001 campaign against the provincial government and especially its mass demonstrations planned for October 16, 2001. Explicitly about local organizing versus summit protest strategies, the debate became overlaid with tactical, identity, and strategic divisions. Despite the heat of this discussion, no serious challenge to the diversity of tactics position emerged. The planned October 16 demonstrations had been billed as "militant and disciplined." Although there was no real deliberation about destroying property at the demonstrations, organizers proposed a "snake march" that would allow demonstrators to disrupt without getting arrested. After the September 11 attacks, however, many argued that the organizers should make clear that the protest would be nonviolent and peaceful. According to one Mob4Glob member, some people were arguing that "diversity of tactics is not just dangerous but suicidal. We have to keep our politics very broad, open to everyone. Keep everything very unified, um. Some people caricatured October 16th as being anti–mass action. It was ultra leftist, it was organized by OCAP. Direct action keeps people away, it's unsafe."

Although the October 16 protests were organized by a coalition led by OCAP, they drew upon many elements of the antiglobalization movement. They provided Toronto activists with the most Seattle-like opportunity to experiment with black bloc and property destruction. Indeed, before the attacks of September 11, such tactics were expected. In an attempt to avoid repression, and for the relational reasons given earlier, Toronto anarchists largely decided not to dress as a black bloc at the protests. In the end, a black bloc largely comprised of Montreal activists participated and some buildings were spray painted. Afterward, discussion about property destruction and black bloc tactics continued but at a lower intensity. At a Toronto-based anticapitalist conference in 2002, a workshop entitled "Protest Tactics and Movement Building" brought CLAC and OCAP and the New Socialists together for a discussion. The workshop description read:

Moving beyond the moralistic debate on violence versus nonviolence, activists need to be asking the political question of how we can build a movement that is both broad and militant, one that aims to be a mass movement but not "legitimate" in the eyes of the state, capital and media. How does the CLAC's idea of "diversity of tactics" or the Ontario Common Front's call for "militant but disciplined" action seek to overcome the falsely posed divide between "militant" and "mass" forms of action, to be effective and dynamic with an eye to drawing broader layers of people into our movements?

It appears however, that only one side of the debate was invited to present on the panel.

As the antiglobalization movement declined in Toronto, discussing Seattle-style black bloc tactics and property destruction seemed inappropriate to the activists with whom I spoke. None of the organizations studied here seriously considered their use. Nonetheless, clusters of youth wearing black masks and hooded sweatshirts continue to occasionally appear at Toronto demonstrations. Often targeted by the police, but rarely attempting to engage in property destruction, they identify with networks of anticapitalist and antiglobalization activists.[6] It wasn't until preparations for Toronto's G20 protests (held in June 2010, more than ten years after Seattle) were underway that sustained discussions about violence or property destruction occurred. There should be little surprise, given the story I've told here, that the Toronto Community Mobilization Network (TCMN) that coordinated the convergence adopted a 'statement of solidarity and respect' that was similar to the diversity of tactics framework and modeled on a statement adopted by organizers against

---

[6] Curiously, other activists and the police often identify these activists as "OCAP activists."

the Republican National Convention in Minneapolis in 2008. The statement read:

We believe that we must embrace honest discussion and debate. We trust that our movement is strong enough, resilient and mature enough to embrace open differences of opinion. We believe that if we are to truly build a socially just world, it will take many different tactics, much creativity and many different approaches. It is this that allows us to work together even when we disagree.

Attempting to avoid the exclusion or public denunciation of anyone's tactical preferences, the statement aimed to keep attention on the issues and avoid divisive tactical debates. The irony was that, even though the statement was formally intended to encourage deliberation, it was also intended to avoid divisive debate. Regardless, various attempts to discuss 'diversity of tactics' or 'solidarity and respect' raged for a few months – but there was little reflexive, open and diverse discussion. Many of the individuals and organizations who had been central to Mob4Glob distanced themselves from the TCMN. When the protests took place, Toronto witnessed both its largest black bloc (over 500) and significant property destruction. Given what I've shown here, it isn't surprising that evidence suggests that this would occur when large numbers of protesters were from outside of Toronto (Stalker and Wood, forthcoming). In the wake of the G20 protests (and massive repression that led to more than 1,000 arrests), there have been ongoing discussions of property destruction and black bloc tactics. While initially, many Toronto activists condemned the black bloc, as repression mounted, these criticisms became quieter. As a result, twelve years after Seattle, although such experiments remain small, Toronto activists are exploring the possibility of using black bloc tactics in their local protests.

CONCLUSION

By smashing Starbucks and Nike stores in Seattle, the black bloc unleashed a wave of debate about the use of property destruction as protest. Since then, dynamics of this debate both online and offline have reverberated between polarization and brokerage. The most polarized discussions in 2000 and 2001 inspired organized black blocs that continue to be active in Washington DC and Montreal. For global justice activists in Toronto and New York, peripheral engagement in and awareness of these debates pushed them to articulate collective identities that refused to condemn activists who destroyed property or formed black blocs. It also led them, whenever possible, to avoid the divisive debates themselves. Until the organizing for the 2010 protests against the G20 in Toronto, the question of property destruction had not been a major topic of debate. Without such discussions, Seattle-style property destruction by black blocs hadn't become part of the local repertoire in either city.

9

Not Like Us

As should be evident by now, even when the conditions for deliberation exist, activists in Toronto and New York do not necessarily adopt the innovation under discussion. In order for the local activists in Toronto and New York to be interested in experimenting with the tactics from the Seattle demonstrations, they needed to see themselves as similar to the demonstrators who were at those protests – who were characterized as militant and creative, as well as white, middle class, young students. As I noted in Chapter 1, McAdam and Rucht note, "All instances of diffusion depend on a minimal identification of an adopter with a transmitter" (McAdam and Rucht 1993, 60; Strang and Meyer 1993). Although activists in both cities distanced themselves from the Seattle protesters as time passed, the activists in New York had a much easier time identifying with the Seattle demonstrators than their Toronto equivalents. This meant that the incorporation of the tactics to their local organizations was easier.

Again, by identification, I mean the process by which an individual or collective sees themselves as having a similar identity to a transmitting individual or collective actor. Sidney Tarrow and Doug McAdam (2005, 130) argue that such a process of identification or "attribution of similarity" is the central mechanism that underlies relational diffusion, the main type we have been examining. However, identification is not simply present or absent. Charles Tilly (2003b) explains that the process of defining one's collective identity takes place through interaction and storytelling, sometimes through deliberation. Identities are constructed through activating us/them boundaries and deactivating other boundaries. "We" tell stories about "us" and about "them." Partly as a result of such stories, "we" begin to interact in different ways with "us" than with "them." "At least some actors on each side of the boundary reify it [an identity] by naming that boundary, attempting to control it, attaching distinctive practices to it, and otherwise creating a shared representation" (Tilly 2003b). The process of identification is tied to more general processes of identity construction by making "us" see ourselves and articulate ourselves as being similar to a particular "them," whose ideas and practices we are much more likely to consider.

McAdam and Rucht specify three conditions that facilitate this process of identification: a common institutional locus, adherents from the same strata, and a common language (1993, 71). Sean Chabot then builds on this list by emphasizing the way that these conditions are enacted: "Identification is most likely when organizations see themselves as compatible, and share common meanings, a mutual sub-cultural language, and are alike in personal and social characteristics" (Chabot and Duyvendak 2002, 699). Such identification occurs most easily between like-minded organizations but may also take place between opponents who value particular skills or attributes like endurance, strategic thinking, or creativity, even when they may be traditional opponents such as protesters and police.[1] Through the dynamics of storytelling, argument, and trust building, identification can be manufactured.

Explicit discussions of identity and identification take place at particular points in movement activity. Similar to the contexts when tactics are discussed, identity only becomes an issue when the existing boundaries of that identity are being challenged or defined. This is most likely when a new possibility is under discussion, whether that possibility is a new challenge, alliance, or tactic. In these moments, discussions of "who we are" and "who we aren't" become much more frequent and central as justifications for or against change. At such moments, discussions around identity often become paramount.

But identities are not fixed, at different times and places, different *we/they* boundaries will have different levels of salience. The shifting salience of these boundaries depends on the relationships and categorical inequalities I discussed earlier. Individual activists may identify primarily with a formal organizational identity at a particular moment, with an ethnic or class identity at another moment, and with an affinity group or style of protest at a third time and place. Activation and deactivation of a particular identity are tied to patterns of interaction. However, as many have pointed out, there are some boundaries that are more influential than others across a wider range of sites of social interaction. In the North American context, I would obviously include among these racial, ethnic, class, gender, and boundaries around sexual orientation, but other identity boundaries, such as those around political ideology or tactical identity, may also be important. Deliberation that supports identification and diffusion generally involves deactivating some previously relevant boundaries – most often during periods of coalition building. This appears to be most likely during periods of increasing mobilization. During these periods, even "thick" boundaries of race and class may temporarily become de-emphasized. It is possible to observe these shifts through examining activist conversations. Ann Mische writes that "identity

---

[1] L. A. Kauffman (2000c) notes that by the time of the protests against the World Bank and IMF in April 2000, activists had adopted paramilitary lingo: tac (meaning tactical), com (meaning communication), scouts, recon (meaning reconnaissance).

qualifying statements" are cues to which aspect of an actor's multiple identities and involvements are active "right now," in a particular set of utterances. Although I do not have detailed transcripts of such conversations, it is also possible to see these post-hoc statements in the explanations activists give for their tactical decisions. McAdam and Paulsen (1993, 656) refer to such cues as "aligning statements" by which actors associate themselves with particular reference groups (Mische 2003).

When I asked the activists about their perception of and their relationship to the Seattle protesters, activists in the local and student organizations from both cities spoke about how they identified with the militancy of those activists. Militancy as an identity helped to explain why some of the ideas and tone of the antiglobalization movement were incorporated into local demonstrations. One SLAM activist argued that there was a natural identification between SLAM and the protesters in Seattle: "SLAM from the beginning was a direct action organization. But then there was this whole movement, a direct action movement that officially had that name, but there wasn't ever a moment that wasn't a natural part of our trajectory."

However, as the days and weeks following Seattle passed and local interactions across class and race boundaries reinforced existing inequalities and identities, poor activists and activists of color within the sample were more likely than middle-class white activists to articulate differences between themselves and the archetypical "Seattle demonstrators." Those in Toronto would often explain why and how any identification with the Seattle protesters had been qualified or had ended because of differences of race, class, strategy, or attitude. In this chapter I am going to use this material to outline the deliberative and rhetorical strategies that activists in Toronto and New York used to identify with and/or distance themselves from the Seattle protesters.

Immediately after the successes of the Seattle protests, poor activists and activists of color in OCAP and SLAM were excited. They found themselves invigorated by these events and wanted to affiliate with what they saw as militant protest. In the interviews with both groups, references to the "militancy" of the Seattle protesters are frequent. These references appear to allow these activists to identify with the protesters and consider their tactics, while de-emphasizing the race and class of the archetypical Seattle activists. By identifying militancy with being poor and being a person of color, they were able to find ways to deliberate and certify the Seattle tactics as appropriate for consideration. This justification was sometimes explicit. One SLAM member explicitly rejected the argument that the Seattle tactics are necessarily white and argued that direct action should be central to people of color organizing:

There is sort of a politics that says that people of color don't do direct action, we're going to get all the white people to be arrested for us. We never understood that. We thought it was sort of patronizing. We wanted to do what DAN was doing, with the masks and stuff.... But then we said, "No, how do people of color get involved and do this? Clearly everybody can't do it, but what do we do then?" So we made a political decision not to do sort of stuff that required wearing a mask that we'd be running from the police per se but to do things so that it would be visible in the media and to other people in the street that young people of color were taking a stand and getting arrested and taking direct action and that we wanted to be visible, so we did it. We didn't want it to be sort of this underground thing where we were doing it, you know, with the mask on and we also didn't want to say "people of color don't get arrested." Because that was not our politics.

In a similar way, one OCAP activist explains how the antiglobalization movement influenced OCAP's antipoverty demonstration of June 15, 2000:

June 15th of course was all on the context of all of the anti-globalization work that was going on and so tactically and in terms of level of militancy and stuff it definitely borrowed from a lot of those things. In terms of the mattresses for instance, although the mattress wasn't something that we had specifically seen in other demonstrations, it was obvious from a lot of other actions, particularly anti-globalization stuff outside of Canada that you had to have some kind of armor against the police if you were going to do anything serious.[2]

Although many of the direct action activists in Toronto and New York could align themselves with the Seattle protesters through the frame of militancy, other boundaries increasingly complicated the process of identification. Boundaries of race, class, and strategy were used to explain why local activists should not experiment with the Seattle tactics. Local activists who were not white or middle class were especially unlikely to see themselves as like the typical "Seattle activist." Some of those same activists argued that because they were poor or people of color, they would be treated differently by the media, police, and other authorities and could not, even if they wanted to, use the Seattle tactics. Activists in both cities also differentiated themselves from the Seattle protesters by emphasizing the boundary between local activist and summit protester, and finally, SLAM, OPIRG, and OCAP activists rejected the particular tactic of blockading by highlighting the boundary between "passive protesters" and "active fighters" and by giving this distinction overtones of class identity. Each of these boundaries disrupted the identification between these activists and the Seattle protesters and, thus, made local experiments with the Seattle tactics less likely. Let us now turn to these discussions of identity and how they helped or blocked the diffusion of the Seattle tactics to New York City or to Toronto.

NOT WHITE, MIDDLE-CLASS COLLEGE STUDENTS

In the vast acreage of published analysis about the splendid victory over the World Trade Organization last November 29–December 3, it is almost impossible to find

---

[2] OCAP activists used mattresses to protect them from police truncheons at their protest on June 15, 2000.

anyone wondering why the 40–50,000 demonstrators were overwhelmingly Anglo. How can that be, when the WTO's main victims around the world are people of color? Understanding the reasons for the low level of color, and what can be learned from it, is absolutely crucial if we are to make Seattle's promise of a new, international movement against imperialist globalization come true.

"Where Was the Color in Seattle?" by Elizabeth (Betita) Martinez (2000)

These words opened one of the most widely read and important internal critiques of the Seattle protests. This piece, published in early 2000, was circulated through listservs, on Web sites and in activist publications. It described the Seattle demonstrations as white dominated and alienating for people of color. Because of this white domination, Martinez suggested that the potential for the emerging movement to be an effective and sustained challenger to neoliberalism was limited. If the movement were to be effective, she continued, it would need to recognize and overcome inequalities of access to resources and proactively prioritize building relationships with people of color. This article and related discussions prompted significant debate. It confirmed the experience and perception of some people of color and white activists, who saw the movement as irredeemably racist or white dominated. These activists distanced themselves from the movement. Others saw the critique as an opening for discussion and became more involved.[3] They attempted to respond by changing movement practices through organizing and promoting antiracism and antioppression trainings, building alliances, and new campaigns and through organizational restructuring.[4] Despite these various attempts, and facilitated by the mass media, the perception of the North American antiglobalization movement as composed of white, middle-class young people spread. This perception understandably limited the spread of the Seattle tactics to activists outside of this identity, except when local activists emphasized the militancy of the Seattle activists and downplayed racial and class differences between themselves and the archetypical "Seattle protester." The impact of Martinez's piece is difficult to determine, but its effects endure – both in the centrality of an antioppression analysis in some sections of the movement and ongoing distrust of the movement by others. Even in 2011, the Martinez piece is still being cited and used as a warning to those who do not recognize the impact of racial inequities on movement organizing. It is also used to explain the collapse of the cycle of protest associated with the Seattle protests. However, it is important to remember that this discussion did not necessarily eliminate the diffusion of the tactics to grassroots organizations led by poor people and people of color. One SLAM member explained how the organization saw itself as interested in the tactics, while remaining demographically unlike the Seattle demonstrators.

---

[3] See *Colorlines* magazine http://www.arc.org/C_Lines/ArcColorLines.html; Of course, many activists ignored the whole controversy.

[4] See Challenging White Supremacy Web site http://www.cwsworkshop.org and Colors of Resistance Web site http://colors.mahost.org, Catalyst Project http://collectiveliberation.org/ See also Starr 2004.

SLAM had made a commitment to doing this Republican Convention [2000] stuff in part because we wanted to get those skills of effective mass civil disobedience and learn how to do it, a la Seattle. And yet we confronted this, and SLAM has consistently confronted it, as a mainly young people of color organization. It means something very different for people to go to jail and so it's what tends to happen and has happened a number of times is that you have the initial enthusiasm for doing this and people are enthusiastic about the action but when it comes down to it, the number of people who are willing to actually go out and get arrested, drops, as people consider their family situations, their job situations and what it means to go through life with a criminal record and its very different if you're, you know, white, middle class, you have certain options. You can take that kind of a hit and a number of SLAM members aren't citizens etc. etc. there are a bunch of things.

This excerpt from the interview shows the way that SLAM activists both identified and distanced themselves from the Seattle protesters, facilitating internal deliberation about and alteration of the Seattle tactics. This may be the result of the explicit discussions about race that SLAM was comfortable in having and the way that they had a people-of-color-led organization that had autonomy from white-dominated political networks. It could decide to engage or disengage, according to the decisions of its members. This complex response facilitated ongoing diffusion of the tactics to New York activists.

In contrast, a Toronto OCAP organizer differentiated her organization from the antiglobalization movement by emphasizing differences of race and class: "The sort of the identification of it with a very, like white middle class youth scene which is not, although it's a piece of OCAP, for sure, it's not where a lot of people are coming from and it's not where we want to go organizationally too." As time passed, other Toronto organizations began to use a characterization of the Seattle protesters as white and middle class to distance themselves from that movement identity. For example, as an organization that was intentionally transforming itself into an antiracist organization, OPIRG distanced itself from the antiglobalization movement.[5] Like OCAP, the attempt to distance themselves from the antiglobalization movement was particularly fervent, partly because both organizations had members who were, demographically, the same white, middle-class students associated with the Seattle protests.

The critique of the Seattle protests as white and middle class limited the identification between Seattle and groups who identified as antiracist and those who identified as working class and/or people of color. As a result, the tactics did not spread easily to those groups. Only when SLAM and OCAP emphasized the militancy of the Seattle protesters or were explicit about altering the tactics could the necessary conversations take place.

One activist of color in SLAM used the racial identity associated with the tactic to explain why, to engage in black bloc tactics, the tactic would need to be altered:

---

[5] During this time, OPIRG Toronto replaced its mostly white board and staff with people of color in an attempt to alter the racial dynamics in the organization.

I don't think that we would ever run with the "white anarchist black bloc." Because basically we see them as yahoos, and unstrategic in the actions they do. As opposed to being strategic about instead of doing a giant march to break a window, sending a few people away from the protest to break a window. Not that that's something that SLAM would do, but understanding the tactical necessity to really examine the situation and what your goal is.

As time passed, activists in both Toronto and New York emphasized the importance of race and class on tactical decisions by speaking about how their poor and people of color members were more likely to be targeted by police repression than the archetypical Seattle activist. This limited the willingness of these activists to experiment with tactics like blockading that increased the possibility of arrest. As one SLAM member explained, "As a mainly young people of color organization, it means something very different for people to go to jail." This argument led to a rejection of particular tactics such as blockades:

I know that for the civil disobedience training, there were very specific things that SLAM members were not going to do. And then we talk about, it was again the white people; people of color thing. The whole bike-lock to a railing: we're looking around the room and going "Hell no, we're not doing that! A cop will hurt us!" We just couldn't imagine putting that much trust in a cop.

OCAP also used stories about class and race to argue that the police treat their members differently than the more privileged middle-class, white anti-globalization protesters who they understood the Seattle protesters to be. One OCAP member explained how jail solidarity appeared to be "a tactic of the privileged." Another continued:

If you're organizing white, middle class youths who haven't been to jail before and you put them into the prison system, it doesn't really worry them so much. They are going to get out the next day. The prison system works that way. Works to keep people like that out of it and put other people in. But we're not organizing the people that it's trying to keep out, just the people it's trying to keep in, and those people who are going to jail, they want to get out as soon as possible and they have every right to be that anxious.

Although initially, OCAP and SLAM activists saw themselves as similar to the Seattle protesters in terms of militancy, increasingly, stories of race and class boundaries became more important.

NOT SUMMIT HOPPERS

Another way that local and student activists in New York City and Toronto distanced themselves from the Seattle protesters was by differentiating themselves in terms of their organizing strategy. Activists from all six organizations emphasized the boundary between those who engaged in local organizing and those who focused on large protest events, or "summit hopping." Indeed, Chapter 7 chronicles the debates around this question and their influence. Especially after the April 16–17, 2000 demonstrations in Washington, DC against the IMF and the World Bank, activists in both cities critiqued the antiglobalization movement for its emphasis on protesting at summits and being unconnected with local struggles and concerns. "If there's one point on which everyone in the movement seems to agree, it's that action-hopping is getting old" (L. A. Kauffman in Dixon 2001).

Activists in Toronto and New York distanced themselves from the Seattle protesters by emphasizing this strategic boundary. One OPIRG activist explained: "I have this criticism of the whole summit hopping thing. Big deal. You rattle their cages for a day or two and then you went home and went back to work."

In a similar fashion, one OCAP activist contrasted the new activists who "went to summits" with those experienced ones who engaged in community organizing:

There is no question that Seattle was part of a process within North America that was occurring on other places as well of an emergence of a whole new grouping of younger activists who wanted to find a way to challenge what was going on. And many of those people went through a period of simply going to summits and big events and protesting but the best people within that new manifestation were concerned about how to actually take it into the communities.

By activating the boundary between summit protesters and community activists, local activists in Toronto and New York limited their identification with the Seattle protesters and, thus, constrained the possibility of tactical experiments with the associated tactics.

NOT PASSIVE RESISTERS

The blockades where activists locked themselves to each other or to lockboxes that disrupted the WTO meetings in Seattle were lauded by many as playing an important role in the mobilization; however, in the post-Seattle period, there was an increasing rejection of forms of civil disobedience that led to arrest. In part, this was a reaction against "old" styles of protest that were framed as ineffective. It was also a response to the recognition that less privileged activists were unwilling to trust the police in such situations and were less likely to be able to emerge unscathed from such an encounter.

In my sample, activists from SLAM and OCAP were most likely to make this distinction. In part, this distancing was tied to the previously discussed racial and class differences in identity. It also highlighted a distinction between "passive resisters" and those who "stood up and fought back." The debate was rooted in the configuration of movement identities and tied to a critique of the blockading tactics used in Seattle. One SLAM activist described a conversation about tactics by showing how its membership saw themselves as different to those who engaged in civil disobedience.

People were like, "I don't want to sit there and get beaten by cops. I think it's great if we can shut down the building. I don't think we need to get arrested to do it. Let's think of how we can take it." I think that's one of the things because SLAM's current membership doesn't come out of the tradition of non-violent direct action or pacifism.

In a similar fashion, one OCAP activist differentiated his approach from the classic civil disobedience strategy:

There is absolutely no hard and fast sort of principled determination here. But in general I think we have tried to elevate the context, the sense of actually fighting back. Resisting, as opposed to methods that have a sense of we're imposing suffering on ourselves. Now the truth is that people locking themselves to something might be a very effective way of shutting something down. It might be employed. But the reservation would be that we prefer to have mobility and a capacity to stand up and resist as opposed to taking a more passive form of, "I'm going to put myself in a position of extreme vulnerability for the cause."

Another OCAP activist talked about why the organization did not experiment with blockading tactics by emphasizing the identity of its membership: "I think people would see it as passive and would see it as something that involves sitting around waiting to be arrested. Especially since so much of our membership just gets arrested daily. I think people would be really uncomfortable with that tactic." By highlighting a boundary between passive protesters and their own members, both SLAM and OCAP activists rejected forms of blockading that limited the mobility of activists. They were not alone in this critique. By the end of 2000, fewer activists were using blockade tactics and more were joining the more mobile "flying squads."

NOT PUPPET PEOPLE

The giant puppets used at the Seattle demonstrations spread rapidly in the post-Seattle context. "Puppetistas" became visible at a wide range of local, national, and global protests. After Seattle, some activists in DAN, Mob4Glob, More Gardens!, SLAM, and OPIRG experimented with the tactic of giant puppets. These activists argued that a model of direct action that used dancing, puppetry, and street theater to disrupt institutions and "business as usual" was both exciting and effective. The strategy became localized in both cities. One Mob4Glob activist explained: "Since Seattle there are at least three or four different sort of giant puppet groups that are now operational in Toronto that were set up by people who cut their political teeth around the anti-globalization movement."

OCAP activists rejected the tactic and distanced themselves from its users. In fact, OCAP and OPIRG Toronto activists had used puppets in the past. During the 1998 Active Resistance Conference in Toronto, activists from the two groups had worked in coalition with activists from the emerging Art and Revolution movement, who, eighteen months later, led the use of puppetry in the Seattle protests. However, many OCAP activists who argued that the tactics trivialized the serious issue of homelessness saw the collaboration as unsuccessful, and argued that those who promoted these tactics were more concerned with aesthetics than with political impact. Due in part to this experience, in the period after Seattle, OCAP activists distanced themselves from those who used the tactic. One member explained:

OCAP's never used puppets [sic]. OCAP wouldn't. There is no tactical use to them. I guess there is a certain amount of, I would say, pride, involved in OCAP. And puppets we'd see as being below us in that they'd make it seem, almost comical, and the situation isn't comical. Or light-hearted. It has this light-hearted feeling about it that isn't appropriate.

Another OCAP activist contrasted the "serious" OCAP approach and aesthetic with a "fun" strategy and aesthetic in the following manner:

[Puppetry] is not serious organizing. It's like some sort of flashy thing that's perhaps designed to make your protest look more appealing or fun or creative or whatever. But there is this very serious attitude of we're not trying to be fun and appealing we're trying to build an actual struggle to change the world and like, if we're going to be serious, let's take it to a serious level…. And sure some people like puppets or whatever but you can't just like build your organization around having these puppets there or whatever.

By differentiating themselves from the "puppet people," OCAP rejected the use of puppetry in their local protests.

CONCLUSION

Unless potential adopters of a particular tactic identify with the users of that tactic, they are unlikely to experiment with that tactic. In the post-Seattle period, discussions about the identity of the Seattle participants were frequent and influential. When I asked activists in Toronto and New York City their opinion of the Seattle tactics of blockading, black bloc, jail solidarity, and puppetry, they often explained their rejection or acceptance using stories about identity.

Initially, many activists identified with the Seattle protesters as militant and creative; however, as the cycle of protest evolved, and deliberation among local activists incorporated critiques of the Seattle activists, identity boundaries were more likely to be activated at the local level. In Toronto, local activists explained how they were different to the Seattle demonstrators in terms of class and organizing style. When such distancing occurred, further deliberation about the utility, appropriateness or effectiveness of a tactic or strategy became unlikely. Sometimes it was repression that activated such boundaries, I'll turn to that now.

10

The Cops and the Courts

I mean, Seattle was one thing where you had a quarter of a million people [sic] in the street and the police were overwhelmed, meetings shut down, it's great. But we were outnumbered by the cops in Windsor, and we had over 3,000 people. And at that point, there was really no point in playing this game anymore. We lost. So I was like, that's the time when you have a meeting and you shift tactics. (Interview conducted in 2003 with OPIRG-Toronto activist about the June 2000 mobilization against the Organization of American States summit in Windsor Ontario)

After police arrested, beat, teargassed, and jailed more than 500 people at the protests against the World Trade Organization summit in Seattle, it seemed logical that observers would hesitate before imitating the tactics of those protesters. However, the protests were declared successful, and for sympathetic observers, the arrests and beatings in that city only seemed to underscore the worthiness of the participants. In the following months, direct-action activists across North America experimented with the protest tactics they had seen used at those protests. Subsequently, at demonstrations in New York City, Toronto, and elsewhere, many of these sympathetic activists themselves experienced pepper spray, arrest, harassment, surveillance, and violence at the hands of the police. As the quote above suggests, such repression led some activists to meet and deliberate and sometimes to adapt or abandon the Seattle tactics; however, some of the time, repression made such deliberation impossible.

Police repression appears to have limited the reception and incorporation of locally new tactics by blocking deliberation in two ways. First, repression interrupted the way that local activists in New York and Toronto identified with the Seattle demonstrators in particular and the global justice movement in general. This limited their interest in discussing the tactics associated with that movement. Second, repression reduced the strategic capacity of the potential

An earlier version of this chapter was published as Lesley J. Wood. 2007. "Breaking the Wave: Repression, Identity, and Seattle Tactics." *Mobilization* 12(4):377–88.

adopters by reducing the availability of human and organizational resources, by fragmenting relationships, and thus by limiting the possibility of deliberation.

REPRESSION'S IMPACT

It is obvious that repression affects the activities of protesters. Arrests, beatings, and surveillance have a strong impact on protesters' perceptions of the state's intentions, strengths, and weaknesses (della Porta 1995). This then affects the level of mobilization. However, the connection between repression and mobilization is complicated. Sometimes repression appears to demobilize protesters, sometimes it mobilizes them, and sometimes it does both (Beissinger 2002; Brockett 2005; Davenport 2005; Gurr 1969; Lichbach and Gurr 1981; Moore 1998; Rasler 1996; Tilly and Wood 2008), depending on the social, political, repressive, and economic contexts. Studies argue that repression absorbs scarce organizational resources (Marx 1977 and others) and fractures social and political solidarity among activists (Gamson 1990; Opp 1994). It is also widely recognized that protesters adapt their tactics in response to police repression (della Porta, Fillieule, and Reiter 1998; Francisco 1996; Lichbach 1987). However, there has been less written on the effect of repression on the diffusion process itself.[1]

As I have discussed in earlier chapters, diffusion is dependent on a number of processes. First, activists need to see themselves as similar to or to identify with the original users of a tactic in order to be interested in experimenting with that same tactic. Second, for diffusion to be possible, the potential adopters must have the strategic capacity to engage in deliberation that would allow for tactical experiments. Marshall Ganz argues that organizations that are able to draw resources from a diversity of salient constituencies and that afford leaders venues for regular, open, and authoritative deliberation are more likely to generate effective strategies than those that do not (2000, 1016). By analyzing activists' accounts of repressive events in the period after Seattle, it quickly becomes apparent how repression interrupted the deliberation that underlay the localization of the Seattle tactics in Toronto and New York City.

LOCAL EXPERIMENTS

After the success of the protests against the World Trade Organization, activists in many cities, including Toronto and New York, engaged in experiments with the Seattle tactics. These experiments sometimes happened in a response to repression. For example, when arrestees including Torontonians were beaten in custody after the April 16, 2000 demonstrations against the International Monetary Fund and World Bank in Washington DC, Toronto activists organized a demonstration in protest. At this event, they used the

---

[1] Moore 1998 and Rasler 1996 are exceptions to this.

Seattle tactics of black blocs and puppetry. These tactics had been used in Toronto in previous demonstrations, but rarely, and they had never been used together. A press release by the organizers showed how many of the Seattle tactics were being tried:

Most protesters wore black to lend support to members of the Black Bloc who according to our reports have been subjected to particularly harsh treatment by the DC police. Banners bearing the slogans "Let Our People Go," "Free Mumia," and "Stop Torturing Canadians in DC" were among the most prominent, while a giant police/pig puppet also made an appearance. As the protest moved away from 52 Division [the closest police station] the police began roughing up protesters for marching on the streets. Pushing and shoving ensued as police began hitting and beating protesters to get on the sidewalk. The protest was peaceful and demonstrators used passive resistance in the face of police brutality. Four people were arrested and one individual was pepper sprayed. Currently a solidarity action is taking place outside of the 52nd Division police HQ demanding the release of the four political prisoners and that the Toronto police distance themselves from the actions of the DC police. (Anarchist Press 2000)

Repression in Washington pushed these Toronto protesters to identify with the global justice movement protesters in Washington DC, and this identification pushed them to experiment with black bloc and puppetry tactics. They were prepared for this solidarity demonstration partly because of training that had been held in the previous weeks in preparation for traveling to the A16 protests. During the same period, New York activists engaged in a similar process of emulation. Activists in New York and Toronto were also beginning to use the tactics locally on other issues. However, in both cities, they argued that when they used the Seattle tactics locally, they attracted increased police repression. This repression made the localization of the Seattle protesters more difficult. By examining four protest events identified by the respondents as significant in this regard, the way that police repression influenced the localization of the Seattle tactics.

Repressive Events

1. May 1, 2000, New York City, Protest for Immigrant Workers' Rights/More Gardens! On May 1, 2000, a global day of action was called by the People's Global Action network, to coincide with International Workers Day, or May Day. Protests planned for this day provided the first opportunity since the Seattle demonstrations for New York activists in the global justice movement to take a leadership role in the city. DAN-NYC worked with the Mexican-American organization Tepeyac and the Coalition for the Human Rights of Immigrants to organize a march and rally advocating for the rights of immigrant workers. Approximately 600 people gathered and prepared to perform street theater using elaborate puppets (Butterfield 2000).

The police had received a briefing from an NYPD "disorder expert" that the crowd could include "WTO-Seattle-type protesters" (Laursen 2001). The police reaction, as a result, was strong and visible. Hundreds of police officers surrounded the gathering point and showed their readiness to arrest the demonstrators by displaying clusters of flex-cuffs. They searched arriving demonstrators and refused to allow most puppets and placards to enter the park, then a police "snatch squad" moved in and arrested nineteen people who were wearing black bloc style masks and charged them with for covering their faces (RTS-NYC 2000). The defendants were held in jail for up to thirty-six hours on a range of charges including the violation of a long unused mask law, which prohibits two or more persons from "congregating" in public while wearing masks to obscure their identities (Laursen 2001).

2. June 3 to 5, 2000, *Windsor, Ontario, Protest vs. Summit of Organization of American States*. From June 3 to 5, 2,500 activists (many affiliated with OPIRG chapters) participated in protests against the OAS summit meeting in Windsor, Ontario, a small city across the U.S. border from Detroit, Michigan. The summit included discussions about the development and implementation of the Free Trade Area of the Americas, thus attracting the attention of the global justice movement. Many of the protest organizers had attended the Washington DC protests in April, and they attempted to replicate the Seattle model (author's field notes 2000).

In the weeks before the OAS summit, protest organizers experienced harassment and intense surveillance by police. One organizer explained: "They had our house bugged, and they'd come up and be like, 'Hey, so I heard your girlfriend is sick.' ... cars circling the house all the time, you see it go down the street, and back down the alleyway, and again twenty minutes later. Always being tailed, looking over your shoulder."

Another protest organizer continued:

The worst one for me was this guy riding down the street with somebody on his bike and all of a sudden a white panel truck pulls up, guys jump out, knock him off his bike, throw him in the back and drive off.... And we didn't see him for about twelve hours. Apparently he came back with a busted lip and a black eye. And he was like, "I was interrogated for eight hours by the RCMP [Royal Canadian Mounted Police]." He said they tried every trick in the book. "They tried to play nice with me. They beat me up, they threw me through the wringer," and he was like, "Oh yeah, and they asked about you, and you, and you, and you, and you," and his finger goes around the room and he points at me, and I was just like, "wow, they are not fucking around."

At the event, 3,700 officers from the RCMP; Ontario Provincial Police (OPP); Peel Regional; and Toronto, Chatham, and Windsor Police Services provided security (deLint 2005, 19). (Other reports have 2,000 to 5,000 police on site). The total cost was $3.34 million (de Lint 2007). The police erected an eight-foot-high fence around the site of the summit, an innovation that police would later replicate for the Summit of the Americas in Quebec City in April 2001.

One OPIRG Toronto activist explained that the protest organizers should have changed their tactics once they had realized how well prepared the police were. "That was the time to really rethink our tactics, and we didn't, we just ploughed ahead and did all the same old stuff." The police strategy made it almost impossible for protesters to disrupt the summit. Seventy-eight people were arrested during the days of action, sixty-three of them for the noncriminal holding charge of breach of the peace (de Lint 2007). Activists reported police beatings and a sexual assault while in custody (Gude 2000). Arrestees tried to use jail solidarity to operate collectively and to protect those with higher charges, but they failed to gain any concessions.

Most participants saw the Windsor protests as a failure. The repression exacerbated internal tensions that ripped apart the organizing body, which never met as a group again.

3. June 15, 2000, Toronto, OCAP Protests vs. Ontario Government. On June 15, 2000, the Ontario Coalition Against Poverty marched to the Ontario Legislature and attempted to have a delegation address the provincial Parliament on the issues of homelessness and poverty. Although not identified with Seattle or the global justice movement, many respondents argued that the event took some of its energy from the increase in protest activity that had taken place in the preceding weeks and months. As in Seattle, activists wore masks and goggles in preparation for tear gas or pepper spray, and teams of activist medics were organized to support injured protesters. When one activist medic was asked in court why organizers had prepared to respond to pepper spray, she answered, "Because of Seattle" (author's field notes, 2002). As one OCAP activist explained: "June 15, of course was all in the context of all of the global justice work that was going on, and so tactically, and in terms of level of militancy and stuff, it definitely borrowed from a lot of those things."

When the demonstrators were refused entry to the Legislature, tensions mounted and the protesters pushed past the barricades. Fifteen hundred people participated in the march on the Ontario Parliament and many in the ensuing battle with the police. Police arrested forty-five people and beat many protesters. Thirty-six protesters reported injuries ranging from broken arms to cracked skulls (Queen's Park Riot Defendants 2001). Forty-two officers reported minor injuries, and nine police horses were injured (ibid.). Police released some of the arrestees on the condition that they not associate with OCAP or its members, and others, especially homeless participants with existing criminal records, spent months in jail. Police charged John Clarke, a leading organizer with OCAP, with "counseling to participate in a riot," and two other OCAP members Gaétan Heroux and Stefan Pilipa with "participating in a riot." Police released all three from jail on the condition that they not associate with OCAP or attend protests for several months. The defendants wrote that "the repression after June 15th was at a level that had not been seen in Ontario for decades ... the attack launched on the organization resulted in approximately 250 charges being laid against its members and allies" (Queen's Park

Riot Defendants 2001). Five years later, after a lengthy jury trial, the courts dismissed or stayed all charges against the leadership of the organization.

4. *August 1, 2000, Philadelphia, Protests vs. Republican National Convention (RNC)*. During the summer of 2000, DAN-NYC and SLAM of New York City were deeply involved in organizing protests against the 2000 Republican National Convention in Philadelphia. In some ways, this was the first "summit-like protest" in which New York activists played a significant leading role. Just as the OAS summit allowed Toronto activists to experiment with the Seattle tactics, the Republican National Convention provided an opportunity for the New York activists.

Philadelphia differed from Seattle in part because the targeted convention was not taking place in the city center; however, activists adopted a strategy for disruption that was similar to the approach taken in Seattle. Activists divided the city into sections, and the organizers of each section of the city strategized about how to disrupt the transportation of conventioneers. They planned to use all of the Seattle tactics: There was a large black bloc, puppets were built, street theater was choreographed, blockades were planned, bicycles were readied for communicating messages, jail solidarity trainings were organized, and the affinity group/spokescouncil model was utilized (author's notes 2000).

As with other protests of the period (Washington DC, New York, Windsor), the police engaged in preemptive arrests and surveillance. In this case, on the morning of the protest, police arrested seventy-five activists at the "Puppet Warehouse" and destroyed all the puppets and signs (Graeber 2004).

When the protests began, groups of activists locked themselves together and blocked intersections and highway entrances. Others roamed in "flying squads" or with the black bloc. Some broke windows, slashed police car tires, and spray painted bank buildings. Theater troupe performances and activist soccer games disrupted traffic. The protests temporarily delayed the delegates from reaching the convention (Pittsburgh Post Gazette 2000). During that day and the days that followed, 420 activists were arrested, 43 of them on felony charges. Those identified as leaders were charged with numerous offenses and held in isolation. Their release required bonds of up to $1 million. The vast majority of arrestees utilized the Seattle tactic of jail solidarity and refused to give their names. Unlike the protesters arrested in Seattle and Washington, DC, activists in custody in Philadelphia were unsuccessful in achieving their demands of anonymous release, medical care for the injured, and reduced charges for those charged with felonies. Activists in police custody reported being beaten, sexually assaulted, refused medication, and bribed into cooperating (Subways 2010). The hundreds of activists who did not cooperate with police remained in custody as "Jane and John Does" for up to two weeks (ACT UP NY 2000; Boghosian 2004, 80). Initially, arrestees who went to trial pleaded guilty in an effort to put pressure on the court system and to get the felony charges dropped. Others fought their charges, and in the end, 97 percent of those arrested had their charges dismissed at trial. Three years later, the last of the arrestees were acquitted (author's field notes 2000; R2K Legal 2004).

These four events show the range of repressive actions that activists identified as significant during the period. That these incidents impacted the direct-action activists in Toronto and New York City is obvious. Activists in both cities were initially interested in experimenting with the Seattle tactics, but repression made many of them reevaluate their utility and reject the tactics. How did this happen? I argue that this effect can be explained at least partly by exploring how they disrupted the processes of identification and deliberation. Both underlay the effective reception of locally new innovations. Let us explore these now.

REPRESSION AND IDENTIFICATION

As discussed earlier, for a potential adopter to be able to incorporate a locally new tactic, that person or group needs to be able to identify with the transmitter of that tactic (McAdam and Rucht 1993, 60; Strang and Meyer 1993). The protests in Seattle inspired direct-action activists in New York City and Toronto, but subsequent repression by the police and courts discouraged identification and emulation.

I asked activists in both New York and Toronto why they abandoned or rejected the Seattle tactics, and repression was quickly cited as a reason by activists in both cities. In particular, New York activists saw the size and strength of the police force as the main reason that their city was unlike Seattle, and why the tactics from those protests did not spread to New York. One DAN activist argued, "It's just too big, there are too many cops. You can do certain tactics, but there are serious limits to what you're doing. You can't shut down the city.... Even if you've got 500,000 people, you can't shut down the city."

There were some experiments with blockading tactics and black blocs in New York, but activists repeatedly argued that "there are just too many police" for those tactics to be effective. Interestingly, the Seattle tactics that did not attract police attention – puppets, affinity groups and spokescouncils – were incorporated by New York activists and continue to be used in 2012.

As repression of the global justice movement and its tactics became evident, some activists distanced themselves from them in particular ways. As I discussed earlier, one way that both OCAP and SLAM activists did this was by emphasizing the differences between the ways repression would impact their members as poor people or people of color as opposed to the profile of the Seattle demonstrators (as white, middle-class students). For example, one OCAP member explained that organization's rejection of the tactic of jail solidarity by describing it as "a tactic of the privileged."

In a similar fashion, one OCAP member explained her rejection of blockading by activating boundaries of identity:

Those symbolic arrests don't work well for people who are going to get fucked when they get arrested and spend the next six months in jail, or what have you.

And because, ultimately, the police are in a position where they can simply beat you down. And with us, and with the constituency that OCAP has, they are not terribly hesitant to do that, so I think if we were doing blockades, they would be more than happy to beat the living hell out of people, arrest them, abuse them in jail. You have to have a certain moral high ground with the police, I think, in part in order for some of those things to be effective and that's difficult with the group of people that we're made up of.

As I mentioned earlier, some members of SLAM made a similar argument about blockades: "The whole bike-lock to a railing? We're looking around the room and going, 'Hell no, we're not doing that. A cop will hurt us.' We just couldn't imagine putting that much trust in a cop."

Activists from other organizations who wished to support the critique of white, middle-class domination within the global justice movement also used this identity based analysis of the disproportionate impact of the police or court repression to limit their identification with the Seattle activists and to reject the Seattle tactics. One activist from the Ontario Public Interest Research Group explained how policing practices that disproportionately impacted vulnerable groups required a rejection of the Seattle tactics:

You get people to show up to demos where there would be a black bloc. Whether they are disabled or transgendered or whatever, and they are sitting there and they are going, "We just showed up to this demo and now it got really hectic. The cops are pulling all sorts of crazy shit and they are fighting back, and there is this huge violence thing. We are caught here, and if someone is going to be beat up, it's going to be us. And if someone gets arrested, you know who's going to be spending longer time in jail? Getting harsher sentences? Getting rougher treatment?" … You start to go, "Who are we (as white people) to be pushing that envelope then? On whose behalf? Under what circumstances?"

Even though members of all six organizations studied here had initially identified with the militancy of the global justice movement in Seattle and had adopted the movement's tactics in the period immediately after the WTO protests, they eventually abandoned many of these tactics. Activists in both cities distanced themselves from the Seattle protesters by emphasizing how police repression disproportionately affected racial minorities, poor people, and transgendered people. In this way, some activists distanced themselves from the Seattle protesters and rejected the associated tactics.

REPRESSION AND DELIBERATION

Effective tactical decision making depends on organizations having sufficient strategic capacity. As already noted, strategic capacity is greater when organizations are able to draw resources from a diversity of salient constituencies and when organizations are able to engage in regular, open, and authoritative deliberation (Ganz 2000, 1005). Respondents in both cities argued that repression reduced the number and diversity of people available to participate in direct action, it fragmented relationships between core and peripheral participants, and it absorbed financial and organizational resources. They also argued that repression limited the way their organizations were able to collectively reevaluate their tactical decisions. Evidence suggests that repression reduced the strategic capacity of the movement organizations and thus limited the ability of the activists to be open to incorporating the Seattle tactics. This was particularly dramatic in the Toronto context.

First, activists argued that repression limited the number of activists willing to protest. When numbers were reduced, the willingness of activists to engage in disruptive tactics declined. One OPIRG activist explained, "I think that police repression really takes a toll on the size of the group and the size of the population of people who are willing to engage in that [disruptive protest]. It [the size of the group] is sort of like the buffer zone against that police repression." One SLAM activist explained how repression of the organization in the mid-1990s led students to withdraw from the organization's activities and consequently led to a de-escalation of tactics: "At Brooklyn College I'd try to get people to go to a rally at City Hall and they would be like, 'I went to your rally, and I got beaten up, I got thrown in jail, I'm not going to any more of your rallies.' So we changed our tactics at Brooklyn College."

Second, activists argued that repression did not simply reduce the number of participants but created divisions between those already affiliated and potential recruits. One OCAP member explained that such divisions were a reason to reject tactics like the black bloc: "You can't get somebody from the streets to come to a whole series of meetings to learn how to be part of a black bloc cell. And I think also, the sort of the identification of it with a very, like, white middle-class youth scene ... it alienates us from our base, and it also alienates us from a lot of support that we absolutely need in order to survive."

Direct-action activists from New York argued in a similar way that the jail solidarity tactic unfairly affected less privileged prisoners and thus damaged alliances between the activists and the other prisoners. As a result, New York City activists abandoned the tactic. One DAN-NYC activist explained:

I was arrested in Philadelphia, and I guess jail solidarity may have achieved some things, but there was a general conversation about how our tactics were affecting other prisoners. What we got, other people were not gaining from it, and it [repression] was coming down harder on them. And what we gained out of it [jail solidarity] was in some cases so little that it didn't seem worth it.... It didn't work so it had to be reconsidered.

Third, repression was perceived to reduce strategic capacity of an organization by fragmenting alliances between targeted organizations and their allies. One OCAP activist explained that the increasing repression against the group in the period after June 15, 2000, was tied to a withdrawal of financial and human support of OCAP by the labor movement.

There was a very overt dividing of forces from things like the [union] flying squads, who had always been willing or eager to participate in our immigration work, withdrawing their support and significantly cutting the number of people that we had to fill immigration offices, and also, the kinds of bodies, burly bodies, that they were, and their flags, etcetera. It had a very serious effect for us.

Fourth, repression was seen to absorb scarce organizational resources, redirecting them from other goal-seeking activities (Cunningham 2004, 153; Davenport 2005, xvi; Marx 1977). One OCAP organizer explained that repression led the organization to change its tactics after June 15, 2000: "We've had to pay a price, we've taken a lot of arrests, we've spent a lot of time in courts, and some people have spent significant amounts of time in jail. And dealing with that has been time-consuming." Another OCAP organizer explained, "Frankly, it forced us to take a big step back from large-scale militant action, at least for a certain time period, because so many people in the organization were facing charges, and also, that the police crackdown on OCAP was so massive that every subsequent thing that we did was very, very difficult."

Organizational resources are absorbed not only when organizations try to avoid police repression at protests, but also through court and legal proceedings. As Koopmans (1997) pointed out, institutional repression can demobilize more than situational or street repression can. Koopmans argues that the reasons for the effectiveness of institutional repression in demobilizing movements include its degree of consistency and legitimacy. One OCAP member explains, "We had a year and a half to two years where we had hundreds of people going through the court system. So going to court, and the court drain, was an ever-present phenomenon, and you have to make a really concerted effort to jump free of that."

In these ways, repression limited the strategic capacity of these activists by reducing the possibility of open and authoritative deliberation. As I have stated earlier, deliberative discourse is characterized by participants' equality, a diversity of viewpoints, claims that are backed up by reasoned arguments, and for some theorists, reflexivity, the ability of participants to question the agenda and the procedures for discussion (Cohen 1989; Dryzek 1990; Fishkin 1991). Such deliberation is crucial for allowing potential receivers to be reflexive, strategic, and sustainable about their tactical decision making (Chabot and Duyvendak 2002, 727; Opp and Ruehl 1990, 526; Rogers 2003, 429). Respondents argued that repression during the post-Seattle period limited the ability of their organizations to bring together diverse perspectives and to be reflexive, thus limiting the possibility of deliberation.

The conditions of release imposed by the court on OCAP members after the demonstration on June 15 made deliberation particularly difficult. Initial conditions of release meant that defendants were prohibited from communicating with other members of the organization (Esmonde 2003, 345). This limited the possibility of accessible diverse deliberation about the tactics of the organization. One OCAP member explained: "For the majority of the time that I've been a member of OCAP, there have been serious restrictions on somebody or other in the executive, the leadership and also the general membership."

Another OCAP member explained that such repression almost destroyed the organization completely by exacerbating differences between members, while simultaneously making it harder to talk about those differences:

There have been a few times since I've been around where it looked like OCAP might end. Partly it's been from people being arrested or on conditions and all that stuff and through the courts ... because also within that situation of people having conditions and arrests and those things, people get worried, and those elements of, that sort of divisions between people sort of grow a little bit at some of those times.

While members of the organization were under restrictions as defendants, it was extremely difficult for the group to collectively reevaluate its strategy.

Repression also limits the reflexive aspect of deliberation. One OPIRG respondent explained the effects of repression on the ability of organizers of the Windsor protests against the OAS to collectively evaluate their experience: "Coming out of that, we all just threw up our hands and were like 'that's that.' And it kind of imploded at that point.... Friendships had fallen apart and people had really been taken for a ride by the whole mindfuck of the CSIS, RCMP, OPP."

Some OCAP members also argued that repression affected the ability of that organization to be reflexive, at least in the short term. One argued:

I think [repression] has really seriously affected the way that we think about things. One of the things that we don't talk about when we talk about the jury trial [is] the effect of having forty-five people take a vicious beating in the court system. Whether it's the big three or whether it's the other forty-two. The things that we don't talk about still are what has happened to the way that we think about the cops and how that affects the way that we organize on the street and how it affects where we put our main organizers and how it affects like, the length to which we're willing to go, to be frank. I think it's a serious discussion that hasn't happened that needs to happen.

By making it more difficult for activist organizations to collectively reevaluate their tactics in Toronto, police repression interrupted the process of deliberation. Interestingly, the New York activists did not argue that repression affected their deliberation. This may be because the level of repression was less intense and more spread out. Possibly supporting Opp and Ruehl's findings about the importance of microprocesses such as deliberation on mobilization, the activists reevaluated and adapted their tactics after experiencing repression. One DAN member explained: "Our not being able to repeat the same kind of tactic [due to police learning], in combination with feedback that we were getting from lots and lots of people ... led to a change in tactic that was more self-reflective in terms of who we were and where we were and maybe more based in our communities."

The testimonies of activists in New York and Toronto suggest that repression limited their strategic capacity by limiting the number of protesters available for disruptive action, by fragmenting alliances between activists and organizations, by absorbing resources, and especially in the case of Toronto activists, by interrupting the process of deliberation.

CONCLUSION

Repression limited the diffusion of the Seattle tactics by interrupting the processes of identification and deliberation among activists, partly through highlighting differences of race and class. Repression also limited the strategic capacity of these potential adopters by limiting the number of participants at their protests; by absorbing scarce organizational resources; by fragmenting relationships between activists, sympathizers, and other organizations; and in Toronto, by making identification and deliberation more difficult. As a result, repression limited the ability and willingness of activists in Toronto and New York to continue to experiment with the Seattle tactics.

11

After 9/11: Rethinking and Reengaging

> After September 11th there was a lot of debate about the politics of protesting the World Economic Forum. But we understood the significance of being able to have a coming out party again in NYC so soon after September 11th and that was not lost on the people here in Toronto ... After September 11th our tactics shifted a lot. We were supposed to be going to Washington for the September 26th demonstrations, immediately after September 11th and we cancelled the buses. Instead we had a demonstration here and it was the tamest thing you've ever seen in your life. Everyone was like "we're not so sure, we're going to get ourselves in trouble for even trying this."
>
> (Mob4Glob activist)

The attacks on September 11, 2001 changed the landscape for direct action politics across North America, but especially in New York City. Those attacks destabilized the ways that activists were used to thinking, speaking, and acting and forced them to reconstruct and rearticulate their relationships to each other, to authorities, and to the wider public. Once the towers fell, the Seattle protests seemed to have taken place in a different era, and incorporating the tactics used there seemed more difficult. The identities of global justice activists as opponents of capitalism and the U.S. government were reexamined. For activists, the questions of "who are we?" "what do we want?" and "who do we work with?" became major topics of discussion. In this new moment, with so much uncertainty, activist strategizing required conversations that were reflexive and relatively open to diverse perspectives. In both cities, activists intentionally tried to set up such deliberative opportunities. The conversations that took place in the wake of the 9/11 attacks both in New York and in Toronto were not always ones in which tactics were being discussed directly, but they were about redefining the identity and strategy of the global justice movement in ways that were connected to tactics.

The global justice movement in the post-9/11 moment prompted at least two major conversations. As time passed and the wave of protest waned, these discussions allowed some of these activists to get back into the streets, do direct action, and adapt and use some, but not all, of the Seattle tactics.

In the days after 9/11, activists in both cities met to grieve, reflect on the meaning of the attacks, evaluate their current trajectory, and discuss what should happen next. Many felt that the existing approaches needed to be reconsidered. Starhawk (2001) recounted that she heard "some of my most political friends say, 'I can't go to another rally. I can't stand hearing one more person tell me in angry tones what the answers are.'" Instead she encouraged activists to gather and talk and listen and reflect on how to move forward.

In the weeks that followed 9/11, activists did engage in both formal and informal conversations. The conversations emerged differently in the two cities, influenced by their preexisting structural, organizational, and movement dynamics. The conversations considered the way forward – many focused on whether or not planned protests in Toronto and Washington DC should take place. As these conversations unfolded and activist identities and strategies fragmented and coalesced, a transformed, smaller, and more risk-averse global justice movement emerged.

I describe the two sets of conversations that took place in the days and weeks after the attacks of 9/11. The first set was conversations that consider the way that race, identity, and inequality operated within the movement. The second set was about the appropriateness of direct action and street protest in the new context. I will follow this up by discussing how these conversations played out in the inclusion of the Seattle tactics in the return to the streets and the emergence of the antiwar movement.

CONVERSATIONS ABOUT WHITE DOMINATION IN THE GLOBAL JUSTICE MOVEMENT

The attacks and the confusion that followed 9/11 led to intense and emotional conversations. Both informal and formal, these conversations were partly attempts to answer questions like: What do the 9/11 attacks mean for our tactics, identity, and strategy? What should we be doing now? Since the attacks, who are we? Who are we against? Who are we with? What do we want? What the heck is going on? In order for the activists to be able to continue to operate, they needed to incorporate the attacks on the World Trade Center and the Pentagon into their frameworks. In this new context, concerns about anti-Arab and anti-Muslim racism, the attacks on Afghanistan, Iraq, and the West Bank, and civil liberties became more central to a broader set of activist frameworks and discussions. These shifts influenced the relationships among new and preexisting movement organizations and thus had an influence on the identity and strategy of the organizations. On the one hand, there was a sense that everything had changed. On the other hand, the moment was seized by some activists as an opportunity for influencing the global justice movement to better address issues of white domination that had long plagued it ...

In the weeks following 9/11, global justice movement activists in both Toronto and New York City hosted community meetings to discuss answers to these questions. There were striking similarities about the ways activists in the global justice movement in both cities attempted to make racial inequalities in the movement a priority in these meetings. Of course, discussions about racism and white domination of the movement were not new. Partly through networks like Colors of Resistance, a section of the movement had developed an analysis of the problem of white domination in the movement and had developed some tools for addressing it. In the reflexivity and openness of the post-9/11 moment, these activists saw an opportunity and a need to ground the movement in a more explicit antiracist politic.

In New York, the meeting took place at the Lower East Side activist center of Charas El Bohio in the days after 9/11. Experienced activists and new arrivals packed the room, wanting to act, to do something. Tragically, the meeting was a shambles. In the hopes that the new moment would provide an opportunity to avoid making the same mistakes as the antiglobalization movement had in New York, facilitators attempted to prioritize the voices of people of color at the meeting, allowing them to speak before other activists. There was also a push to get people to commit to a statement of unity that incorporated an explicit antiracist framework before discussing concrete projects. However, the unfamiliar language of antioppression and antiracist politics, fueled by anger about long-standing white domination in local movements, was alienating for many of the people who attended the meeting. New arrivals were unfamiliar with the language and culture on display, and some white activists were hostile to the intervention. Many participants in this meeting never returned.

One DAN activist of color, sympathetic to antiracism but frustrated with the way white domination in the movement was addressed at this meeting explained:

After September 11th, mostly people who were in DAN called a meeting to get an umbrella group together to work on the fallout from September 11th and a small group of people, from one group or another decided that they were going to push this thing that was supposedly in the interests of people of color as far as points of unity goes. They basically started so much shit and were so obnoxious about the whole thing that out of the 300 people there the first night, by the third meeting, there was half of that. So all these new people that like, finally got off their asses because a building got blown up in New York who were potential organizers were gone because they were forced to be involved in a conversation that they have no language for and didn't know even where the fuck it was coming from. So, you know, it didn't make anybody a better organizer and a lot of people dropped out because of it and basically it was a totally fucked up way – basically you do shit my way or leave, and we'll force you out kind of stuff.

Even though the attempt to address concerns about white domination of the movement was lauded by many, some were concerned about the way these activists tried to address the problem. Others argued that this attempt was inevitable, given the ongoing frustration by activists of color and their allies. The confusion of the post-9/11 moment and the frustration about the inadequacy of popular responses to the moment led to internal divisions, fragmenting the movement further and demobilizing many activists.

In Toronto, as in New York, some of the activists who had been involved in the global justice movement but had concerns about white domination in that movement organized community meetings after 9/11. Helen Luu, an organizer who had been involved in the Windsor protests, was involved. She explains:

At our first community meeting, which drew about 250 people, we tried to address the internal dynamics of oppression that exist even within progressive groups by implementing a speakers' list that would allow people of color (especially women) to speak before white people (especially men). Reflecting on this later, I know that the method we haphazardly chose was not the best way to tackle the issue, but the crowd that came to the meeting reacted in a way that made me again see how many supposedly progressive people refuse to critically look at themselves as possible agents of oppression, no matter how good their intentions may be. Rather than engaging in a critical dialogue with everyone about their concerns, some chose instead to yell that we were "racists" and that "[we] just don't get it." (Luu 2004)

In both cities, the attacks of September 11 and recognition that the context had changed pushed global justice movement activists to meet and to attempt to rearticulate the movement's identity and strategy in a way that would build a strong foundation for ongoing work. The concern about white domination of the global justice movement, along with a related concern about being unconnected to local concerns and issues became central to these discussions. The post-9/11 context also prompted many activists to discuss the appropriateness and effectiveness of direct action, and the Seattle tactics in the new era.

CONVERSATIONS ABOUT TACTICS AND STRATEGY AFTER 9/11

Activists in both cities were confused about how to act in a context whose political opportunity for protesting neoliberalism had seemingly closed. In both cities, the initial shock and paralysis led some to demobilize, others to continue unabated, and still others be driven to do "something useful" that would correspond with their desire to make a better world. These routes were manifested in different ways. Activists in New York City discussed how they could translate their commitment to "direct action" and justice into helping locals who had been affected by the attacks. DAN and SLAM members went down to Ground Zero hoping to offer the medical skills that had been honed in direct action protests. Others set out across the boroughs, armed with buckets of paint, intent on covering up racist graffiti. When the expected graffiti was scant, one group decided that the best way to engage was one on one, so they spread out to talk to ordinary people about what had taken place in the hopes of encouraging reflection and discussion. Such discussions were seen as a way of reengaging with the public and a way of offering a political vision that differed from the militarism and nationalism of most mass media. Some direct action activists spent time in Union Square, where those who had lost loved ones were joining other New Yorkers in lighting candles and grieving.

In Toronto, there was a similar desire to respond to the crisis in a practical manner that reflected their identity as "people working for justice." Helen Luu, who was involved with OPIRG, explains that after September 11, she and other activists of color contacted Arab and South Asian community groups, organizations, and mosques to find out how to help (Luu 2004, 418). Mob4Glob also turned inward after September 11, questioning their strategy, tactics, vision, and identity (Rutherford 2003).

This shift away from transgressive street protest toward local community projects and reflection is not surprising. Many activists were scared of the consequences of challenging or criticizing capitalism or the state during those first post-9/11 weeks. One DAN activist expressed his frustration: "I think people are too afraid to experiment... As soon as those towers were hit, bam. All of this stuff [tactical experiments] was completely dropped."

The question of tactics and strategy for a movement that wanted to use direct action to challenge neoliberalism, if not capitalism and the U.S. government did not disappear. As mobilizations against war, civil liberties restrictions, sweeps of immigrants, and government action began to be planned, questions of identity and strategy returned with a vengeance. In both cities, many direct action activists wanted to rearticulate their definition of who *we* – who also opposed the global capitalist system but in a different way than the 9/11 attackers – were. One DAN activist describes the way that this attempt to redefine identity in a way that would limit risk, led to a rejection of certain tactics:

Anything that could be considered militant, or could be spun as being terrorist [was rejected]. There was a lot of worry about that. I don't think it kept people from wanting to do it [direct action]. It was just like, a temporary thing. The sense was that everyone is going to be looking at us with a lot more scrutiny. They'll be misinterpreting a lot of things, [mis-] construing a lot of things, just to arrest us.

This reconstructed identity of the global justice movement was one that saw itself as more vulnerable than before 9/11. In a context in which the police were enjoying record levels of support and admiration, there was a reluctance to engage in any tactic that might lead to confrontation. Public support for police, it was thought, would likely mean more repression of dissent. Discussing a protest against the Carlyle group, one DAN member explained:

What was interesting to me was one major shift after 9/11 was that almost everyone was like, 'they'll cut my arm off, they don't care about me in contrast to the confidence that people, that privileged people had before at the anti-globalization protests, and before September 11th ... September 11, took away some sense of security based on race and class privilege in protesting. It just made tangible another thing that was justifiable to be violent to people about.

Activists feared that this new militarized and patriotic context would mean that the public would be intolerant of any protest that challenged existing authorities. In this environment, tensions between more and less confrontational groups increased. Alliances were reconfigured, and there was a retreat from more controversial tactics including black bloc, property destruction, and civil disobedience and blockading. One SLAM member explains:

I think it affected the movement. It divided a lot of groups. I don't know about splitting groups up, but that's another thing that caused people to rethink the tactics. Not just the direct action thing, but just to think about what they were doing and what it was going to look like, which I don't think a lot of people really gave a shit about before.

Civil liberties and surveillance became an increasing concern. One SLAM activist explained:

I think that September 11th threw fear into a lot of people. The PATRIOT ACT came out, and it's only been used twice. I mean we don't know about no tap warrants. Those could be used left and right, we don't know. But September 11th really scared a lot of people. I mean it also, some people got excited, saying the chickens have come home to roost. But no one I know could be cavalier about killing all those people.

In SLAM, the September 11 attacks coincided with a shift in the membership of its organization and a shift toward issues of student survival and university accessibility. One SLAM member explained that "the on campus group gets very involved in antiwar stuff, opposition to the repression directed at Muslims and South Asians and opposition to the war in Afghanistan. There is not a strong direct action component; it was right after September 11th. A lot of people were not interested in confronting the state."

The direct action activists in Toronto were less dramatically affected by the 9/11 attacks, but there too, the incident changed the context, affecting the issues, relationships, and discussions that pushed activists to reevaluate and rearticulate their identities and strategies away from confrontational protest. On September 15, 2001, members of Mob4Glob Toronto participated in a national conference of global justice activists in Hull, Quebec, that allowed the group to discuss how to respond to the attacks. Other groups met to discuss the new context and how to respond. In this new context, many argued that there should be a retreat from street protest. The Canadian Auto Worker president Buzz Hargrove wrote a letter to the Canadian Labour Congress arguing that the labor movement should cancel the upcoming protests planned for the global day of action against the World Trade Organization.

As you are aware, the ICFTU had planned a world-wide demonstration for November 9 this year against the free trade agreements being signed without democratic input or protections for the world's poorest. I would call on you, as president of the CLC, to urge the ICFTU to suspend this day of protest as a symbolic act to signify our movement's outrage and our condemnation of terrorist acts as well as all senseless acts of violence against any of the world's people. (Hargrove 2001)

Similarly, one of the immediate discussions for activists in Toronto after 9/11 was whether or not to go forward with the Ontario Common Front (OCF) day of action, planned for October 15, 2001. The planning for the protests against the incumbent provincial Conservative government and its' Premier Mike Harris had been underway all summer, with organizers traveling throughout the province. The day of action was planned to address Harris's ongoing neoliberal agenda and cuts to social spending. Although not explicitly about global justice, the plans had attracted the attention and support of many young activists who had experienced the global justice protests of the previous years. The Common Front was organized as a coalition, initiated by the Ontario Coalition Against Poverty, and included antipoverty groups across the province, Mobilization for Global Justice, First Nations groups, and unions.

In the days after the September 11 attacks, the OCF organizers acknowledged the way that the September 11 attacks had influenced the situation but, after internal discussion, argued that the events must continue. OCAP organizer John Clarke explained:

We felt that certainly there were immediate questions on how people organize, on how people presented themselves that had to be taken seriously, but we also realized that in many ways September 11 and the horrible events of that day would serve to intensify the very agenda we were challenging and that is certainly true in terms of Harris.

Clarke continued, "The reality is that [September 11] didn't – as far as we are concerned – create a reason to put our struggle on hold; in fact it made it more important than ever" (Teetaert 2001).

One of the most widely cited defenses of the protest was by York University professor David McNally, who in a piece written in the week following the attacks argued:

It is clear that the climate of military saber-rattling and crackdowns on civil rights requires some sober reflection on our part. We are operating in a changed context, and it would be foolhardy not to recognize it as much. At the same time, we cannot afford to surrender our agenda of mobilizing for social change. Now more than ever, we need to raise our voices and take to the streets in our campaigns for global justice, even if we do so with a renewed sense of self-discipline. (McNally 2001)

This "self-discipline" involved long discussions about how to return to the streets with dignity, but avoiding confrontation with the police.

The attacks of September 11 dramatically changed the context for deliberation and for street protest in both cities, affecting the ongoing use of direct action tactics. Activists gathered together to discuss the new context: renegotiating and rearticulating the identity and strategy of the global justice movement. The commitment activists showed to these discussions was impressive. Many published their thoughts; others organized both closed and open meetings of affinity groups, organizations, and networks. Online discussions flourished. Such collective deliberation allowed sections of the global justice movement in Canada and the United States to reorient itself to the new context – and for some to keep mobilizing for large-scale events like the protests against the IMF and World Bank planned for September 2001. However, the changed context of the 9/11 attacks activated and drew attention to differences in privilege, resources, goals, and ideology. These boundaries made deliberation and direct action more difficult. In the months that followed, those who returned to the streets were fewer, more isolated, and often more cautious.

BACK INTO THE STREETS

People returned to the streets in both Toronto and New York within the month, but there was a decline in the size, frequency, and transgression of protest in both cities. When I compare protests in 2001 in Toronto covered by the *Toronto Star*, I find that before September 11, in 2001 there were thirty-nine demonstrations, averaging almost five per month. In contrast, in the months after September 11, there were only ten demos in Toronto (an average of two per month). This was even more dramatic in New York City, with thirty-three protests reported in the *New York Times* before September 11, an average of just over four per month. After September 11, there was slightly more than one protest per month.

Things were clearly different than they had been in Seattle in 1999. There was a great deal of uncertainty about how to move forward. Some activists returned to the models and organizations they had used before the Seattle demonstrations. Others stayed committed to the Seattle model. Still others formed new coalitions and began to see themselves as part of an antiwar movement. One Mob4Glob activist explains:

Mob4Glob did actually have the first demonstration I think in Canada against the war in Afghanistan. We transformed what was supposed to be a trip to Washington [to protest the IMF and World Bank], and instead rolled that into a march for peace and justice, just cause we didn't know what to do. We just assumed that we wouldn't get into the US, and didn't know what was happening.

In Toronto, despite demonization from politicians and in the press, the Ontario Common Front activists protested on October 16, 2001. The crowds were smaller than anticipated and less interested in confronting the police than before 9/11. However, the protesters faced a significant police response as they tried to gather. Carrying goggles to protect myself from tear-gas, I, like a dozen others, was arrested on the suspicion that I was going to participate in an unlawful protest, and was held until the demonstrations were over. Buses of protesters from Montreal and Quebec City were also initially detained by police who refused to allow them to join the demonstrations. Such pre-emptive policing appeared widely sanctioned in the new context.

During the protests, approximately 1500 protesters roved through the financial district, drumming, and chanting, with some pagans dressed as a "Living River," a tactic used at the FTAA protests in Quebec City. The protests ended at the U.S. Consulate, where several speakers denounced the U.S.-led attacks on Afghanistan and people chanted "Stop the war on the poor – at home and abroad!" (Bacque 2001b).

In the street, the conversations about the identity and strategy of the movement in relation to September 11 continued. One activist caught hold of an American flag, sprayed "Stop Murder" on it, and set it alight. According to the coverage in the *Toronto Star*, a good number in the crowd were horrified and gasped "oh no, oh no." Discussions among the marchers ensued about the appropriateness of flag burning in the post-9/11 moment. Journalist Royson James reports that the majority complained about the incident, arguing "This is not what we are about. That's not the message we want to send" (James 2001).

Despite the involvement of many global justice activists, there were only scattered references to the Seattle demonstrations in the OCF protests. This was due in part to the central role played by OCAP, but also because of an interpretation of the new context, with its increased fear of repression and isolation. There were general assemblies rather than spokescouncils and snake marches instead of black blocs. There were few puppets and affinity groups.

In New York City, too, direct action activists returned to the streets relatively quickly. After participating in peace vigils and discussions in Union Square, when the bombs started dropping on Afghanistan on October 14, 2001, they marched for the first time since 9/11. Many people were uncertain about how the protest would be received by New Yorkers. The march left from Union Square, where ongoing memorials to those who had died in the World Trade Center attacks remained, and marched to Times Square. Despite the fears of participants, the crowd was applauded by many passersby. The mood of the crowd was determined, but cautious. Indeed, activists smiled and nodded at police, and when a fire truck passed by, presumably on its way to "Ground Zero," many in the crowd applauded.

When it was announced that fall that the World Economic Forum (WEF) would be meeting in New York City at the end of January 2002, direct action activists from DAN-NYC discussed how to respond and initiated a new coalition called Another World Is Possible (AWIP). These activists faced a dilemma. As the hosts for these protests, they were carrying on within a trajectory of annual global justice protests that had taken place in Davos, Switzerland. The World Economic Forum was a target that shared similarities with the World Trade Organization. In many ways, it was the perfect opportunity to use the Seattle tactics. Still, the location of New York City only six months after the attacks on the World Trade Center meant that local global justice activists feared being isolated by other organizations and targeted by the police if they engaged in actions that were seen as confrontational or anti-American. The headline of the January 24, 2002 article by Sarah Ferguson in *Mother Jones* just before the protests made the conundrum clear: "Testing Protest in New York: Could Seattle Tactics Backfire in New York?" The question was stated: "How can a movement which has relied on provocative street actions to sustain its momentum stage protests in a still-shaken city without alienating the public at large?"

It was a good question. Of course the activists knew that the organizers of the WEF were hoping that this conundrum would paralyze the protesters. The WEF had chosen to move their event to New York in part to escape the direct action tactics of European militants. Bringing it to New York City was seen as a dare and a trap by New York activists. "It's a brilliant PR move, to essentially dare the globalization movement to do anything in confrontation with the NYPD," said Mike Dolan, deputy director of Public Citizen's Global Trade Watch. "And I think it's a potential PR disaster if we don't agree on rules of engagement that are explicitly non-violent. The minute a provocateur puts a brick through a window in midtown Manhattan, the media will grab onto it and that'll be the story. In the post 9/11 climate, this is a trap" (Dolan in Ferguson 2002). His organization and others planned educational activities instead of protests. Other key figures from the Seattle demonstrations were similarly wary. John Sellers, the executive director of the Ruckus Society, the direct action training organization central to the Seattle protests, explained: "Don't get me wrong, I am extremely supportive of the people who will be protesting in New York, but I don't trust the media to make us look anything but ugly and unreasonable, particularly when we'd be standing across the barricades from New York's finest, the heroes of Sept. 11" (Strom and Uchitelle 2002).

Long discussions about strategy ensued. Even though the NYC activists understood that they needed to be careful, they were unwilling to ignore the WEF's challenge. They felt that they had to reaffirm their existence, and the right to protest in the new context. As Brooke Lehman, an organizer from DAN in Seattle who had been central to DAN-NYC and the spin-off coalition Another World Is Possible, explained, "If we back down now, we'll send the message that the globalization movement has been scared quiet. I think it's more important to come together and put our message out, knowing full well the media may spin it in such a way that's unfavorable, but that's a chance I think we have to take" (Usborne 2002). David Graeber of the Anti-Capitalist Convergence, DAN-NYC and AWIP agreed, saying, "We feel like we're under some obligation to do something, and to show that if you can do it now, in New York, you can do it anywhere. It's scary, they're going to kick our asses, but we've got to do it anyway" (Usborne 2002).

During this period, the media featured large photographs of police, armed with machine guns, protecting the Waldorf Astoria Hotel, where the meetings were to be held, from the protesters. Right-wing pundits and police spokespeople made the analogy between the antiglobalization protesters and the attackers of the World Trade Center. Every Starbucks and McDonalds restaurant in lower Manhattan had police stationed outside. The atmosphere was completely hostile to activism in general and direct action protest in particular. As a result, there were widespread fears about a lack of public support for the protests. The new context pushed the activists to repeatedly differentiate themselves from "violent terrorists." Careful media work was prioritized, as activists attempted to be clear and explicit about the message of their protests.

This meant that strategies were chosen to minimize repression and isolation. To the consternation of some militants, the AWIP organizers decided to obtain a legal permit from the police to march against the World Economic Forum.

Despite the permit, even in the post-9/11 environment, the protest was largely organized within the Seattle framework of spokescouncils, affinity groups, puppetry, and black blocs. As one SLAM activist explained: "We did participate in the WEF thing, we went to that big thing. However, we made that decision like the vast majority of people in New York that it was not the moment for mass civil disobedience ... but there was a desire to keep the anti-globalization stuff alive." Key figures from the Seattle protests traveled to New York to support the mobilization. David Solnit, a central organizer involved in making puppets a large part of the Seattle protests, set up a puppet-making space and helped build puppets for the protests. Global justice trainers from California like Starhawk and Lisa Fithian, both of whom had been central in the preparations for Seattle, trained new and experienced activists. Medical teams, legal observers, and communications teams from the global justice movement were organized. There were radical cheerleaders, groups dressed up in Statue of Liberty costumes, and a great deal of creative protest. Reclaim the Streets satirized the fearmongering about the black bloc by organizing a "tango bloc." There was even a black bloc. This group arrived with shields and masked up for the big march. The police arrested them immediately. There was also evidence of some post-Seattle innovations. Borrowing from the Toronto OCF protests of October 2001, there was a snake march in the Lower East Side. Like the black bloc, the group was quickly surrounded by police and arrested.

The WEF protests were heavily policed, with the march completely contained within barricades. Anyone engaging in disruptive protest was quickly arrested. Nonetheless, many of the DAN/AWIP activists argued that simply holding the event was a success, given the post-9/11 context in New York.

By the spring of 2002, the paralysis of the immediate post-911 period had been shaken off, and a new (albeit less confrontational) chapter of protest had begun. In the wake of the WEF, AWIP disbanded, DAN-NYC regrouped as a smaller organization, with many New York direct action activists joining preexisting global organizations like Rainforest Action Network or shifting into local activism around immigrant rights, solidarity with Palestinian sovereignty, movements defending community gardening, and on environmental and prisoner justice. For most, there was less of an emphasis on "corporate globalization" than there had been in the past. Fewer activists embraced the identity of an antiglobalization or global justice activist.

In Toronto, the decline of the global justice movement was more gradual. Mobilization for Global Justice activists continued to meet and mobilized for the "Take the Capital" protests planned for Ottawa in June 2002 and the G8 summit in Kananaskis, Alberta, the following month. Still, September 11 had changed the tone, tactics, and goals of these events. In Ottawa, even though there were squats and a black bloc, activists who had previously put their energy toward decentralized direct action organized a family-friendly "No One Is Illegal" march. Similarly, the G8 summit in Alberta featured little direct action but plenty of puppets. The momentum and confrontational nature of the global justice movement had slowed. By the fall of 2002, both Mobilization for Global Justice in Toronto and DAN-NYC had stopped meeting. The antiglobalization identity had lost its sheen and its large coalitions had collapsed, and with it, a large number of activists demobilized.

Those who did not took the experience of those successful protests and elements of the strategy and tactics from the global justice movement with them into future mobilizations. These spin-off movements included an immigrant rights movement that challenged both the nation-state and global capitalism, a Palestine solidarity movement, and most obviously, a new, globally networked antiwar movement.

SPILLING OVER INTO THE ANTIWAR MOVEMENT

In the last few months, getting people out has been hard. After 11 September 2001, the anti-globalization movement in Europe morphed seamlessly into an antiwar movement, with huge rallies in European capital cities drawing hundreds of thousands of people each. But here in North America, the global justice protests dissipated, unable to resolve their internal tensions, unable to clarify their politics, and too weak to challenge the naked opportunism of the Bush administration in the wake of the attacks. The Bush administration's bloody-minded fixation on war against Iraq has changed that.... On Saturday, we witnessed the rebirth of two movements: the peace movement, so long quiescent, and the North American anti-globalization movement. With the experience of anti-Vietnam protesters, the energy and drive of the young global justice movement, the credibility and moral power of organized religion and the resources of organized labor, we may be able to stop this war. It's possible again to feel the heady optimism of Seattle. It feels like the dawn, after a long, dark, winter night.

Corvin Russell, Toronto activist (Ashman 2003)

As Russell explains, the attacks on Afghanistan began and those in Iraq began to appear imminent, and an antiwar movement began to emerge. In Toronto and New York City, this movement took some energy and tactics from the Seattle protesters but combined these with the strategies and organizations of activists from earlier protest cycles. Antiwar activists from the Gulf War, antinuclear, and anti-Vietnam struggles, along with various socialist organizations became much more central in the new moment.

In Toronto, the antiwar movement was spearheaded by the Toronto Coalition to Stop the War – a coalition that involved many of the larger organizations involved in Mob4Glob, along with some community organizations from Arab and Middle Eastern communities. In New York City, two main antiwar coalitions emerged: United for Peace and Justice and ANSWER.

David Meyer and Nancy Whittier's (1994) study of the effect of the U.S. women's movement on the peace movement has shown us how earlier movements influence the frames, tactics, organizational forms, and participation of later movements. They have this influence because of shared membership, participating in the same coalitions, having overlapping communities, and being affected by shared external changes and shifts. These channels facilitated the diffusion of the Seattle tactics into the movement against the wars on Iraq and Afghanistan; however, such spillover was only partial – partly a result of differences between the makeup, approach and goals of the different movements and partly a result of the perception by activists of the closed political opportunity (Hadden and Tarrow 2007).

The limits of this spillover also reflected preexisting differences between the antiwar and antiglobalization identities and strategies. Some antiwar organizers were suspicious of the tactics and identity of global justice movement, often emphasizing the way such protests attracted repression or were dominated by young, white, countercultural students. Other veteran activists were committed pacifists and wanted to avoid discussing questions of violence and nonviolence within the new movement. In response, many global justice activists critiqued the approach of the antiwar movement as ineffective, outdated, and timid. The boundary between the two activist generations quickly began to harden (see Whittier 1997). In global justice movement parlance, *we* became those who were used to operating in a decentralized manner within affinity groups, using puppets, music, and new technologies and subscribed to a "diversity of tactics" approach. *They* were seen as timid, hierarchical, bureaucratic, moneyed, dogmatic, and simply "old."

The activation of this identity boundary meant that there was limited spillover between the global justice movement and the antiwar movement. Still, as the antiwar movement emerged in both cities, global justice movement activists became involved in a number of ways. In New York and Toronto, some DAN and Mob4Glob activists joined the new antiwar coalitions. Some of these activists argued that it was important to use the moment to build a broader movement against an impending war. Others saw it as a way to move forward and escape ongoing conflicts and confusion within the global justice movement. One Mob4Glob activist who joined Coalition to Stop the War after 9/11 argued that discussions in the antiwar movement were much more productive, and that the movement was more diverse and rooted in local communities. The stated ability to avoid white domination of the movement was identified as an important improvement over the global justice movement; however, other global justice activists who tried to become involved in the antiwar movement argued that they had been intentionally cut out of the planning meetings because they were too interested in direct action. One Mob4Glob activist argued that:

For the first few months the Stop the War coalition had completely closed meetings so nobody could attend them.... It wasn't until after February 15th, 2003 that Stop the War [sic] coalition started having open meetings that people could attend. So the organizing culture [of the antiwar movement] was completely different [than the global justice movement] in Toronto. It was closed, it was very bureaucratic, it was top down, the politics were watered down.... In the antiwar movement, direct action was shunned; there was no room for it at all. It was interesting the politics of it all ... there was a real attempt in Toronto to marginalize that conception of direct action and to re-conceptualize it as a tactic that you only use in certain circumstances. There was a real effort to malign direct action and actually to conceptualize it as an angry, alienated white kid, privileged type of organizing and action.

This respondent claimed that the International Socialists and the Canadian Peace Alliance were behind this strategy to link concerns about white domination to concerns about direct action. Nevertheless, he argued that the collective memory of the antiglobalization movement remained as an important, albeit informal, resource to the burgeoning antiwar movement.

There were similar criticisms of the new antiwar coalitions in New York, primarily around a lack of open, democratic decision making. Decisions in United for Peace and Justice (UFPJ) were officially made in open meetings, but the agenda for those meetings was decided in advance by a smaller group. Critics argued that this was rooted in the biographies and political ideologies of key members of that coalition. Similar critiques were made of the ANSWER coalition, which made fewer claims about consensus decision making and participatory democracy (Weinberg 2005). These groups were not particularly interested in the Seattle approach, believing that large, permitted rallies and marches would be more strategic. This frustrated many global justice protesters, who argued that because of limited openness at the meetings, there was limited opportunity to introduce more confrontational tactics or strategies. One DAN activist argued:

It's really hard, you had this really fresh, invigorated thing pop up right after Seattle, and then this old guard still holding on, and then it's almost like things were almost ready to come to a head but they didn't because of 9/11. And so now the old guard is back in position. I'm talking about UFPJ, I'm talking about ANSWER. And this new innovative kind of stuff has completely fallen off the radar.

In an attempt to keep the direct action tactics in the repertoire, some members of the DAN-NYC formed the short-lived No Blood for Oil Coalition, which described itself in a way that reflected its roots in the global justice movement: "Our mission is to bring direct action into the movement against the war. We're not organized around holding large rallies; our focus is more around civil resistance: facilitating affinity groups, organizing guerrilla action and other visible ways that show we're ready to put our bodies in line to speak against this war."

In 2004, a similar formation emerged as Toronto's June 30th Organizing Committee, contrasting itself to the Toronto Coalition to Stop the War in its emphasis on the connections between war and corporations, anti-imperialist language, youthful membership, and its direct-action strategy. Both streams of the antiwar movement defended their choices and argued that the urgency of the situation allowed no time for such debates.

On February 15, 2003, a global day of action was planned against the impending war on Iraq. The strategy in both cities was largely determined by the coalitions who planned large, permitted marches and rallies, rejecting a more decentralized Seattle approach and direct action as elitist and inappropriate.[1] Nonetheless, in both Toronto and especially in New York City, direct-action activists were deeply involved in the preparations. Some DAN-NYC members became part of the leading UFPJ coalition, working on media strategy, outreach, and other areas. Others decided to set up the support infrastructure for the protest, including volunteer security and medical and legal observer teams.

At the time, I worked with a group of global justice activists who had banded together to provide radio communication at the WEF and protests against the Republican National Convention in Philadelphia, as well as local community garden protests and Critical Mass rides. At each of these events the team spread throughout the crowd, communicating any need for medical or legal support to the appropriate group or communicating the movement of protesters and police to the crowd. The approach was intended to facilitate decentralized forms of mobilization by sharing information widely. Our "comms" group explained our plan to UFPJ, who agreed to provide funds to rent equipment and a space to work from; however, it quickly became apparent that their priority was the rally site, and they had little interest in or the ability to support those outside that area, especially those involved in direct action or confrontations with the police. When, during the protest we told organizers about arrests and confrontations outside of the rally area, they responded that because it was not part of the permitted rally, providing support in those locations was not their priority. This attitude was condemned by some activists from DAN-NYC and SLAM. One SLAM activist resisted the conflation of direct action with white youth by emphasizing how people of color were using direct action, and how these activists were not being supported by the leadership in the antiwar movement:

> I think there is a lot of disappointment in the organizers for not supporting people taking the street and those not being "bad protesters." Those not being "black bloc people" like that they described. But them being 40 year old women and men and people with babies and people of color and white people.

On February 15, in New York City, dozens of feeder marches attempted to gain access to the rally site and were blocked by police barricades. A crowd of activists was charged by police horses, and many activists were arrested. Other groups of activists decided to flood Times Square and other sites, engaging in sit-ins and blocking roads. Even though such decentralized, disruptive protest was not a central strategy in New York's antiwar movement, the

---

[1] San Francisco activists pursued a Seattle-style approach for the same day of action, which was organized by a coalition called Direct Action Against the War.

infrastructure and deliberations from the previous period played a crucial role in the antiwar mobilizations of the period.

A similar dynamic took place in Toronto at demonstrations from December 2002 through March 2003. A call by the Rhubarb Collective (2002) for an antiwar spokescouncil that would discuss direct action in Toronto in December 2002 was introduced by the following lines:

> When bombs first rained down on Iraq,
> we marched and listened to speeches.
> When bombs rained down on Yugoslavia,
> we marched and listened to speeches.
> When bombs rained down on Afghanistan,
> we marched and listened to speeches.
> ~~What are we going to do this time?~~

Global justice activists perceived that they had been intentionally excluded from the antiwar decision-making meetings, and that antiwar activists appeared interested in emphasizing the distinction between pre- and post-9/11 practices. As a result, the divisions between the two streams were maintained.

Despite Corvin Russell's hope that the antiwar movement and the global justice movement might merge into a new, vibrant antiwar movement, in both Toronto and New York in the years after the attacks on the World Trade Center, there was more marching and listening to speeches than there was decentralized direct action of the Seattle variety. Although there were plenty of ways the tactics could have spread from one movement and moment to the other, without an interest in and opportunity for deliberating about the Seattle tactics in the mainstream antiwar movement, there was limited spillover. Within the global justice movement itself, however, the tactics persisted – but that movement was narrower, more isolated and more cautious. The moment and the movement had clearly changed.

12

Conclusion

A discussion in which different types of people with different ideas think and talk creatively, reflexively, and relatively equally about taking action in a new way is a rare and precious thing. Such moments and spaces allow groups of people to play with new ideas. They can discuss (and argue about) whether they identify with the past users of these ideas, whether they can abstract those ideas from their original context, and if the conversation moves in the appropriate direction, whether they can imagine how these innovations might be adapted for and used by their own organization.

If we understand that such conversations lie beneath collective action by social movements, we build on existing insights about diffusion (Tarrow 2005, 2010). We already know that social movement organizations have more strategic capacity when they bring together people from diverse communities, who have access to different experiences and ideas and can discuss them in a relatively equal, reflexive, and open way (Ganz 2000). When such organizations meet, they are more likely to be able to identify with a wide range of other actors, consider their ideas, adapt, and experiment with them. However, when we look at the meetings and conversations in which activists discuss new tactics, we see that most of the time, this does not happen. Inequalities in power, resources, and capacity rooted in political economy, political networks, and organization can make deliberation – and thus diffusion – extremely unlikely. As a result, movement organizations, like other types of organizations or groups, keep doing what they have done in the past, or lock themselves onto innovations without adequately deliberating and adapting them to their own context.

This does not mean that deliberation should always result in the incorporation of a new tactic. Most of the time, an innovation may not be suitable, appropriate, or strategic for a particular task or time and place. Moments of deliberation allow groups to think more clearly and creatively about past and future practices, and can lead activists to incorporate, adapt, or reject a new tactic. Because social movement organizations are so often voluntary, operating with fuzzy goals, high levels of risk, and limited resources, such deliberation is more important for diffusion among them than it is among other types of organizations. Because social movements are engaged in challenging authorities that have more power and influence, they need to be able to deliberate relatively frequently about the effectiveness and meaning of their actions. More than other types of organizations, social movement organizations that try to decentralize decision making and value deliberation are vulnerable to the divisive effects of repression, resource inequalities, and cultural difference. For these organizations to be able to have deliberative conversations about street protest requires a certain level of trust and relative equality, but both external changes and internal dynamics can limit such conversations. First, external shifts and shocks like repression, revolutions, events like 9/11, governmental change, economic crises, or alterations of social structure, can bring people together in new ways or can activate boundaries between those with different access to resources or stakes in the new context changing the likelihood of deliberation.

These external dynamics influence internal processes. Internal struggles over how to interpret of the external context and how to effect change, as well as struggles over power and resources, when trust and equality break down, can also block deliberation. Without deliberation, strategic capacity is limited, and with that limitation, the possibility of incorporating, adapting or rejecting innovations is reduced.

The connections between relational context, deliberation and diffusion that I show in the preceding pages builds on existing theories of diffusion, but highlights the role of microlevel interactions in the receiving context and the influence of relational context on those interactions. In the receiving context, inequalities of race and class, the structure of political networks and organizational dynamics influence diffusion among organizations by facilitating or constraining deliberation among potential adopters. Building on Sean Chabot's (2010) emphasis on the role of dialogue in diffusion, I argue that for collective actors who struggle together over the meaning of innovations, we need to look at patterns of interaction and deliberation, but how these patterns are inevitably influenced by local, national, and global political economies and regime dynamics.

Although I think this explanation points us in the right direction, I know that there is still more work to be done. The explanation I offer still cannot explain the relative importance of the organizational, local, national, and global contexts; it cannot show why categorical inequalities block identification at some times and not at others. It cannot show how online and offline, informal and formal, internal and external conversations relate to each other as each influence deliberation. I suspect that timing, duration, and sequence are crucial here, but more research – research that is able to map these things more accurately – is needed.

Twelve years after the WTO protests in Seattle, that initial moment of experimentation and collaboration seems like ancient history. Even though many activists inspired during that wave are still engaged in struggles around poverty, war, First Nations solidarity, climate change, immigration, and housing, many others are gone. The activists who were twenty-five years old in 1999 are now thirty-seven. The wave of protest associated with the Seattle protests has waned. It waned for reasons like the attacks of September 11, 2001, the elections (and reelections) of Bush, Harper, and Obama, increasingly militarized and preemptive policing, the wars in Iraq and Afghanistan, successes in stalling agreements like the Free Trade Area of the Americas, and the World Trade Organization, and now the effects of economic crisis. Each of these events altered the political context and forced activists and social movement organizations to respond and adapt their strategies, tactics, and identities. The wave also waned for internal reasons, as all waves do. The struggles over how to sustain organizations, to incorporate new people, to sustain momentum, to obtain resources, to prioritize targets and tactics, and to deal with internal inequalities, personalities, and emotions all take their toll.

The direct-action activists who mobilized in the period after Seattle now look back with mixed emotions. Some are nostalgic for the optimism of that time, while others look back with disdain and regret. Still others are bringing their stories and practices from those protests into the wave of protest associated with Occupy Wall Street in 2011 and 2012.

One can see this influence in some of the hundreds of occupations in cities and towns across Canada and the United States. These recent protests are both a product of and distinct from the 1999–2001 wave of protest. The tactics and forms of organization from the Seattle protests are seen occasionally and in particular places. As I write this on December 5, 2011, Occupy activists use black bloc tactics in a march in Oakland, California. Others use giant puppets at Occupy Wall Street and Occupy DC. Soft blockades continue to be widespread, but PVC-style "lockboxes" have only been used once, at a bank occupation done by Occupy Seattle. Similarly, there have been no reports of activists refusing to give their names as part of a jail solidarity action. Spokescouncils have been adopted by Occupy Wall Street and Occupy Portland, and affinity groups have been incorporated widely. As this research might suggest, New York City's Occupy Wall Street appears to be one of the Occupy sites where the most Seattle tactics have been incorporated, but even Occupy Wall Street activists clearly distance themselves from the earlier wave of protests.

Although the cluster of Seattle tactics studied here did spread to new users in networks across the United States, Canada, and beyond, it is clear that diffusion was not widespread. Now each place where they continue to be used offers a new opportunity for diffusion. Occupy Oakland's use of the black bloc tactic launched debates that echoed, and in some cases replicated, the debates about violence and property destruction that took place after the Seattle protests. Occupy Wall Street's shift from a "general assembly" to a spokescouncil form of decision making recoded and retransmitted the practice. Its spread, this time like the last, is dependent both on the external context and the local relational conditions as they impact the possibility of reflexive, egalitarian discussions among diverse actors with diverse perspectives.

This study began with a puzzle. When the Seattle demonstrations occurred, the tactics associated with that success spread widely, but not everywhere. They were incorporated in some cities, by some activists, and not by others. I wanted to understand why some Toronto activists abandoned the Seattle tactics less than a year after those protests, while their equivalents in New York continued to experiment with them. I used a comparison of two cases to make a larger claim. More research will be needed to see whether the conditions for deliberation appear to affect diffusion in other contexts. It will be important to specify whether these dynamics around tactical diffusion are the same in other parts of the world and to think more deeply about how global inequalities play into diffusion processes. More work also needs to be done to specify more closely the relative importance of equality, difference, reflexivity, and diversity of participants in deliberation, and their effect on diffusion. Future research will also need to evaluate whether deliberation is as important for the diffusion of other types of innovations as it is central to the diffusion of protest tactics.

For those of us who study social movements, this argument pushes us to look closely at our models of mobilization and contention and to consider the influence of sites beyond the boundaries of organizations, movements, and nations as relevant. It suggests that to understand diffusion in social movements, as elsewhere, one needs to look more broadly at organizational dynamics, cultural and interpretive processes of meaning making, and the interplay of political networks at different scales. If one is able to do this, it will help us to understand the ways processes of globalization and transnational integration are playing out within and beyond local contexts.

Although written for an academic audience, this book is also intended to be useful to activists engaged in organizing. What I found here pushes me to emphasize how important it is for social movement organizations to stay open and reflexive about new ideas, to avoid isolation, to be conscious of decision-making processes, and to be aware of how repression, inequalities, and patterns of interaction can affect the decision making and strategic capacity of their organization. It also argues that meeting processes and conversational dynamics are deeply tied to the ability of movements to be strategic and effective. So, in part, this is a warning to my fellow activists about the ways that repression and power inequalities affect strategizing and praxis. This does not mean that incorporation of new tactics is always good. Indeed, the Seattle tactics are not useful in the vast majority of contexts. Deliberation does not allow only the incorporation of a new tactic but should allow for its alteration to the new context, or even its rejection. Without deliberation, movements are less strategic and effective.

It is often said that the Seattle protests launched a wave of protests that involved an increased level of direct action, and that the 9/11 attacks ended that wave. The explanation of how these events influence waves of protest is less clear. We know it involves emotions; people feel hope, or fear, or anger. We know it involves changing political opportunities at local, state, or global levels and the interpretation of these opportunities by activists and organizers. We know it involves the patterns of interaction as people gather together, or distance themselves from each other. It also involves innovation, new tactics, emulation, and experimentation.

This study shows that direct-action movements within participatory democracy, involve all of these things, all processed through collective discussion. Tactical decisions and movement strategies develop as enthusiastic or tired people, who may love or loathe one another, talk together, think, evaluate, reason, tell stories, pressure and cajole each other with humor or with bitter warnings. It is these conversations that underlie both the incorporation and rejection of new tactics and the ebbs and flows of cycles of protest.

As I finish work on this manuscript, I receive an announcement for a global day of action by the Occupy Movement. Will this new wave of protest, spreading across Europe, the Middle East, and North America, with its revitalized and innovative tactics, and ways of organizing, alter the form of local struggles? It will depend, it seems, partly on whether activists in different local contexts are able to transcend historical differences and inequalities to gather, deliberate, and strategize about how to bring the movement home.

Appendix

Direct Action Tactic Project

Interview #
Date
Location
Organization

First, I am going to ask you some questions about the organization and your place in it.

1. When did you get involved with (organization name)?
2. When did you stop being involved?
3. Can you describe your role or involvement in the organization?
4. What sort of activism had you done before you became involved with this organization?
5. I have here a timeline of the events that (organization name) participated in between 1998 and the end of 2001.
6. What were the biggest changes in the organization during this period?
7. Did any other organizations influence the tactics the organization used during this period? If so, what were they, and how did they influence the organization?

    Let us go through each major event in turn. (Adding to or revising timeline, we will discuss the tactics used at events and ask the following questions.)

8. Are the tactics used in each event correct?
9. Were any new tactics used at this event?
10. Where did the new tactic come from?
11. Why was it used?
12. Was it successful? Why or why not?
13. Did the group or participants in the group ever consider using any of the following tactics? (Some tactics will have already been discussed.)

14. Why or why not? When would you use them?
    a. Black bloc
    b. Puppets
    c. Blockading/ lockboxes
    c. Street Party/Reclaim the Streets
    d. Bicycles
    e. Jail solidarity
    f. Legal collectives
    g. Ya Basta!
    h. Cacerlolazo
15. What about police response? How much and when does that affect the tactics that you use?

    Finally, I want to ask a few questions about the Seattle protests that took place in the middle of our time period.

16. Did you attend the Seattle protests against the WTO?
17. Did anyone in your organization attend the Seattle protests?
18. Did anyone you know attend the Seattle protests?
19. If you did not attend, and if you know people who did, did they tell you much about the protests?
20. Did you see videos about the protests?
21. What did you think when you heard about the protests?
22. How did they affect your participation in protest activity?
23. Did the protests affect your organization in any way? How?
24. Did the protests affect the tactics your organization engaged in any way? How?
25. Did the protests affect activism in New York/Toronto in any way? How?

References

Abrahamson, Eric. 1991. "Managerial Fads and Fashions: The Diffusion and Rejection of Innovations." *The Academy of Management Review* 16(3): 586–612.

ACLU Washington State. 2000. "In Second Lawsuit, ACLU Challenges Seattle's WTO No Protest Zone." March 7, 2000. Accessed December 5, 2011. http://www.aclu. org/free-speech/second-lawsuit-aclu-challenges-seattles-wto-no-protest-zone-behalf-seven-local-people

ACME. 1999. "N30 Black Bloc Communiqué: A Communiqué from One Section of the Black Bloc of N30 in Seattle." Accessed December 5, 2011. http://www. urban75.com/Action/seattle9.html

ACT UP NY. 2000. "Brutal Treatment Continues Against Jailed Protesters." Accessed December 5, 2011. http://www.actupny.org/reports/rnc-updates6.html

Albert, Michael. 1999. "On Trashing and Movement Building." *Z Magazine.* Accessed December 5, 2011. http://www.zcommunications.org/on-trashing-and-movement-building-by-michael-albert

Amabile, Theresa M. 1996. *Creativity in Context.* Boulder, CO: Westview Press.

Amoore, Louise. 2005. "Introduction: Global Resistance, Global Politics." In *The Global Resistance Reader,* edited by Louise Amoore, 1–12. New York: Routledge.

Anarchist Press. 2000. "Urgent Call to Action: Toronto DC Solidarity March Attacked by Police." Press release. Accessed December 5, 2011. http://dc.indymedia.org/newswire/display/2763

Anderson, Scott. 1998. "Peppered With Questions." *Now Magazine,* September 24–30. Toronto.

Ansell, Christopher. 1997. "Symbolic Networks: The Realignment of the French Working Class." *American Journal of Sociology* 103(2): 359–90.

Antibody, Spazz, Sketch & Entropy. 2000. "Letter From Four Persons who were in the D2K Black Bloc." In *The Black Bloc Papers,* edited by David Van Deusen and Xavier Massot, 82–3. Shawnee Mission, Kansas: Breaking Glass Press.

Area Connect. 2000. "New York City, New York Statistics and Demographics US Census." Accessed December 5, 2011. http://newyork.areaconnect.com/statistics. htm

Ashman, Sam. 2003. "The Anti-Capitalist Movement and the War." *International Socialism.* Accessed December 11, 2011. http://pubs.socialistreviewindex.org.uk/isj98/ashman.htm#18

Ayres, Jeffrey M. 1998. *Defying Conventional Wisdom: Popular Movements and Popular Contention Against North American Free Trade.* Toronto: University of Toronto Press.

Bacque, Graeme. 2001a. "Reclaim the Streets Event Invaded by Police on Horseback." Accessed December 5, 2011. http://members.fortunecity.com/brutalitycanada/rts2001.html

——— 2001b. "O16: Economic Disruption Hits Canada's Capitalist Heartland." Accessed December 5, 2011. http://www.mail-archive.com/kominform@lists.eunet.fi/msg09617.html

Bearman, Peter and Kevin D. Everett. 1993. "The Structure of Social Protest, 1961–1983." *Social Networks* 15: 171–200.

Beaverstock, J.V., R.G. Smith and P.J. Taylor. 1999. "A Roster of World Cities." *Cities* 16 (6): 445–58.

Beckwith, Karen. 2000. "Hinges in Collective Action: Strategic Innovation in the Pittston Coal Strike." *Mobilization* 5: 179–200.

Beissinger, Mark. 2002. *Nationalist Mobilization and the Collapse of the Soviet State.* Cambridge: Cambridge University Press [Comparative Politics Series].

Benjamin, Medea. 2000. "The Debate Over Tactics." In *Globalize This! The Battle Against the World Trade Organization and Corporate Rule.* Edited by Kevin Danaher et al. 67–72. Monroe, ME: Common Courage Press.

Bennett, Lance. 2003. "Communicating Global Activism: Strengths and Vulnerabilities of Networked Politics." *Information, Communication & Society* 6(2): 143–68.

Beveridge, Andrew. 2003. "How Different Is New York City From The United States? Demographics New York." *Gotham Gazette.* May 14, 2003. Accessed December 5, 2011. http://www.gothamgazette.com/article/Demographics/20030514/5/388

Boghosian, Heidi. 2004. "The Assault on the Free Speech, Public Assembly, and Dissent: A National Lawyers Guild Report." Accessed December 5, 2011. http://www.nlg.org/publications/the-assault-on-free-speech-public-assembly-and-dissent/

Bohman, James and William Rehg. 1997. *Deliberative Democracy: Essays on Reason and Politics.* Cambridge, MA: MIT Press.

Bourdieu, Pierre and Loic Wacquant. 1992. *Invitation for a Reflexive Sociology.* Chicago: University of Chicago Press.

Brockett, Charles D. 2005. *Political Movements and Violence in Central America.* New York: Cambridge University Press.

Brown, Shona L. and Katheleen M. Eisenhardt. 1997. "The Art of Continuous Change: Linking Complexity Theory and Time-Paced Evolution in Relentlessly Shifting Organizations." *Administrative Science Quarterly* 42(10): 34–56.

Burt, Ronald S. 1980. "Innovation as a Structural Interest: Rethinking the Impact of Network Position on Innovation Adoption." *Social Networks* 2(4): 327–55.

——— 1987. "Social Contagion and Innovation: Cohesion versus Structural Equivalence." *American Journal of Sociology* 92: 1287–35.

——— 1999. "The Social Capital of Opinion Leaders." *Annals of the American Academy of Political and Social Science* 566(1): 37–54

Butterfield, Greg. 2000. "Police attack youths as May Day march demands immigrant rights." *Workers World.* May 11, 2000. Accessed December 4, 2011. http://www.workers.org/ww/2000/undoco511.php

Captain Vegetable. 2002. "Canada, Toronto – Direct Action Training/Conference, May 24–26." Accessed December 5, 2011. http://www.ainfos.ca/02/may/ainfos00385.html

Carlsson, Chris and Jim Swanson, editors. 1997. "Five Years Old – Critical Mass!" Accessed December 5, 2011. http://www.scorcher.org/cmhistory/pdf/crit5a16. pdf

Chabot, Sean. 2000. "Transnational Diffusion and the African American Reinvention of the Gandhian Repertoire." *Mobilization* 5: 201–16.

———. 2010. "'Dialogue Matters' Beyond the Transmission Model of Transnational Diffusion between Social Movements." In *The Diffusion of Social Movements: Actors, Mechanisms and Political Effects*, edited by Rebecca Kolins Givan, Kenneth M. Roberts, and Sarah A. Soule, 99–124 New York: Cambridge University Press.

Chabot, Sean and Jan Willem Duyvendak. 2002. "Globalization and Transnational Diffusion between Social Movements: Reconceptualizing the Dissemination of the Gandhian Repertoire and the 'Coming Out' Routine." *Theory and Society* 31: 697–740.

Churchill, Ward. 1998. *Pacifism as Pathology*. Winnipeg: Arbeiter Ring.

Clemens, Elisabeth. 1997. *The People's Lobby*. Chicago: University of Chicago Press.

Cohen, Joshua. 1989. "Deliberation and Democratic Legitimacy." In *The Good Polity*, edited by Alan Hamlin and Philip Pettit, 17–34. Oxford: Blackwell.

Coleman, James, Elihu Katz and Herbert Menzel. 1957. "The Diffusion of an Innovation Among Physicians." *Sociometry* 20(4): 253–70

———. 1966. *Medical Innovation*. New York: Bobs-Merrill.

Collier, Robert. 1999. "Turmoil in Seattle Streets / Protesters force cancellation of trade summit's opening session." *San Francisco Chronicle*, December 1, 1999.

Conell, Carol and Samuel Cohn. 1995. "Learning from Other Peoples Actions: Environmental Variation and Diffusion in French Coal Mining Strikes, 1890–1935." *American Journal of Sociology* 101(2): 366–403.

Conway, Janet. 2003. "Civil Resistance and the 'Diversity of Tactics' in the Anti-Globalization Movement: Problems of Violence, Silence and Solidarity in Activist Politics." *Osgoode Hall Law Journal* 41(2&3): 505–29.

Couch Potato Revolution. 2008. "Pink and Black Block at New York City's Pride." June 25, 2008. Accessed December 5, 2011. http://couchpotatorevolution.blog-spot.com/2008/06/pink-and-black-block-at-new-york-citys.html

Cunningham, David. 2004. *There's Something Happening Here: The New Left, the Klan, and FBI Counterintelligence*. Berkeley: University of California Press.

Czepiel, John A. 1974. "Word-of-Mouth Processes in the Diffusion of a Major Technological Innovation." *Journal of Marketing Research* 11(2): 172–80.

Danaher, Kevin and Roger Barbach. 2000. *Globalize This!* Monroe, ME: Common Courage Press.

Davenport, Christian. 2005. "Introduction." In *Repression and Mobilization*, edited by Christian Davenport, Hank Johnston, and Carol Mueller, vii–xli. Minneapolis: University of Minnesota Press.

Davis, Joseph. 2002. *Stories of Change: Narratives and Social Movements*. Albany: SUNY Press.

de Lint, Willem. 2007. "Policing Public Order in Canada: An Analysis of Recent Events." *Ipperwash Inquiry*, Hon. Sydney Linden, Commissioner. Research Submission. Accessed August 31, 2011. http://www.attorneygeneral.jus.gov.on.ca/inquiries/ipperwash/policy_part/research/pdf/deLint.pdf

Debord, Guy. 2004. *Society of the Spectacle*. London: Rebel Press.

Deffuant, G., S. Huet and F. Amblard. 2005. "An Individual-Based Model of Innovation Diffusion Mixing Social Value and Individual Benefit." *American Journal of Sociology* 110(4): 1041–69.

della Porta, Donatella. 1995. *Social Movements, Political Violence and the State*. Cambridge: Cambridge University Press.

della Porta, Donatella, Olivier Fillieule, and Herbert Reiter. 1998. "Policing Protest in France and Italy: From Intimidation to Cooperation?" In *The Social Movement Society*, edited by David S. Meyer and Sidney Tarrow, Chapter 5. New York: Rowman & Littlefield.

della Porta, Donatella, Abby Peterson, and Herbert Reiter, editors. 2006. *The Policing of Transnational Protest*. Aldershot: Ashgate.

della Porta, Donatella and Sidney Tarrow. 2006. *Transnational Protest and Global Activism*. New York: Rowman and Littlefield.

DiMaggio, Paul and W. Walter Powell. 1983. "The Iron Cage Revisited: Institutional Isomorphism and Collective Rationality in Organizational Fields." *American Sociological Review* 48: 147–60.

Dixon, Chris. 2001. "Finding Hope After Seattle: Rethinking Radical Activism and Building a Movement." Accessed December 4, 2011. http://theanarchistlibrary. org/HTML/Chris_Dixon__Finding_Hope_After_Seattle__Rethinking_Radical_ Activism_and_Building_a_Movement.html

Dolan, Michael. 2002. "Activists Plan Upcoming WEF Protests." Scott Harris interviews Michael Dolan. Accessed December 5, 2011. http://www.alternet.org/ story/12261/activists_plan_upcoming_wef_protests?page=3

Dominick, Brian. 1999. "Anarchy, Non/Violence and the Seattle Actions." *Z Magazine*. December 6, 1999. Accessed December 5, 2011. http://www.zcommunications. org/anarchy-nonviolence-and-the-seattle-demonstrations-by-brian-dominick

Dryzek, John S. 1990. *Discursive Democracy: Politics, Policy, and Political Science*. New York: Cambridge University Press.

Dunbar-Ortiz, Roxanne. 1999. "The Tyranny of Democracy" *San Francisco Bay Guardian*, December 16, 1999. Accessed December 5, 2011. http://www.driftline. org/cgi-bin/archive/archive_msg.cgi?file=spoon-archives/anarchy-list.archive/ anarchy-list_1999/anarchy-list.9912&msgnum=719&start=50373&end=50470

Dupuis-Deri, Francis. 2003. "Black Blocs. Bas Les Masques." Un article publié dans la revue *Mouvements des idées et des luttes*, No. 25. Accessed August 2, 2011. http://classiques.uqac.ca/contemporains/dupuis_deri_francis/black_blocs_bas_ les_masques/black_blocs_bas_les_masques.pdf

Dwyer, Katherine. 2001. "Lessons of Quebec City." *International Socialist Review*, June–July 2001. Accessed December 3, 2011. http://www.isreview.org/issues/18/ lessons_of_quebec.shtml

Earth First! 2011. "About Earth First!" Accessed December 3, 2011. http://www. earthfirst.org/about.htm

Ekvall, Goran. 1996. "Organizational Climate for Creativity and Innovation." *European Journal of Work and Organizational Psychology* 5(1): 105–23.

Erickson, Thomas. 1999. "Persistent Conversation: An Introduction." *Journal of Computer Mediated Communication*, 4. Accessed December 5, 2011. http:// jcmc.indiana.edu/vol4/issue4/ericksonintro.html

Esmonde, Jacquie. 2003. "Bail, Global Justice and the Limits of Dissent." *Osgoode Hall Law Journal* 41(2–3): 323–59.

Ferguson, Sarah. 2002. "Testing Protest in New York: Could Seattle Tactics Backfire in New York?" *Mother Jones*. January 24, 2002. Accessed December 5, 2011. http://motherjones.com/politics/2002/01/testing-protest-new-york

Fiori, Gerry. 2002. "Thousands Protest World Economic Forum." *Socialist Action*. Accessed December 5, 2011. http://www.socialistaction.org/news/200202/forum.html

Fishkin, J. S. 1991. *Democracy and Deliberation*. New Haven: Yale University Press.

Francisco, Ronald A. 1996. "Coercion and Protest: An Empirical Test in Two Democratic States." *American Journal of Political Science* 40(4): 1179–204.

Frankel, Jeffrey A. and Peter R. Orszag. 2002. *American Economic Policy in the 1990s*. Boston: MIT Press.

Freedom Road Socialist Organization. 2006. "Some Thoughts on the History of CUNY *SLAM*." Accessed December 5, 2011. http://www.frso.org/about/pamphlets/cunyslam2007.pdf

Freeman, Jo (AKA Joreen). 1970. "The Tyranny of Structurelessness." Accessed November 29, 2011. http://www.jofreeman.com/joreen/tyranny.htm

Friedman, Thomas. 1999. "On Being Senseless in Seattle." *New York Times*. December 1, 1999.

From Somewhere in the Mid-West. 2001. "A Communiqué On Tactics And Organization To The Black Bloc." Accessed December 3, 2011. http://www.sheffieldmayday.ukf.net/articles/blackbloc.htm

Gamson, William. 1975. *The Strategy of Social Protest*. Homewood, IL: The Dorsey Press.

———. 1990. *The Strategy of Social Protest*, 2nd edition. Belmont, CA: Wadsworth Publishers.

Ganz, Marshall. 2000. "Resources and Resourcefulness: Strategic Capacity in the Unionization of California Agriculture, 1959–1966." *American Journal of Sociology* 105(4): 1003–62.

Ghosal, Sumantra and Christopher A. Bartlett. 1988. "Creation, Adoption and Diffusion of Innovations by Subsidiaries of Multinational Corporations." *Journal of International Business Studies* 19(3): 365–88.

Gitlin, Todd. 2003. "The Media in the Unmaking of the New Left." In *The Social Movements Reader: Cases and Concepts*, edited by Jeff Goodwin and James Jasper, 301–12. Wiley Blackwell.

Gould, Roger V. 1991 "Multiple Networks and Mobilization in the Paris Commune 1871." *American Sociological Review* 56: 716–29.

———. 1995. *Insurgent Identities*. Chicago: University of Chicago Press.

Government of Canada. 2001. *2001 Census*. Statistics Canada.

Graeber, David. 2004. "On the Phenomenology of Giant Puppets: Broken Windows, Imaginary Jars of Urine, and the Cosmological Role of the Police in American Culture." Accessed December 5, 2011. http://balkansnet.org/zcl/puppets.pdf

———. 2009. *Direct Action: An Ethnography*. Oakland, CA: AK Press.

Granovetter, Mark. 1973. "The Strength of Weak Ties." *American Journal of Sociology* 78: 1360–80.

———. 1978. "Threshold models of collective behavior." *American Journal of Sociology* 83: 1420–43.

———. 1983. "The Strength of Weak Ties: A Network Theory Revisited." *Sociological Theory* 1: 210–33.

Greenhalgh, Trisha, Glenn Robert, Fraser Macfarlane, Paul Bate, Olympia Kyriakidou, and Richard Peacock. 2005. "Storylines of Research in Diffusion of Innovation: A Metanarrative Approach to Systematic Review." *Social Science and Medicine* 61(2): 417–30.

Gude, Stephanie. 2000. "Canada, Windsor, Hunger Striking Political Prisoners Still Being Jailed in Windsor June 7, 2000." Accessed December 4, 2011. http://www.ainfos.ca/oo/jun/ainfos00142.html

Gumbel, Andrew. 1999. "WTO Protest – The Apathy Generation Finally has a Reason to be Angry." *The Independent (London)*, December 2. Accessed December 6, 2011. http://www.independent.co.uk/news/wto-protest-the-apathy-generation-finally-has-a-reason-to-be-angry-1125328.html

Gurr, Ted. 1969. *Violence in America*. New York: Bantam Books.

Guttman, Amy and Dennis Thompson. 1996. *Democracy and Disagreement*. Cambridge, MA: Belknap Press of Harvard University Press.

Habermas, Jürgen. 1984/1987. *The Theory of Communicative Action*, translated by Thomas McCarthy. Cambridge: Polity.

Hackman, J. R. 1990. "Creating More Effective Work Groups in Organizations." In *Groups That Work*, edited by J. R. Hackman, 479–504. San Francisco: Jossey-Bass.

Hadden, Jennifer and Sidney Tarrow. 2007. "Spillover or Spillout? The Global Justice Movement in the United States After 9/11." *Mobilization* 12(4): 359–76.

Hardt, Michael. 2002. "Porto Alegre: Today's Bandung?" *New Left Review* 14: 112–118.

Hargrove, Buzz. 2001. "Letter to CLC president Ken Georgetti." September 16, 2001. Accessed December 5, 2011. http://www.caw.ca/en/4214.htm

Hedstrom, Peter. 1994. "Contagious Collectivities: On the Spatial Diffusion of Swedish Trade Unions 1890–1940." *American Journal of Sociology* 99(5): 1157–79.

Hedstrom, Peter, Rickard Sandell, and Charlotta Stern. 2000. "Mesolevel Networks and the Diffusion of the Swedish Social Democratic Party." *American Journal of Sociology* 106: 145–72.

Highleyman, Liz. 2002. "The Black Bloc: Behind the Mask." Accessed December 5, 2011. http://www.black-rose.com/articles-liz/blackbloc.html

Hirsch, P. M. 1972. "Processing Fads and Fashions: An Organizational Set Analysis of Cultural Industry Systems." *American Journal of Sociology* 77: 639–59.

Holden, Robert T. 1986. "The Contagiousness of Aircraft Hijacking." *American Journal of Sociology* 91(4): 874–904.

Hurl, Chris. 2005. *Diversity of Tactics: Coalescing as New Combinations*. Unpublished MA Thesis, University of Victoria. Accessed December 5, 2011. https://dspace.library.uvic.ca:8443/bitstream/handle/1828/849/hurl_2005.pdf?sequence=1

Hutchins, Edwin. 1991. "The Social Organization of Distributed Cognition." In *Perspective on Socially Shared Cognition*, edited by L. B. Resnick, J. M. Levine and S. D. Teasley, 283–307. Washington, DC: American Psychological Association.

Ikegami, Eiko. 2005. *Bonds of Civility: Aesthetic Networks and the Political Origins of Japanese Culture*. Cambridge: Cambridge University Press.

Indymedia Seattle. 2011. "History." Accessed November 29, 2011. http://seattle.indymedia.org/about-us

James, Royson. 2001. Column. *Toronto Star*, October 17, 2001.

Jasper, James. 1999. *The Art of Moral Protest: Culture, Biography, and Creativity in Social Movements*. Chicago: University of Chicago Press.

Josiahag. 2000. Blog posting. Accessed May 2003. http://www.goshen.edu/~josiahag/r2k/3.html

Just Cause. 2004. "How to Use Jail/Court Solidarity." Accessed December 5, 2011. http://www.lawcollective.org/article.php?id=187

Katz, Elihu. 1968. "Diffusion (Interpersonal Influence)." In Vol. 4, *International Encyclopedia of the Social Sciences*, edited by David L. Shils, 78–85. London: Macmillan and Free Press.

1999. "Theorizing Diffusion: Tarde and Sorokin Revisited." In *The Annals of the American Academy of Political and Social Science*, edited by Paul Lopes and Mary Durfee, 144–55. Thousand Oaks: Sage Publication.

Kauffman, L. A. 2000a. "Whose Movement?" *Alternet*, April 1. Accessed December 5, 2011. http://www.alternet.org/story/9072/

2000b. "Black Comeback: An Interview with Kai Lumumba Barrow." *Free Radical: Chronicle of the New Unrest*, 11, Accessed December 5, 2011. http://www.anarchistpanther.net/others/other1.html

2000c. "We the Peeps." *Alternet*, April 2000. Accessed December 5, 2011. http://www.alternet.org/story/11/

2001. "All has Changed." *Free Radical*, 19, September 17. Accessed December 5, 2011. http://www.peoplesgeographyproject.org/changed.html

2002. "Who Are Those Masked Anarchists?" In *The Battle of Seattle*, edited by Eddie Yuen, George Katsiaficas and Daniel Burton Rose, 125–29. New York: Soft Skull.

2011. "After the Action." *n+1*. 16 December, 2011. Accessed February 4, 2012. http://nplusonemag.com/after-the-action

Keck, Margaret and Kathryn Sikkink. 1998. *Activists across Borders*. Ithaca: Cornell University Press.

Katsiaficas, George. 1987. *The Imagination of the New Left: A Global Analysis of 1968*. Cambridge MA: South End Press.

Kolins Givan, Rebecca, Kenneth M. Roberts, and Sarah A. Soule, Editors. 2010. *The Diffusion of Social Movements: Actors, Mechanism and Political Effects*. Cambridge: Cambridge University Press.

Koopmans, Ruud. 1997. "Dynamics of Repression and Mobilization: The German Extreme Right in the 1990s." *Mobilization* 2(2): 149–64.

1993. "The Dynamics of Protest Waves: West Germany, 1965 to 1989." *American Sociological Review* 58(5): 637–58

La Botz, Dan. 2011. "Ontario's 'Days of Action': Citywide Political Strikes." *Troublemakers Website*. Accessed December 3, 2011. http://www.troublemakershandbook.org/Text/Strikes/La%20Botz%20Days%20of%20Action.htm

Lakey, George. 2002. "Mass Action Since Seattle." In *Battle of Seattle*, edited by Eddie Yuen, George Katsiaficas and Daniel Burton Rose, 153–71. New York: Soft Skull Press.

Laursen, Eric. 2001. "Who is that Masked Man?" *In These Times*, September 3. Accessed December 5, 2011. http://www.inthesetimes.com/article/1643/who_is_that_masked_man/

Lazarsfeld, Paul F., Bernard Berelson, and Hazel Gaudet. 1944/1948/1968. *The People's Choice: How the Voter Makes Up His Mind in a Presidential Election*. New York: Duell, Sloan and Pearce/Columbia University Press.

Lichbach, Mark. 2003. "Global Order and Local Resistance: Structure, Culture and Rationality in the Battle of Seattle." Unpublished paper. April 21.

1987. "Deterrence or Escalation? The Puzzle of Aggregate Studies of Repression and Dissent." *Journal of Conflict Resolution* 31(2): 266–97.

Lichbach, Mark I. and Ted Gurr. 1981. "The Conflict Process: A Formal Model." *Journal of Conflict Resolution* 25(1): 3–29.

Luu, Helen. 2004. "Discovering a Different Space of Resistance: Personal Reflections on Anti-Racist Organizing." In *Globalize Liberation: How to Uproot the System and Build a Better World*, edited by David Solnit, 411–26. San Francisco: City Lights Books.

Majahan, V. and R. Peterson. 1985. *Models for Innovation Diffusion*. Beverly Hills, CA: Sage

Marco. 2001. "S-Top Hopping." *Summit Hopping* Web site. Accessed June 24, 2011. http://tao.ca/~ridefree/summithop/

Martinez, E. B. 2000. "Where Was the Color in Seattle?" In *Globalize This!*, edited by Kevin Danaher et al., 74–81. Monroe, ME: Common Courage Press.

Marx, Gary. 1977. "External Efforts to Damage or Facilitate Social Movements: Some Patterns, Explanations, Outcomes and Complications." In *The Dynamics of Social Movements*, edited by M. Zald and J. McCarthy, 94–125. Cambridge, MA: Winthrop Publishers

McAdam, Doug. 1982. *The Political Process and the Development of Black Insurgency*. Chicago: University of Chicago Press.

————. 1995. "'Initiator' and 'Spin-Off' Movements: Diffusion Processes in Protest Cycles." In *Repertoires and Cycles of Collective Action*, edited by Mark Traugott, 217–39. Durham: Duke University Press.

McAdam, Doug and Ronnelle Paulsen. 1993. "Social Ties and Recruitment: Toward a Specification of the Relationship." *American Journal of Sociology* 99: 640–67.

McAdam, Doug and Dieter Rucht. 1993. "Cross National Diffusion of Social Movement Ideas." *The Annals of the American Academy of Political and Social Science* 528: 56–74.

McCarthy, John, Clark McPhail and Jackie Smith. 1996. "Images of Protest: Dimensions of Selection Bias in Media Coverage of Washington Demonstrations, 1982 and 1991." *American Sociological Review* 61: 478–99.

McDonald, Kevin. 2006. *Global Movements: Action and Culture*. Malden, MA: Blackwell.

McLeod, P. L. 1992. "The Effects of Ethnic Diversity on Idea Generation in Small Groups." Unpublished paper presented at the Academy of Management Convention, Las Vegas.

McNally, David. 2001. "The Ontario Common Front after September 11." *Infoshop News*. Accessed December 5, 2011. http://news.infoshop.org/article.php?story=01/09/26/0806435

Meyer, D. S. and Nancy Whittier. 1994. "Social Movement Spillover." *Social Problems* 41(2): 277–98.

Mikalbrown, Kerstin. 2002. "Saving Esperanza Garden: The Struggle Over Community Gardens in New York City." In *From ACT UP to the WTO*, edited by Ben Shepard and Ron Hayduk, 229–33. London: Verso.

Mische, Ann. 2003. "Crosstalk in Movements: Reconstructing the Culture-Network Link." In *Social Movements and Networks: Relational Approaches to Collective Action*, edited by Mario Diani and Doug McAdam, 258–80. New York: Oxford University Press.

Moore, Will H. 1998. "Repression and Dissent: Substitution, Context and Timing." *American Journal of Political Science* 42(3): 851–73.

More Gardens! Coalition. Undated. "Description of More Gardens! Coalition" *Tisch Community Connections*. Accessed November 30, 2011. http://community.tisch.nyu.edu/object/OCC_gardens.html

Morris, Aldon. 1981. "Black Southern Student Sit-In Movement: An Analysis of Internal Organization." *American Sociological Review* 46: 744–67.

Myers, Daniel J. 2000. "The Diffusion of Collective Violence: Infectiousness, Susceptibility, and Mass Media Networks." *American Journal of Sociology* 106(1): 178–208.

N30 Global Day of Action Collective. 1999. *Do or Die* 9:112–113. Accessed December 5, 2011. http://www.eco-action.org/dod/no9/seattle_proposal.html

Nemeth, C. J. and B. M. Staw. 1989. "The Tradeoffs of Social Control and Innovation in Groups and Organizations." In *Advances in Experimental Social Psychology*, 22, edited by L. Berkowitz, 722–30. New York: Academic Press.

New York City Bar. 2001. "Welfare Reform in New York City: The Measure of Success." Accessed February 4, 2012. http://www2.nycbar.org/Publications/reports/show_html.php?rid=41

Next Left Notes. 2007. "44 Arrested Protesting Wall Street War Profiteers." March 20. Accessed December 4, 2011. http://antiauthoritarian.net/NLN/?p=192

No Compromise. 1999. "1999 Fur Season Recap." *No Compromise*, 15. Accessed December 5, 2011. http://www.nocompromise.org/issues/15fur_season99.html

Oliver, Pamela and Doug J. Myers. 1998. "Diffusion Models of Cycles of Protest as a Theory of Social Movements." Accessed December 4, 2011.http://www.nd.edu/~dmyers/cbsm/vol3/olmy.pdf

OPIRG. 2000. "Skills weekend." email comunication. Accessed January 4, 2012. http://owner-OPIRG-events@sandelman.ottawa.on.ca

Opp, Karl-Dieter. 1994. "Repression and Revolutionary Action." *Rationality and Society* 6(1): 101–38.

Opp, Karl-Dieter and Wolfgang Ruehl. 1990. "Repression, Micromobilization and Political Protest." *Social Forces* 69: 521–47.

Parrish, Geov. 2002. "Imagine." In *The Battle of Seattle*, edited by Eddie Yuen, George Katsiaficas and Daniel Burton Rose, 121–4. New York: Soft Skull Press.

2004. "Is This What Failure Looks Like?" *The Seattle Weekly*. November 24, 2004.

Parsons, Talcott and Edward Shils. 1951. *Toward a General Theory of Action*. New York: Harper and Row.

Pittsburgh Post Gazette. 2000. August 2, 2000. Accessed December 3, 2011. http://groups.yahoo.com/group/tenabolition/message/679

Polletta, Francesca. 2001a. "Collective Identity and Social Movements." *Annual Review of Sociology* 27: 283–306.

2001b. "'This is What Democracy Looks Like': The Direct Action Network." *Social Policy* 31: 25–30.

2002. *Freedom is an Endless Meeting*. Chicago: University of Chicago Press.

2006. *It Was Like a Fever*. Chicago: University of Chicago Press.

Queen's Park Riot Defendants. 2001. *June 13 1/2*. Toronto: Self-published.

R2K Legal. 2004. "Legal Statistics." Accessed December 5, 2011. http://r2klegal.protestarchive.org/r2klegal/stats.html

Rasler, Karen. 1996. "Concessions, Repression and Political Protest in the Iranian Revolution." *American Sociological Review* 61(1): 132–52.

Renz, Katie. 2005. "People Power: An Interview With David Solnit." *Mother Jones* March 22, 2005.

Rhubarb, Collective. 2002. "Topic: 1st Toronto Anti-War Spokescouncil – Dec 1, 2002." e-mail communication. Accessed December 5, 2011. http://archive.rabble.ca/babble/ultimatebb.cgi?ubb=get_topic&f=5&t=000579

Ridefree. 2001. "Stop Hopping". Accessed December 5, 2011. http://tao.ca/~ridefree/summithop/

RNC Welcoming Committee. 2007. "Frequently Asked Questions." Accessed December 5, 2011. http://web.archive.org/web/20080711020359/http://www.nornc.org/

Rogers, E. M. 1962. *Diffusion of Innovation*. New York: Free Press.

———. 1995. *Diffusion of Innovations*, 4th ed. New York: Free Press.

———. 2003. *Diffusion of Innovations*, 5th ed. New York: Free Press.

Rose, Fred. 2000. *Coalitions Across the Class Divide: Lessons from the Labour, Peace, and Environmental Movements*. Ithaca: Cornell University Press.

RTS-NYC. 2000. "Mayday2k-New York: Report and Update." Accessed June 23, 2011. http://www.urban75.org/mayday/018.html

Rucht, Dieter. 2001. "Lobbying or Protest? Strategies to Influence EU Environmental Policies." In *Contentious Europeans: Protest and Politics in an Emerging Polity*, edited by Doug Imig and Sidney Tarrow, 125–42. Lanham, MD: Rowman & Littlefield.

Rude, George F. E. 1964. *The Crowd in History: A Study of Popular Disturbances in France and England 1730–1848*. New York: Wiley.

Rutherford, Stephanie. 2003. "Manufacturing Discontent: Knowledge Construction in the Global Justice Movement." Unpublished dissertation, York University.

Sassen, Saskia. 1991. *The Global City: New York, London, Tokyo*. Princeton University Press: Princeton.

Shalom, Stephen R. 2000. "The Diallo Case, March 4 2000." Accessed December 5, 2011. http://www.zcommunications.org/the-diallo-case-by-stephen1-shalom

Shapcott, Michael. 2001. Ontario Alternative Budget 2001: Made In Ontario Housing Crisis, Technical Paper #12. Accessed December 3, 2011. http://www.urbancenter.utoronto.ca/pdfs/curp/ShapcottOntario.pdf

Shepard, Benjamin. 2004. "A Short, Personal History of the Global Justice Movement (from New York's community gardens, to Seattle's tear gas, Quebec's fences, the 9/11 backlash, and beyond). An interview with L.A. Kauffman." In Confronting Capitalism, edited by E. Yuen, D. Burton-Rose, and G. Katsiaficas, 375–88. Brooklyn, NY: Soft Skull Press.

Shepard, Benjamin. 2010. *Play, Creativity, and Social Movements: If I Can't DANce, It's Not My Revolution*. New York: Routledge.

Shepard, Benjamin and Hayduk R. 2002. *From ACT UP to the WTO*. London: Verso.

Silverberg, Gerald, Giovanni Dosi, Luigi Orsenigo. 1988. "Innovation, Diversity and Diffusion: A Self-Organisation Model." *The Economic Journal* 98(393): 1032–54.

Smith, Jackie. 2001a. "Introduction to Special Issue: Globalization and Resistance." *Mobilization* 6(1): i–vii.

———. 2001b. "Globalizing Resistance: The Battle of Seattle and the Future of Social Movements." *Mobilization* 6(1): 1–20.

———. 2008. *Social Movements for Global Democracy*. Baltimore: Johns Hopkins University Press.

Smith, Jackie and Hank Johnston, Editors. 2002. *Globalization and Resistance: Transnational Dimensions of Social Movements*. Lanham, MD: Rowman and Littlefield.

Smith, Neil. 1996. *The New Urban Frontier: Gentrification and the Revanchist City*. New York: Routledge.

Smith Nightingale, Demetra et al., 2002. *Work and Welfare Reform in New York City During the Giuliani Administration: A Study of Program Implementation.* The Urban Institute Policy and Labour Center. Accessed December 3, 2011. http://www.urban.org/uploadedPDF/NYC_welfare.pdf

Snow, David A., E. Burke Rochford, Jr., Steven K. Worden, and Robert D. Benford. 1986. "Frame Alignment Processes, Micromobilization, and Movement Participation." *American Sociological Review* 51(4): 464–81.

Solnit, David. 2004. *Globalize Liberation: How to Uproot the System and Build a Better World.* San Francisco: City Lights Books.

Solstice. 2000. "A16 – An Analysis of Our Tactics." *Earth First Journal* 6. Accessed December 6, 2011. http://www.earthfirstjournal.org/article.php?id=47

Soule, Sarah A. 1997. "The Student Divestment Movement in the United States and Tactical Diffusion: The Shantytown Protest." *Social Forces* 75(3): 855–83.

Spalter-Roth, Roberta, Norman Fortenberry, and Barbara Lovitts. 2007. *What Sociologists Know About the Acceptance and Diffusion of Innovation: The Case of Engineering Education.* Washington, DC: American Sociological Association.

Staggenborg, Suzanne. 1988. "The Consequences of Professionalization and Formalization in the Pro-Choice Movement." *American Sociological Review* 53: 585–606.

Starhawk. 1999. "How We Shut Down the WTO." *Z Magazine,* February 2000. Accessed June 23, 2011 http://www.starhawk.org/activism/activism-writings/shutdownWTO.html

——— 2001a. "Quebec City: Beyond Violence and Nonviolence." Accessed June 23, 2011. http://www.starhawk.org/activism/activism-writings/quebeclessons.html

——— 2001b. "Only Poetry Can Address Grief: Moving Forward after 911." Accessed December 4, 2011. http://www.starhawk.org/activism/activism-writings/moving-forward.html

——— 2002. *Webs of Power: Notes from the Global Uprising.* Gabriola Island: New Society Publishers.

Starr, Amory. 2000. *Naming the Enemy: Anti-Corporate Movements Confront Globalization.* New York: St. Martins Press.

——— 2004. "How Can Anti-Imperialism Not Be Anti-Racist? The North American Anti-Globalization Movement." *Journal of World Systems Theory* 10(1): 119–51.

Steinberg, Marc. 1999a. "The Talk and Back Talk of Collective Action: A Dialogic Analysis of Repertoires of Discourse among Nineteenth Century English Cotton Spinners." *American Journal of Sociology* 105: 736–80.

——— 1999b. *Fighting Words: Working-Class Formation, Collective Action, and Discourse in Early Nineteenth-Century England.* Ithaca, NY: Cornell University Press.

Stilborn, Jack. 1997. *National Standards and Social Programs: What the Federal Government Can Do.* Political and Social Affairs Division. Library of Parliament, September.

Strang, David and Dong-Il Jung. 2005. "Organizational Change as an Orchestrated Social Movement: Recruitment to a `Quality Initiative.'" In *Social Movements and Organization Theory,* edited by G. F. Davis, D. McAdam, W. R. Scott, and M. N. Zald, 280–309. Cambridge: Cambridge University Press.

Strang, David and John Meyer. 1993. "Institutional Conditions for Diffusion." *Theory and Society* 22(4): 487–511.

Strang, David and Sarah A. Soule. 1998. "Diffusion in Organizations and Social Movements: From Hybrid Corn to Poison Pills." *Annual Review of Sociology* 24: 265–90.

Strang, David and Nancy B. Tuma. 1993. "Spatial and Temporal Heterogeneity in Diffusion." *American Journal of Sociology* 99: 614–39.

Strom, Stephanie and Louis Uchitelle. 2002. "A Global Icon Retools For Meaner Streets." *New York Times,* January 27. Accessed December 5, 2011. http://www.nytimes.com/2002/01/27/business/a-global-icon-retools-for-meaner-streets.html

Subways, Suzy. 2010. *We Shut the City Down: Six Former Student Liberation Action Movement (SLAM) Members Reflect on the Mass Direct Actions Against the 2000 RNC in Philadelphia.* Self-published zine. Accessed June 23, 2011. http://suzy.defenestrator.org/SLAM%20Herstory%20Project/R2K%20interviews/SLAM%20R2k%20for%20distro_spreads.pdf

Tarrow, Sidney. 1998. *Power in Movement,* 2nd ed. New York: Cambridge University Press.

——— 2005. *The New Transnational Activists.* New York: Cambridge University Press.

——— 2010. "Dynamics of Diffusion: Mechanisms, Institutions and Scale Shift." In *The Diffusion of Social Movements: Actors, Mechanisms and Political Effects,* edited by Rebecca Kolins Givan, Kenneth M. Roberts, and Sarah A. Soule, 204–20. New York: Cambridge University Press.

Tarrow, Sidney and Doug Imig. 2001. *Contentious Europeans: Protest and Politics in an Emerging Polity.* Lanham, MD: Rowman & Littlefield.

Tarrow, Sidney and Doug McAdam. 2005. "Scale Shift in Transnational Contention." In *Transnational Protest and Global Activism,* edited by Donatella Della Porta, Sidney G. Tarrow, 121–48. Lanham, MD: Rowman and Littlefield.

Teetaert, Vince. 2001. "Disrupting the Economy of Capitalism. Anti-Poverty Groups Challenge Ontario's Corporate Elite." *The Manitoban.* Accessed June 2007. http://www.themanitoban.com/2001-2002/1017/features_index.shtml

Thompson, A. K. 2010. *Black Bloc, White Riot: Antiglobalization and the Genealogy of Dissent.* Oakland: AK Press.

Thompson, Beverly Yuen. 2007. "The Global Justice Movement's Use of 'Jail Solidarity' as a Response to Police Repression and Arrest." *Qualitative Inquiry* 13(1): 141–59.

Thompson, J. D. 1967. *Organizations in Action.* New York: McGraw Hill.

Tilly, Charles. 1995. *Popular Contention in Great Britain.* Boston: Harvard University Press.

——— 1997. "Parliamentarization of Popular Contention in Great Britain 1758–1834." *Theory and Society* 26: 245–73.

——— 2003a. "Invention, Diffusion and Transformation of the Social Movement Repertoire." Unpublished paper. Conference on Political Transfer, Groningen University.

——— 2003b. "WUNC." In *Crowds,* edited by Jeffrey T. Schnapp and Matthew Tiews, 289. Stanford: Stanford University Press.

——— 2008. *Contentious Performances.* New York: Cambridge University Press.

Tilly, Charles and Lesley J. Wood. 2008. *Social Movements 1768–2008.* Boulder: Paradigm Publishers.

Tolbert, Pamela S. and L. G. Zucker. 1983. "Institutional Sources of Change in the Formal Structure of Organizations: The Diffusion of Civil Service Reform, 1880–1935." *Administrative Science Quarterly* 28(1): 22–39.

Toronto, City of. 2011. *Toronto's Racial Diversity.* Accessed December 3, 2011. http://www.toronto.ca/toronto_facts/diversity.htm

Toronto and York Region Labour Council. 2002. *Statistics on Rates of Unionized Labour.*

Traugott, M. 1995. *Repertoires and Cycles of Collective Action*. Durham: Duke University Press.

Trudeau, P.E. 1969. "Address to the American Press Club, Washington D.C." (March 25, 1969).

Usborne, David. 2002. "Go on, Punks, Make Our Day ... New York Awaits Anti-Globalisers." *The Independent*, January 30.

Van de Ven, Andrew H. 1986. "Central Problems in the Management of Innovation." *Management Science* 32(5): 590–607.

Van de Ven, Andrew H. and Everett M. Rogers. 1988. "Innovations and Organizations: Critical Perspectives." *Communication Research* 15(5): 632–51.

Van Deusen, David and Xavier Massot. eds. 2010. *The Black Bloc Papers*. Shawnee Mission, Kansas: Breaking Glass Press. Accessed December 2, 2011. http://www.infoshop.org/amp/bgp/BlackBlockPapers2.pdf

Von Blum, Paul. 2006. "The Democratic National Convention Protests in Los Angeles: August 12–17, 2000." *Guild Practitioner* 63: 47–55. Accessed June 2011. http://www.nlgminnesota.org/node/25

Walker, Jack L. 1969. "The Diffusion of Innovations among American States." *The American Political Science Review* 63(3): 880–99.

Walton, John and David Seddon. 1994. *Free Markets and Food Riots*. Oxford: Blackwell.

Watts, Ronald L. 1987. "The American Constitution in Comparative Perspective: A Comparison of Federalism in the United States and Canada." *The Journal of American History*, The Constitution and American Life: A Special Issue, 74(3): 769–92.

Weber, Max. 1947. *The Theory of Social and Economic Organization*. Translated by A. M. Henderson and Talcott Parsons. London: Collier Macmillan Publishers.

Weil, David. 1994. *Turning the Tide*. New York: Lexington Books.

Weinberg, Bill. 2005. "The Politics of the Anti-War Movement and the Intractable Dilemma of International ANSWER." World War 4 Report. Accessed February 4, 2012. http://ww4report.com/node/1337 Dec. 1, 2005.

Whittier, Nancy. 1997. "Political Generations, Micro-Cohorts and the Transformation of Social Movements." *American Sociological Review* 62(5): 776–8.

Will, Brad. 2003. "Cultivating Hope: the Community Gardens of New York City." In *We Are Everywhere: The Irresistible Rise of Global Anti-Capitalism*, 134–9. New York: Verso.

Wood, Lesley J. 2000–2011. Author's notes, unpublished.

    2004. "Breaking the Bank and Taking to the Streets." *Journal of World-Systems Research*. Special issue: Global Social Movements Before and After 9/11. 3–23.

    2005. "Taking to the Streets Against Neo-liberalism: Global Days of Action and Other Strategies." In *Transforming Globalization: Challenges and Opportunities in the Post 9/11 Era*, edited by Bruce Podobnik and Thomas Reifer, 69–82. Leiden, NL: Brill Academic Press.

    2007. "Breaking the Wave: Repression, Identity and the Seattle Tactics." *Mobilization* 12(4): 377–88.

Wood, Lesley J. and Kelly Moore. 2002. "Target Practice." In *ACT UP to the WTO: Urban Protest and Community Building in the Era of Globalization*, edited by Ben Shepard and Ron Hayduk, 21–34. London: Verso.

Working, Russell. 1999. "The WTO Protests: Pardon Me if I'm Rusty on the Meaning of Protests." *The Oregonian*, December 5.

Young, Daniel Dylan. 2000. "Masking Up And The Black Bloc: A Pre-Seattle History."
Accessed December 5, 2011. http://groups.yahoo.com/group/smygo/message/865

Yuen, Eddie, George Katsiaficas, and Daniel Burton Rose, Editors. 2004. *Confronting Capitalism: Dispatches from a Global Movement.* New York: Soft Skull Press.

Zmud, R. W. 1982. "Diffusion of Modern Software Practices: Influence of Centralization and Formalization." *Management Science* 28(12): 1421–31.

ZNet. 2004. "Vision and Strategy Pages." Accessed December 5, 2011. http://www.zcommunications.org/topics/vision-strategy

Index

CAMBRIDGE STUDIES IN CONTENTIOUS POLITICS
(*continued from page iii*)

CPSIA information can be obtained at www.ICGtesting.com
Printed in the USA
LVOW08s0005100816

499677LV00004B/202/P